For my sisters and brother-in-law, who lent support when it was most needed.
And for uncommon help and inspiration from Gabrielle Goodchild,
Liz Thomson, and Clare Pedrick … deep thanks.

— **R S, LONDON, 1986**

STERLING
New York

An Imprint of Sterling Publishing Co., Inc.
122 Fifth Avenue
New York, NY 10011

ISBN 978-1-4549-4265-8

Distributed in Canada by Sterling Publishing Co., Inc.
c/o Canadian Manda Group, 664 Annette, Street
Toronto, Ontario, Canada M6S 2C8

For information about custom editions, special sales, and premium and corporate purchases,
please contact Sterling Special Sales at 800-805-5489 or specialsales@sterlingpublishing.com.

Manufactured in China

2 4 6 8 10 9 7 5 3 1

www.sterlingpublishing.com

Design by Palazzo Editions
Credits see page 304

BOB DYLAN

NO DIRECTION HOME

Robert Shelton

Revised Illustrated Edition
Edited with a New Foreword and Afterword
by Elizabeth Thomson

STERLING
New York

CONTENTS

FOREWORD

PREVIOUS PAGES

High sixties:

Bob Dylan, 1966.

OPPOSITE

Columbia Studio A, early

sixties and bound for glory.

On September 29, 1961, a review appeared in the *New York Times* that ultimately changed the course of popular culture. "A bright new face in folk music is appearing at Gerde's Folk City," it began. "Although only twenty years old, Bob Dylan is one of the most distinctive stylists to play a Manhattan cabaret in months." His work bore "the mark of originality and inspiration, all the more noteworthy for his youth."

The critic was Robert Shelton, who had begun work at the *Times* a decade earlier, hired as a copy boy and trained as a reader. Like any ambitious young graduate, he wrote stories on the side, and by the time the dull gray of Eisenhower's fifties turned into sixties Technicolor with the election as president of the young John F. Kennedy, he had made quite a name for himself as a chronicler of popular music, a catch-all phrase that included pretty much everything outside the conservatoire. Shelton was at the first Newport Folk Festival in 1959, when Joan Baez made her unannounced debut, writing in the *Times* of her "achingly pure soprano," a quote that would forever follow her. The folk revival was gaining ground, and in an article on November 17, 1960, Shelton noted: "Folk music is leaving the imprint of its big country boots on the nightlife of New York in unparalleled fashion, from the grimiest Greenwich Village espresso joint to the crook-fingered elegance of the Waldorf Astoria."

Bob Dylan arrived in New York from Minneapolis in January 1961. He'd given up all pretense of university to head east in search of his idol, Woody Guthrie, drawn also (he would later admit) by Baez, whose voice he likened to "that of a siren from off some Greek island." He was soon in Greenwich Village, the center of the New York folk revival and much besides—jazz of course, but also art, literature, poetry, drama, and progressive social politics. The Village was "a Coney Island of the mind" where "everything started except Prohibition," as some wit once put it. A place of low rent and high art. There was "music in the cafés at night and revolution in the air" long before Dylan blew in, making a beeline for the Folklore Center and playing early gigs at the Café Wha? and the

Gaslight, all of them on MacDougal Street.

The Village in the sixties was "a scene," and Shelton, who lived at 191 Waverly Place—equidistant between Gerde's and the fabled White Horse Tavern, in what realtors now call the West Village—was as much a part of it as the musicians about whom he wrote. It seems extraordinary now how much space the *New York Times* devoted to young unknowns playing on makeshift stages downtown. In those heady days it was the closest America came to a national newspaper, and much of its content was syndicated. Shelton was writing not just for local music fans, nor even for the citizens of the five boroughs, but for the general reader, the coast-to-coast record-buying public. And for the first time, those readers were invited to follow Shelton into smoke-filled coffeehouses much as they followed his classical counterpart, the great Harold C. Schonberg, into the uptown splendor of Carnegie Hall and the Metropolitan Opera.

When Shelton died in December 1995, Jon Pareles wrote in the *Times* that he had been both "catalyst and chronicler of the 1960s folk boom," though he also wrote about rock, jazz, country music and what we now call world music. Janis Ian, whose fifteen-year-old talent he championed, told me he was "absolutely the father of rock journalism. There was Shelton in the *Times*—and that was it. He gave it credibility."

For a few heady years in the Village, Shelton and Dylan were buddies; hanging out, often with their respective girlfriends—Suze Rotolo and Baez in Dylan's case. The friendship did not prevent Shelton from being critical, in person and in print, sometimes to Dylan's annoyance. But he was fair-minded and he understood from the moment he first heard him perform at a Gerde's hootenanny in June 1961 that Dylan mattered, that his was a talent like no other. His review led to a contract with Columbia Records. The biography he proposed over dinner on New Year's Eve 1965 was never intended as a potboiler—but neither was it intended that it would take twenty years to write.

Shelton talked to *everyone*—childhood friends from Hibbing, including Echo Helstrom and Bonnie Beecher, the real "Girl from the North Country." To fellow students from whom Dylan begged, stole, and borrowed money, records, and songs as he passed briefly through university in Minneapolis. To the vast coterie of musicians and poets who scuffled for dimes in now legendary Greenwich Village clubs and hung out in Washington Square Park. He studied all the poets, and seers, and mystics who had influenced Dylan. And Shelton was *there*, a witness to all the crucial moments of Dylan's formative years: at Newport '63, and at the celebrated Philharmonic Hall concert of Halloween 1964. At Newport '65, when Dylan went electric. On the

April 1965,
press conference
at London's
Heathrow
Airport. Dylan
and his party,
including
manager Albert
Grossman and
Joan Baez,
had flown
from Seattle-
Tacoma Airport
aboard a Trans
World Royal
Ambassador
flight. On arrival
he was mobbed.

pivotal 1966 tour with the Hawks. At the Woody Guthrie memorial in 1968, and the Isle of Wight in 1969. They chatted for hours in Manhattan in 1971, during Dylan's withdrawal from public life, and long into the night in London during the 1978 world tour.

No Direction Home: The Life and Music of Bob Dylan was eventually published in 1986, when Dylan's career was at a low ebb. Shelton always said it had been "abridged over troubled waters," a characteristic pun. He hoped one day to revisit the book that had become his lifetime's work, but he died prematurely in 1995, at just sixty-nine. In 2011, for Dylan's seventieth birthday, a much fuller version was published: the book as Shelton had wanted it in 1979, before rows with his publisher over both length and aesthetics. At its heart was the only first-hand account of Dylan's formative Village years, restored in all its pointillist vibrancy. It also restored the interview with his parents, Abe and Beatty Zimmerman—Shelton was the only journalist to whom they talked, the man they called when news broke of Dylan's motorcycle accident—and the remarkable freewheeling conversation between author and subject during a late-night flight amid the *sturm und drang* of Dylan's 1966 world tour.

This new edition, marking Dylan's eightieth birthday, will be read by a young audience for whom the sixties are ancient history, and who cannot appreciate the extent to which Dylan's music—listened to on twelve-inch vinyl, not in a pick 'n' mix of streamed tracks—defined a community. The heart of *No Direction Home* remains Shelton's unique eyewitness account, which brings the Village and Dylan himself vividly to life. This edition retains all the crucial elements of the original text, but trims some of the exhaustive (and at times exhausting) detail about Dylan's student life, the history of Woodstock as an arts colony, and the extensive highways and byways where Shelton explored and explained the lives of Dylan's countless *confrères*. The signposts remain for those seeking to learn more, from albums and further reading, and the 2011 edition can still be found. For serious scholars, there's now The Bob Dylan Archive at the University of Tulsa, Oklahoma.

What *has* been excised from this new edition is Shelton's album-by-album commentary, and the lengthy exegesis on Dylan as poet, which drew extensively on the emerging field of Dylan studies taking root on American campuses during the seventies. Even in 1986, Shelton was still battling to make the case for Dylan as "an extraordinary poet" and "an artist of transcendent historical importance." Dylan was, Shelton argued, "a new species of poet remarrying speech and song," and he sought witnesses for the defence.

That he was then acclaimed by some outliers as the American Yevtushenko, the American Brecht, or Homer in denim, is now neither here nor there. For in 2016, Bob Dylan was awarded the Nobel Prize for Literature "for having created new poetic expressions with the great American song tradition." To his last breath, Shelton felt he had to make the case for Dylan as a serious creative artist in the great twentieth-century pantheon, alongside Chaplin, Picasso, Beckett, Welles, and Brando. It's now clear that the final arguments have been successfully made, the case closed. How sad Shelton did not live long enough to see the cultural benediction.

Sceptics aghast at Dylan's Nobel laurels should listen—*really* listen—to the mighty handful of albums he recorded between 1962 and 1966, and to *Blood on the Tracks* (1975), to hear songs that have become part of our cultural DNA, to the phrases that are as much a part of today's lingua franca as Shakespeare. Dylan articulated our grievances and our grieving, taking poetry off the bookshelves and loading it onto the jukebox. He wrote songs that were timely yet also timeless. "With God on Our Side" and "A Hard Rain's a-Gonna Fall," Dylan's own nightmare war vision sung by Patti Smith as she accepted his Nobel Prize, remain powerfully resonant and relevant today—almost sixty years after they were written, in ten-cent notebooks in Greenwich Village coffeehouses.

No Direction Home leaves Dylan at the not-quite halfway point of his life, old friends chatting in the warm afterglow of his acclaimed Earls Court concert series in London, in June 1978. Ahead lay Dylan's born-again period, and four decades in which his curiosity and restless creativity have found new and sometimes surprising means of expression. As Dylan growled in the second of three songs slipped out in spring 2020 during the world's dark and dislocating period of lockdown, "I Contain Multitudes." An allusion to Walt Whitman, no stranger to Greenwich Village, and a poet without whom, it is said, we cannot understand America. Without Bob Dylan, we cannot fully understand the twentieth-century.

Presenting Dylan with the Presidential Medal of Freedom in May 2012, Barack Obama talked of the "weight" and "unique gravelly power" of his voice, his "redefining not just of what music sounded like, but the message it carried and how it made people feel." The man who'd told senators and congressman not to impede youthful progress, and who sang of presidents standing naked, looked on impassively as Obama concluded: "There is not a bigger giant in the history of American music."

Elizabeth Thomson
London, May 2020

OPPOSITE

Dylan in Embankment Gardens, outside the Savoy Hotel, London, May 1965.

PRELUDE:
THE TIMES CHANGED

This is a story about a poet and musician who was born and reborn time again, who "died" several "deaths" and yet continued to live. It is the story of a popular hero who denied his own heroism, a rebel who so eloquently challenged his culture that he helped build a counterculture, and who then turned against the excesses of what he'd helped create. This is an attempt to tell the truth about a myth-maker, a myth-taker and a myth-breaker, who mythologized the dreams and nightmares of a generation.

The quest of Bob Dylan is riddled with ironies and contradictions, shadowed with seven types of ambiguity, scorched with stage-light glare, heightened with scabrous humor and darkened with his pain, and ours. Dylan wore a score of masks, assumed a legion of personas, invented a galaxy of characters we recognize as friends and foes. "There's so many sides to Dylan, he's round," said a Woodstock friend. "He's a dozen different people," said Kris Kristofferson. "Just let me be me," Dylan wrote in 1964.

His career has been a personal search, a constant flight along an endless spiritual highway. Like every artist, he had a vision of the future: "Someday, everything is gonna be smooth like a rhapsody/When I paint my masterpiece."

Dylan songs have orchestrated our time—known, loved and studied by an army of Dylanites, Dylanologists, Dylantantes, Dylan interpreters, fans, freaks and followers. Among them were two men named Carter—one called Hurricane, who once lived in the jailhouse, and another called Jimmy, who once lived in the White House. The convict Carter called Dylan "a man that was for life and living, not for death and dying." The president-to-be Carter accepted his nomination exhorting America to heed Dylan's line: "he not busy being born is busy dying."

However deeply Dylan is immersed in show business, its glamour, cruelties and shams are only a portion of his landscape. He has entered classic American folklore, pop lore and mythology—"myth" not as "false belief," but for those archetypal symbols and stories that express a culture's dreams, attitudes and values.

As early as 1964, he knew the dangers of defining his views, writing, sardonically: "do not create anything, it will be misinterpreted, it will not change. It will follow you the rest of your life." I think Dylan always wanted to keep his options open. In 1966 he said: "I define nothing. Not beauty, not patriotism. I take each thing as it is, without prior rules about what it should be." In 1976, he said he didn't "comprehend the values most people operate under. … I can't understand the values of definition and confinement. Definition destroys. Besides, there's nothing definite in this world." Despite his ambiguity, defiance and rhetorical flourishes, Dylan has defined and redefined himself often and unequivocally, but the definitions were always subject to change. Since the day I first met him in 1961, he has come closer to defining the shape, course, moral order and texture of our time than any artist I've encountered.

Yet by 1968, having written the biblically infused and moralistic *John Wesley Harding*, he was ready to say that "we are all moralists." Dylan's ability to change was an implicit critique of a rigid educational system that yields "useless and pointless knowledge." Defiantly, he dropped out of college, finding then that the universities and museums were among the institutions where "Lifelessness is the Great Enemy." But in the value-shifting sixties, he became a hero to collegians and intellectuals. Some named him "Public Writer No. 1." By the beginning of the eighties, Dylan, the self-taught writer-musician, had become a suitable subject for study. Princeton University gave him an honorary doctorate.

ABOVE LEFT

Jet magazine cover with President John F. Kennedy at the International Civil Rights Center & Museum in Greensboro, North Carolina, where a student sit-in in 1960 lead to desegregation during the US civil rights struggle.

ABOVE MIDDLE

"Diamonds
and Rust" and
Rolling Thunder:
Dylan and Baez,
Clearwater,
Florida,
April 22, 1976.

ABOVE RIGHT

With Ronee
Blakley at Rolling
Thunder's Clinton
Correctional
Institute show,
December 7,
1975.

A basically quiet man, he's been blisteringly articulate. An international communicator, he has often been unable to communicate directly to those around him. As moods of dark and light colored his personality, silences alternated with pistol shots or geyser blasts of words. What sure aim he had in this line: "I'm helpless, like a rich man's child."

Using language elliptically, he wasted few words in writing about pity, terror, release, longing, vulnerability, liberation, responsibility, cages, traps, and injustice. He was a quintessential writer of this period. His chief form was the song lyric. He wrote, often with his extraordinary twist of black humor, about the arrogance of power and authority, utopianism and its deceits, existential freedom and the modern apocalypse, the search for identity, commitment and lack of it, love and its

many faces, about all the false beliefs that hold us prisoner, and the truths that can set us free. Always, he asked challenging questions. As he sang of his quest for answers and for new questions, the songs set the tempo for our own quests. We grew up, or stayed young, with Dylan. Often misunderstood, he demanded to know: "how come you're so afraid of things that don't make any sense to you?" He knew a lot about fear: "experience teaches that silence terrifies people the most." He knew as well as Rimbaud ("I am the master of silence") how to master silence and turn it into a protective fence around wisdom.

As friend, reporter, critic and biographer, I was often able get behind that fence. Sometimes he provided the key, sometimes I found a door myself. It was marvelous when he'd really open up. Once

he told me: "Everybody has something to do. I just can't believe that people are born and die without reason." He told me repeatedly how he hated labels: "I don't know what I am, truthfully speaking. When people believe that I am this or that, already there is a misunderstanding, a barrier, between them and me." He's said a lot to me down the years, but he also says a lot to people who've never met him, if they really listen to his songs.

However sardonically, Dylan stressed his role as entertainer, as "song and dance man." He deflated his role as teacher, yet he taught us much about love and loss, society's flaws and powers, alchemy and redemption, the border country between life and death. Like Jung, he was often astounded at the creativity that came out of him. Of his success he once said: "I'm there only because of time and

chance. There are a million 'me's' all over the United States. And they are all hung up, but they cannot split from where they are."

Almost single-handedly, Dylan took poetry off dusty shelves and put it on the jukebox. Still, he was often uncomfortable at being labeled a "poet." He once exploded at me: "That's such a huge, God-damn word for someone to call themselves. 'A Poet!' I think a poet is anybody who wouldn't call himself a poet. When people started calling me a poet, it didn't make me any happier."

By disdaining the title "poet," he protected himself from those unaware of the grand tradition of folk and popular poetry, those who couldn't see the artistry in his borrowing and reshaping everyday speech, those who rejected the possibilities of a literature of the jukebox. Dylan began with the

ABOVE
Zeppelinfeld,
Nuremberg,
July 1, 1978:
the last of three
German dates.

OPPOSITE ABOVE
Madison Square
Garden, New
York, August 1,
1971: The Concert
for Bangladesh–
the first major rock
fundraiser.

language of folk say, then he flowered into sophisticated city expression. His determined use of the syntax, vocabulary and rhythms of colloquial speech, his reliance on popular song-form, and his disavowal that he was a poet—all retarded his serious acceptance as a literary figure. Why is Dylan an extraordinary poet? I can call attention to his concise formulations and aphorisms; his ability to say several things simultaneously; his audacious use of metaphor, simile and symbol; his evocative imagery; his cunning use of rhyme and near rhyme, the sounds and colors of his words; the surprising contexts and combinations of felicitous phrases that touch and unsettle the listener and the musical bend and sway of his lines. For many, Dylan's art is an aural/oral expression that needs the nuance and emphasis of song. Yet once known, his lyrics come alive on the page, music resounding in the mind's ear.

As literary acceptance of Dylan grew, he winced less at being regarded as a visionary poet who'd made vast contributions to modernist poetics. When commentators saw him as a Whitman with a guitar or a Rimbaud with a recording contract, Dylan could stop pretending he didn't know the difference between a quatrain and a freight train. Definitions of "literature" had to be expanded in new ways to encompass Dylan's art.

Central to Dylan's nimbus of genius is his art of concealing art. He often gave the impression of being only the spontaneous, intuitive wordsmith, the casual minstrel. He sheltered the purposeful, highly conscious designs that weave throughout his work from the storm of critical overkill. Because his indictments of social ills and human failings were so severe, his listeners felt guilt, and some were quick to strike back. He was called arrogant, manipulative, ambitious, paranoid, and egotistical. He's frequently admitted that his sudden fame threw him, that he wished he hadn't said quite so many harsh things about associates.

This romantic, angry, passionate, delightful, and maddening man—who, many thought, could not maintain any close relationship for long—is, he freely admits, contradictory. Yet, there was no confusion about his compassion for the victims he recognized in all of us—victims of social lies, of deceptions, of manipulations by government, media or the music world. He heard apocalyptic voices and distant bells tolling in the storm.

As he matured, his catechism went beyond the simplistics of good and evil. He changed from activist critic to observer to evangelist. He sometimes played the part of visionary and of satanic jester who knew that life was tragic for those who felt too much, and an absurdist comedy for those who think too much. His work oscillated between tears and laughter. He often lived to excess. Then, as moderate man he reveled in balance and order. As Blake wrote: "The road of excess leads to the palace of wisdom." Soon, he was back in emotional turmoil again, living to excess, refining it all into song. What he seemed most deeply to accept was the constancy of change itself. "There's nothing so stable as change," he said in 1964.

"No artist can accept reality," Nietzsche wrote. Dylan challenged the larger realities and his own. Because some of his own actualities were too mundane and literal for his romantic vision, he changed them a dozen times. Thinking mythically, he often lived mythically. Yet, here was a most vulnerable, sensitive writer who longed, repeatedly, for obscurity and its blessings, even though the other part of him needed to surpass, triumph and conquer. He tried to protect his inner core by becoming increasingly distant, elusive and unreachable. Yet he repeatedly bared his soul in song. We knew that even if he wrote about he, or she, or them, or it, or any of a large cast of characters, he was never far from himself, or the many selves that roared in debate inside him. In our minds, he became some of the characters he created.

So here is a man as elusive as a Garbo or Brando, simultaneously exposing to strangers his experiences, thoughts and feelings. He was there—visible and tangible; yet he was nowhere—spectral and hidden. The more the public clamored to know the inner Dylan, the less he revealed. He could use words as a screen. As Talleyrand said: "Man invented speech to conceal his thoughts." Dylan developed new forms of popular song in which both to reveal, and conceal, his thoughts. The lonely artist in America is a sad legend. Dylan is part not only of the old tradition that doomed Hart Crane and John Berryman, but he also pioneered a new tradition in which the poet could find larger audiences than ever. Some of his alienation was social, some was that of the writer who agonizes over the discrepancy between the way things are and the way they ought to be.

The power of Dylan's leadership, the force of his personality and talent, the bardic stance and the self-perpetuating aura of legend—all this led some to try to deify him. Dylan backed away from much of the power the public wanted to bestow upon him, although the temptations were great. Saint or sinner, he discarded the messianic clock and the devil's pitchfork, and just sang: "Don't follow leaders."

Despite his efforts to shrug off "mystique" and "charisma," those words seemed coined for him. Those who felt Dylan's strong gravitational pull were often unable to describe his special magic. Some have found him "just very sexy." "Mystic force," others would say, or, "he seems to live out a lot of my dreams." With this magnetism, Dylan became one of the most influential artists of his time. If he recorded a song one day, it was sung the next in Prague or Tel Aviv, discussed at Oxford, disputed at Antioch, imitated in Los Angeles, or copied in Nashville. Of course, the influence was centered in pop music.

"I was doing new things in 1959. I was pretty raggy then, but I was doing things that haven't been heard since. Listen to my records before 1965, and you won't hear anything that sounds like that."

He made the topical-protest song "respectable." When he sired "folk rock" and other styles, the whole music world followed him. Groups named Blonde on Blonde, Judas Priest, and Starry-Eyed and Laughing echoed his titles and characters. Critics, novelists and poets echoed Dylanisms in book titles such as *Something Happened*, *Hard Rain Falling*, *Busy Being Born*, *Outlaw Blues*, and *Gates of Eden*.

Dylan is typically ambivalent about his pre-eminence. He knew if he acceded to his place on a pedestal, detractors would point to his feet of flesh. Beneath his many public faces, Dylan has always been an easy mark for critics. In those early years, that affecting singing voice was ridiculed, called "tubercular," like that of an animal in a trap. "It makes me think I'm not being heard," Dylan once said. Yet those who loved that distinctive voice felt it was the perfect vehicle for the anguish, wit and anger it articulated.

Even granting his errors, excesses and contradictions, the case can be made for placing Dylan among the greatest of twentieth-century artists. Dylan arguably did for the popular song-form what Picasso did for the visual arts, Stravinsky for "serious" music, Chaplin for film and Joyce for the novel. Those unable to savor the heights to which he took popular song-poetry might regard such homage as a biographer's myopia or tunnel vision, a friend's hyperbole. Theirs is the loss.

Those who lionized him were not just star-struck "kids," but seasoned "cultured" commentators, as well. I was scoffed at in 1963 when I dubbed Dylan "the singing poet laureate of young America." Since then, a chorus of assent has grown steadily. John Clellon Holmes: "No one, years hence, will be able to understand just what it was like to live in this time without attending to what this astonishingly gifted young man has already achieved." In *The Greening of America*, Charles Reich saw Dylan as "a true prophet of the new consciousness." John Peel regarded him as "the single most important force in maturing our popular music," and Allen Ginsberg saw him as "a space-age genius minstrel." The acceptance of Dylan as a literary voice has grown enormously. Professor Christopher Ricks wrote: "A great amuser, a great entertainer, who belongs with the artists who've looked for the widest popular constituency, like Dickens and Shakespeare." Frank Kermode thought him "a virtuoso" with "no close rival." Dylan's work has been compared to Whitman, Yeats, Eliot, the Kabbalah and the Bible.

Conversely, some would argue that Dylan was a flawed genius, an unfinished musician, an erratic songwriter, a bewildered surrogate-messiah, an uneven performer. This book will try to show Dylan as a very human being, but equally an artist of transcendent historical importance. He is, I submit, a threshold-figure to our grasp of the contemporary fabric of American ideals and society. I see him as a new type of artist and entertainer, a new breed of superstar, a new species of poet remarrying speech and song. He is a new culture hero and anti-hero. I find his self-education and quest that of an archetypal American Dreamer. He is an incarnation of the Young Man from the Provinces, who fought to gain recognition in the city. A born combatant, opposing everything that looks untrue, unfair or distorted to his vision, his journey became emblematic of the sixties.

For all the lionization, for all the riches, Dylan has been mistreated often by the public and press. He made his voice heard as he kept moving abrasively against the tides. He was luckier than Joe Hill, the radical union singer who was executed; luckier than those eighteenth century Scots protest singers hanged for their defiance. Dylan fared better than poet-balladeer Wolf Biermann, forced into exile in November 1976 by East German communists who didn't like his dissident tune. Dylan prospered better than Prague rock stars put on trial for their anti–Big Brother independence. And, he's luckier than those "subversive" singer-poet-dissidents in the Soviet Union, who faced jail or psychiatric hospital for their underground tapes. Yet, for all his wealth and honor, Dylan was often denied the acceptance and respect his work deserved. For a lot of us, the time since 1960 will be etched in memory as "the age of Dylan." Many others still don't know who he is, what he signifies.

We start, then, with a controversialist—just a songwriter and pop star to some, but the "hero with a thousand faces" to many others. Some wanted Dylan to be *Time*'s "Man of the Year," and *Rolling Stone* talked of "Dylan for President." Slowly, even grudgingly, the academy, the politicians, and the media acknowledged Dylan's signature on these changed times. Dylan personifies the spirit of his period in the way Byron and Fitzgerald represented theirs.

There is scarcely a popular music form Dylan didn't infuse with new possibilities. A master politician as well as influencer, he befriended and affected the Beatles, Peter, Paul and Mary, Joan Baez, the Band, the Byrds, Johnny Cash, and a roster of singer-writers often referred to as "new Dylans." He wouldn't stand still, or lock himself into a single pander-to-the-audience style, so he was always losing admirers as he gained others. His sixties work seemed to categorize itself into early, middle and late "periods," but he kept turning in new directions and soon there were many more "periods." He is still changing and growing, and proving just how much that change disturbs.

Dylan's life-style and death-style were so widely imitated that he became the precursor of nearly every major youth culture trend for two decades. Often, the influence ran far beyond his command. A sub-industry in his bootleg tapes and records sprang up around the world. The self-destructing Weathermen took their name from his line: "You don't need a weather man/To know which way the wind blows." Demonstrators at the Chicago Democratic Convention in 1968 chanted "The whole world is watching," a paraphrase of another Dylan line. Admen, copy editors, headline writers and columnists borrowed or adapted his lines and titles: "My Back Pages," "Bringing It All Back Home," "Visions of Johannesburg." Classified property ads in *The Times* of London were once sold under the heading "Subterranean Homesick Blues!" Dylan's rhythms, cadences and images have re-entered our everyday speech from which he refined them—he has so affected the loam of our speech we can forget where his lines end and our own begin.

Every cult figure stands on the shoulders of those who came before. Dylan, the great assimilator, amalgamated a legion of types and styles—Dean and Brando from film, Woody Guthrie and a dozen ballad-makers, bluesmen, and others from music. Changing form and style, changing his looks,

"Another friend
of mine …
someone we all
know": at George
Harrison's
Concert for
Bangladesh,
Madison Square
Garden, New
York, August 1,
1971.

RIGHT

Woodstock East:
Dylan at the Isle
of Wight Festival,
August 31, 1969.

changing his expression, Dylan is Osiris one day and Proteus the next. One moment he was The Magician from a Tarot pack, the next, Pierrot in whiteface. The style of it all was cool and mysterious, for to explain just what he was doing would violate the part left unsaid that we, the listener, had to complete. As Oscar Wilde wrote in *The Picture of Dorian Gray*: "He knew the precise psychological moment when to say nothing."

From 1961 on, Dylan spoke to us in riddles and paradoxes, epigrams and metaphors. He loved to make us laugh, at first, and then he seemed to love to mystify us. There was always that mixed sense of nearness and distance in which one Dylan was beside us and another was outside, watching each drama unfold. He seemed, at first, aching to be recognized. "I was hungry and it was your world," he later wrote. What really impressed us most about him was that he wouldn't compromise. He seemed part of us and yet always detached, always elusive, sometimes even to himself. We envied his drive, yet we knew about the loneliness of the long-distance runner, and we didn't envy him that loneliness.

Then, from mid-summer of 1966 until late 1973, he stopped running. He built up to an incredible three-year onslaught of concert, film and recording activity. Then, he stopped running again. Each time, he'd outdistanced all other runners. During the first hiatus, he did what he always said he'd wanted to do—sit with a big family in a big house and write. The second pause, with that family life in disarray, he pondered his next moves. Whether in action or repose, in front of me or distanced, Dylan astonished me with his sense of intense life, and astonished me further by not burning himself out. We saw him dying young, like poets and stars are "supposed" to do. He beat the rap, a writer who decided he'd rather be read than dead.

Where can I begin his story? I'd need a movie camera to show the flashing chains of visual images: Dylan in Chicago starting Tour '74 to a thunderclap ovation? Or at London's Albert Hall and Paris's Olympia in May 1966, resisting audience hostility to his new music? Dylan playing to 250,000 at Blackbushe in 1978, or way back at Folk City in 1961, in his black Huck Finn corduroy cap? Or turban-headed on national TV in 1976? Jamming on Sunday afternoons in his hometown, Hibbing, or tumbling through the New Orleans Mardi Gras madness? Delighting or shocking the audiences at the Newport Folk Festivals? Contemplating a house that wasn't a home on the Pacific Coast, or strumming his guitar on the streets of Woodstock? A magnetic performer in so many settings, his whole life seemed a performance.

Or, do I begin at the midpoint, with the turbulent sixties behind him and the unexplored seventies still ahead? About a decade after I'd befriended him, he came to visit me at the Henry Hudson Hotel on Manhattan's West Side. I hadn't seen him since he appeared at the Isle of Wight Festival eighteen months earlier. I'd been living in England, sifting and assembling the facts and the truths-behind-facts of his career. I'd been seeking absolute truth, though I knew relative truth was the best I could hope for. I wanted to unlock the door of his creative mysteries. I told him that he held the key but didn't own the lock. He is often not his best explicator. He had written his masterpieces, told his turbulent tale piecemeal in songs, poems, interviews and arguments. I wanted to piece it together partly because I thought he was a far more remarkable character than

any novelist could invent. I had interviewed scores of people who thought they knew him. Usually, they said they knew only a part of the picture, and they would give me a jagged piece of experience, insight or anecdote to fit into the mosaic. Nearly everyone I interviewed had as many questions for me as I had for them, including his parents and brother. I had felt like the reporter in *Citizen Kane*, looking for Rosebud. But there were dozens of Rosebuds.

As he came up the hotel corridor, he looked different again—very healthy, even a bit of color in his cheeks. Fringe beard, heavy workman country boots, cord slacks, an old country undershirt peeking out beneath his leather jacket. Would the meeting be an anti-climax, I wondered, or would it be like all the other times—a few jokes, a sense of imminent drama, a dash of mystery, a flash of anger? No man is a hero to his biographer, nor is he an anti-hero, either. Why did this man I knew so well always intrigue me? After all, he was offstage now; why should I be keyed up as if the curtains were parting? How would he be today—mercurial, chimerical, tense, or gamey? Which of his many pseudonyms would he be wearing?

"How're you doin'?" I asked, and he said with a warm smile as we shook hands, "Oh, gettin' along, I guess."

Bob entered my room and began a minute examination of its every detail. He had repose written all over his face. He looked like *New Morning* that morning. We compared experiences about where we were living. "Woodstock turned into a bad joke. Why, they were running tours up there. There were people up there trying to pick up a piece of the earth, a piece of the lawn or of the shrubs." His "Eden" had turned into a zoo, he made that clear. Why had he returned to the Village? "I'll be able to let you know about that better after we're not living in the Village anymore. We're just passing through. A lot of the time, you just have to go down many roads to get where you are going. The important thing is to keep moving. Or else to stop by the side of the road every once in a while, and build a house. I guess that's about the best thing anyone can do." Was it a question of finding some place to hide from the notoriety and fame? "No," Bob replied, "I really don't want to hide from anything." The speaking voice was so calm, its tempo

matching the serenity of his mood. But soon he was telling me he was embattled again.

One self-styled "Dylanologist" had been systematically plundering his garbage pail for "clues" to the "real Dylan." Not every superstar had to pay that price of fame. Why was he still so worshipped and castigated?

"The media created the trouble for me. They blew me out of proportion. My thing was just for a crowd of people who were on the same wavelength that I was on. What I was doing wasn't really for a mass audience. The mass audience was all shuck, all hype. I'm not a Shea Stadium type of performer, I never was. The slogan that was going around was 'the Beatles, Dylan, and the Stones were the kings.' I never said that. I never called myself the king, or anything like it. The promotion men did all that. The media did all that. I never rejected the title of 'king' because I never accepted it in the first place." That's how it looked to him then, before he was ready to go back into the marketplace with Tour '74. If he wanted to blame the media, which he could play like a harp, one just listened.

I told him how depressing it was, after he'd stamped intelligence on to pop music, that there was still such a lot of trivia being hawked. How could top-forty radio continue with such poor quality when he had actually changed the face of pop music? "Changing the face of pop music is not necessarily changing its metabolism. I didn't change the metabolism. All I did was just open up a whole lot of doors. But, you have to admit, the influence—my influence—is there, all over, even in country music. Now you can hear the street sound in pop music almost anywhere. The influence is there."

We talked about some old mutual friends we didn't see much anymore. Bob could be nostalgic about those old times, then, and he would later try

> **Everybody has something to do. I just can't believe that people are born and die without reason.**

to bring it all back home with the *Rolling Thunder Revue*. "Those were wonderful days, all right. It was a movement then, a real movement. But it was probably the last movement. Say," he exclaimed, "that would make a good song title wouldn't it?" Bob resumed, sadly: "The dream is gone. That feeling is gone now. It's meaningless to try to grasp what's passed. I see no similarity between what the people are trying to do today and what happened in the early sixties. Those early days in the Village were great, and the days in Dinkytown were even greater. Now, things are depressing. The Village is depressing. Neon and cheapness. Today, it seems as if thousands of years of experience are being compressed into a year. What is going on now doesn't surprise me. Do you see the sort of books and records and junk they are rushing out every day? It's unbelievable."

Couldn't he find any encouragement in the activities of the New Left? "The New Left has no policy, no program, no philosophy, really, when you come right down to it. There really isn't a New Left. Those people who march for peace are just interested in peace, but that doesn't make them part of any New Left. It is not like the Old Left, or what we had in the early years. The Old Left had a program and a policy and a place, and things like that. The Old Left had some reason behind it. When you come right down to it, there is no youth culture, and there is no New Left, and, as far as the music business is concerned, it's just a toy, nothing but a toy."

The words seemed cynical, but his tone wasn't. I asked him what he'd been reading lately. It was the sort of question he wouldn't have answered when he arrived in New York, when he was devouring everything he could lay his eyes upon. Even in the late sixties, when he kept a large open Bible on a reading stand in Woodstock, he would have thought it pretentious to tell anyone. (In early 1977, the *Times Literary Supplement* asked Dylan, among a roster of literary heavies, which he regarded as the most underrated and overrated books of the century. To both questions he puckishly answered: "The Bible.")

Bob told me: "It's a very heavy responsibility for me to say what it is I'm reading, because too many people would regard that as some kind of endorsement. Some of them would run right out and start reading the same thing and I don't want to do that. That happened once when I said I was interested in the *I Ching*." He relented, and told me he was reading novels by Isaac Bashevis Singer and Chaim Potok. "They make a lot more sense to me these days than all that Maharishi stuff or the Indian mystic thing." Bob was about to go on a private visit to Israel but, again, beyond his command, it was to be publicized out of shape "I went to a Hasid wedding last week," he told me, weighing, I thought, my reaction. "The Jewish thing in this city is becoming very heavy," he said.

Bob knew I'd spent years contacting old friends of his to piece together a comprehensive biography. I told him I'd finally tracked down a good Hibbing friend, John Bucklen. Bob smiled. "Where in the hell did you find him?" I told him he was a disc jockey in Wisconsin. "John was really my buddy, my best buddy." He regretted that when he'd last seen Bucklen "I was terribly rushed, terribly busy. I went back to Hibbing for the class reunion." That tenth anniversary of high school graduation had been a moment of elation. He continued: "When I was fifteen, I said to myself: 'They treat me pretty low down here now, but I'll be back one day and then they'll all run up to shake my hand.' It's true, that I said that

A man called Alias: filming *Pat Garrett and Billy the Kid*,
Durango, 1972–73. "He's got a presence on him like
Charlie Chaplin," said Kris Kristofferson, who
persuaded him to join the film.

to myself. I said: 'I'm gonna come back here and have people look up to me.' I made that deal with myself. And it actually came true, in the summer of 1969. I sat there in Hibbing and signed autographs for an hour, more than an hour. … Yes, Echo was there, too.

"You've seen Hibbing," Bob continued. "You've seen that great ugly hole in the ground, where that open-pit mine was. They actually think, up there, that it's beautiful. They think it is a scenery place. Well, they are doing that now to the whole country. I didn't really look at Hibbing, when I went back. I just went for the graduation party. I don't need to be reminded of what it was like. I'll never forget it." His face was impassive, but a shudder seemed to run through him. It reminded me of his book *Tarantula*, where he said he'd make a Faustian pact with the devil to get away from the wasteland vacuum of Middle America. "I'm sick of cavity," he wrote, and the big hole in the ground in Hibbing was a metaphor for all the sickening cavities he saw around him.

We talked about his recordings. Dylan was embattled then, and since, by bootleggers, scavengers, and by the writers he didn't know or respect who'd threatened their way into his life. Bob clearly was ambivalent about the honors some had shown him, but he disdained the sales-mill approach toward instant popular culture, the grinding out of posters, bootleg tapes, pseudo-biographies, magazine pieces, ill-considered reviews.

I tried to assure Dylan that I could end up with a portrait in which he could retain dignity and respect as an artist. He had known me long enough, I hoped, not to bracket me with the reporters who think denuding celebrities is a respectable way of earning a living. Dylan suggested some people I might try tracking down. A name or two from Minneapolis came up and I asked how they might be helpful. Bob smiled: "It's just a clue."

In the early years in New York he'd started out charming, then gradually became tenser, warier, more difficult. But here was the moderate man about, finally, to sever his links with his long-time manager, Albert Grossman. "He had me signed up for ten years, for part of my records, for part of my everything. But I'll be out of that next month. I finally had to sue him. I got me a lawyer and was going to sue him, but Albert wanted it quiet and, because of that, he settled out of court. A lot of people would go out of their way to run Albert down, but I wouldn't." Bob went on to tell me that a lot of deals he'd made with Grossman, such as his first song-publishing contract, had proved better for Grossman than himself. It had a sticky, five-year on-and-off divorce that had been painful to both parties.

Dylan was one of the few contemporary artists of the era who had shifted partial control in the music business away from the fat cats to the artists themselves. He had often told me of troubles he'd had with the businessmen, the record company executives, agents, box-office people. He called his own tune as soon as he was strong enough to do so. What sort of a hostile world was this for a poet to be working in? He needed a shield. When things were going well with his manager, Bob lauded him to the skies, but even now he held back in attacking Albert. He had his complaints, yet he wasn't vengeful. The international music business is a colossus, and Dylan had to put a saddle on it to ride it. He knew its rewards, defeats, and hypocrisies.

Bob and I talked on for hours. If I probed too close to the bone, he stood up, looked out the window, as if leaving. If I released the pressure of questions, he sat down again. Sometimes he spoke in aphorisms: "There's no place to go. There are guys in prison that just can't afford to get out." We joked about how he was never the most organized person in retaining his own mementoes. "I used to write songs on napkins, just like Woody did, and then I used the napkins to wipe my mouth with," he recalled, smiling. "I was doing new things in 1959. I was pretty raggy then, but I was doing things that haven't been heard since. Listen to my records before 1965, and you won't hear anything that sounds like that." Did songs still flow out as quickly? "A few years ago, when I was in the very heart of it all, I would write a song in two hours, or maybe two days, at the most. Now, it can be two weeks, maybe longer." I tried to sound him out about social action but, at that point, the angry fires seemed banked. We agreed that America was in trouble again, the masters of war still in power. Bob made no comment then about how, or if, he might get back on the barricades again. Yet, when he said to me "they're not going to get away with it," there was much steely resolve in his voice. I knew it was only matter of time until he picked up his cudgels against "them."

We drifted downstairs and stood beside the swimming pool a few minutes, then chatted our way out to his new lime-green station wagon. We passed a few people along West 57th Street, but no one took any notice of him.

Dylan and his wife were to fly to Israel in two days. I was to stay on in New York to refresh memories of Greenwich Village and Woodstock. I was living in the past then, turning the time back to those great days of the early sixties. "Folk City is just a parking lot now," Bob had told me, and there at the corner it was, just torn down and paved over. Mike Porco had moved the club to West 3rd Street. I walked past Dylan's old apartment on West 4th Street, across the street from the Hip Bagel, then inched my way along to his new place down the road. Sara Dylan, behind sunglasses, was coming out the doorway, furtively looking both ways, wrapped in a raincoat, taking her little white dog for a walk. New York wasn't even fit for dogs, I thought. There wasn't room to breathe. Bleecker Street was slummier than ever— tired, dirty, sad cafés. Pizza shops and espresso joints still thrived, but it had all slid downhill. The New York in which Dylan had arrived late in 1960 was the concrete jungle of vitality and struggle it'd always been—a lure to all the young men and women of the provinces who'd used up the sparse resources of their hometowns.

1960: that's another point where the story begins.

There had seemed so much hope back in 1960. John F. Kennedy had won the presidency by a hair's-breadth from Nixon. In the South, 1960 was the start of the integration sit-ins in Greensboro, North Carolina. Castro was consolidating the Cuban revolution. Americans were reading *To Kill a Mockingbird*, *Born Free*, and *The Rise and Fall of the Third Reich*. Many were getting ready to celebrate the Civil War centennial. Broadway hits included *A Taste of Honey* and *Bye Bye Birdie*. Paul Newman was emerging as a new screen cult figure. Hitchcock scared the hell out of us with *Psycho*. Oscar Hammerstein II died at sixty-five. Emily Post died at eighty-six, and American manners never quite survived the shock. Hank Ballard's "The Twist" was about to be turned into a dance craze by Chubby Checker. The biggest excitement in popular music was coming from folk music, a revival that was to set the tempo for the early sixties.

> " I define nothing. Not beauty, not patriotism. I take each thing as it is, without prior rules about what it should be. "

In 1960, America stood poised with a young man in the White House who we hoped was an idealist. We tried to believe "the New Frontier" was more than a slogan. Before the Cuban Missile Crisis and before assassins' bullets and Vietnam turned all that promise into sorrow, it was a great time to be young and starting out. Before Martin Luther King Jr.'s passive resistance ran into a stone wall, it was even a time to be black and young and hopeful.

1960 was after Joe McCarthy, before Eugene McCarthy. After the Beats, before the hippies. After the Old Left, before the New Left. After Campbell's Soup, before Andy Warhol. After Dada, before camp. After the *Village Voice*, before the *East Village Other*. After Marshall Field, before Marshall McLuhan. After Trotsky, before Yippie.

1960 was post–Thomas Wolfe, ante–Tom Wolfe. Post-Presley, ante-Beatles. After tea, before pot. After apathy, before cool. After the Angry Young Men, before the protest singers. After the Red Cross, before the Red Guard. After Billy Graham, before Bill Graham. After momism, before popism. After the Establishment, before street people. 1960 was a time of promise. For a garland of reasons, world youth was beginning to breathe and stir after the silence and apathy of the fifties. Pope John XXIII was budging the Catholic Church into the twentieth-century. Castro and Guevara were trying to bring color back to a revolution that had turned bureaucratic and stifling. The Kennedy "Camelot" was bringing some youth, culture and style to a Babbitized Washington.

1960 was before Bob Dylan got to New York town.

GREETINGS FROM HIBBING MINN.

MAHONING MINE, LARGEST OPEN PIT MINE IN THE WORLD, HIBBING, MINN.

86870

01

"DON'T RAISE YOUR VOICE AROUND HERE!"

Daily Cross Word
This popular feature is found on
Page 2 today.

The Hibbing Daily Tribune

NRA

VOLUME 36
NUMBER 40

HIBBING, MINNESOTA, FRIDAY EVENING, AUGUST 16, 1935.

PRICE
THREE CENTS

ROGERS, POST DIE IN PLANE CRASH

Federal Relief in Minnesota Picks up Momentum Today

HIBBING WORK LISTED AMONG THE PROJECTS

St. Louis County Given Large Share of Grants

FIX LOCAL AIRPORT

Appropriation for the Completion of Airfield Included

(By The Associated Press)

ST. PAUL, Aug. 16.—Relief in Minnesota picked up momentum today as Victor Christgau, state administrator, announced President Roosevelt's approval of an $8,327,275 outlay for this state.

Bringing the delayed works program to a total of $22,000,055 in expenditures, the works program 254 projects show "good start" for the state, Christgau said, but he again urged speed in further recommendations from counties.

The 254 projects, Christgau said, will provide work for 1,617 persons for a year in the 54 counties concerned. Warning that federal funds will stop reaching Minnesota after Nov. 1, he emphasized a need for early applications.

On the total outlay in the 644 projects approved to date, labor will receive $10,856,027 with the remainder to expenses and materials.

Largest of the new projects is a $2,065,565 park improvement program in Minneapolis. St. Louis county shares heavily with 44 projects at a cost of $1,554,708 in the government and $257,957 to the county.

A more than $500,000 portion of the $8,327,275 goes to sewing projects in 12 counties aiming to meet clothing needs of relief clients and employing 500 seamstresses.

Unless communities wish to "shoulder the whole program of relief," Christgau said, "it is urged that they rush work projects into their offices immediately."

"There are no short cuts in the procedure for securing approval. We can only urge immediate action," he said.

Projects approved by Christgau, listing federal and sponsor's respective contributions, by counties and communities include:

Itasca county: County-wide gravel and reshaping roads, federal funds $31,425, sponsor $5,635. Cohasset — Gravel streets, federal funds $565, sponsor $270.

St. Louis county: Virginia—Building creek garden, federal funds $14,700, sponsor $3,600; curbing, federal funds $6,999, sponsor $1,200; widening runway, federal funds $28,183, sponsor $6,912.

Buhl—Road maintenance federal funds $4,705, sponsor $1,299; road maintenance, federal funds $3,748, sponsor $162.11.

Eveleth — Addition to hippodrome federal funds $3,827, sponsor $13,698. Hibbing—Construction of storm heat line, federal funds $2,750, sponsor $2,673; completing airport federal funds $23,676, sponsor $8,410. Balkan—Deepening creek, federal funds $13,450, sponsor $2,400. Stuntz—Repairing sink-hole, federal funds $8,975, sponsor $13,322.

Probably Showers

MINNESOTA: Showers probable tonight and Saturday cooler tonight and in southeast portion Saturday.

Boston	68	78
Calgary	56	82
Chicago	70	90
Duluth	67	84
Kansas City	76	94
Los Angeles	63	74
Miami	80	89
Minneapolis	68	97
New Orleans	76	88
Winnipeg	54	80

HIBBING'S WEATHER VANS

3 p.m.	90
6 p.m.	91
9 p.m.	84
12 p.m.	73
24 Hour Maximum	
24 Hour Minimum	67

Local temperatures are from the recording of a thermometer on the established under government regulations at the Hibbing Water and Light plant.

AAA AMENDMENT TO PRESIDENT

Passes Both Houses This Week

(By The Associated Press)

WASHINGTON, Aug. 16.—Secretary Wallace today declared emphatically that the AAA "has not and will not change its goal." The concept from the beginning," Wallace said, "has been to produce a normal supply per capita for the American consumer and not to produce a surplus which could find a market which has been lost."

(By The Associated Press)

WASHINGTON, Aug. 16. — New deal officials, expressing satisfaction because congress finally has passed the AAA amendments designed to strengthen their crop adjustment program, looked today for quick presidential approval of the legislation.

Anticipating the new powers, justice department lawyers planned to seek distribution of 500 temporary injunctions restraining the government from collecting AAA processing taxes. Manufacturers, packers, millers and other processors have filed 1,112 suits against the taxes.

The senate and house completed congressional action on the amendments late yesterday. They have two major purposes: To give the secretary of agriculture added powers in prosecuting the farm program and to erect bulwarks around the program against the time it meets its crucial test in the supreme court.

One of the most controversial points was the section barring suits by processors to recover processing taxes in the event the levies are held unconstitutional.

Under house-senate the compromise, the processors can sue for recovery, but, first they must submit their claims to the commissioner of internal revenue who will place his findings before the court. On these will be taxed the final decision whether recovery should be granted. The processors must show they have not passed the taxes along. The amendments also specifically seek to validate the processing taxes.

Among other things, the bill:

Permits the secretary of agriculture to draft marketing agreements with the consent of the majority of producers or processors. Lists the commodities: Milk, fruits (except apples), tobacco, vegetables, soybeans, pecans, walnuts and naval stores. Vegetables and fruits for canning are exempt.

Life-Long Cronies Killed

Will Rogers, famous humorist, whose articles appear daily in the Hibbing Tribune and Wiley Post, noted aviator, were killed in a plane wreck in Alaska.

Streicher Keeps Up His Campaign Against 'Enemies'

Whips People into Fervor in Talk

(By The Associated Press)

BERLIN, Aug. 16.—A more intensive phase of the Nazi anti-semitism drive was foreseen today for Germany on the basis of Julius Streicher's denunciation of Jewry as the nation's racist economic betrayers.

Streicher viciously outspoken in his advocacy of "wipe against the racial disgrace of mixed marriages" between Jews and Aryans.

"We are proceeding into a great German future," he said, "which will again save all humanity from the Jewish race."

In denouncing the foreign press reports of anti-Jewish disturbances, Streicher demanded that the press reports "from justice in America." His reference to a menace of Dodd's family was made to his comment on the heading of a woman through the streets placarded 'racial traitor.'

"Prevent at the time this incident occurred," he said, "was I, believe, the wife of the American ambassador, who was shocked. The American press said that in Nuremberg Jews and girls were led through the streets with placards 'racial traitor' on their breasts."

Bear River Boosters Ask Hibbing to Send Delegation to Bear River Fair, Aug 21st

Hibbing Chamber of Commerce boosters were requested today by the management of the Bear River fair to send a local delegation to participate in the exposition to be held Aug. 21 at the Bear River school and grounds.

A complete display of agricultural, home economics and 4-H club products will feature the exposition.

Events, with chairmen for each committee, follow:

Valley ball, Arne Lahko; horseshoe, Max Frank, Allen Sheckley; track and field, David Matteson; baseball, Howard Rein; novelty events, Dorothy Matteson.

A dance will be held in the evening.

THREE LEADERS MEET TODAY TO STUDY DISPUTE

Laval, Aloisi and Eden at Paris

(By The Associated Press)

PARIS, Aug. 16.—Three men met today in a secret session which may result in the alteration of the map of Ethiopia and a change in the African empire's economic life.

The men were Premier Laval of France, Baron Pompeo Aloisi of Italy and Anthony Eden of Great Britain. They conducted their talk in the antechamber of the clock room of the foreign ministry where the countries in 1928, signed the Kellogg-Briand pact "outlawing war."

Their avowed intention is to prevent war between Italy and Ethiopia.

At noon, Premier Laval came out from the room alone and said: "We have no declaration to make. We worked hard all morning and will continue throughout the afternoon."

Premier Mussolini's demand for occupation of Ethiopia to enforce his concessions given Italy decreased in scope and the tripartite conference representatives that they would be unable to prevent war in East Africa.

Uncertain Factor.

Emperor Haile Selassie, not represented at the parleys, remained an uncertain factor upon whose moving problems is to find a way of making Italian conquest of Ethiopia acceptable to him.

Their hopes lay in the possibility that he would accept Mussolini's minimum demand when he is convinced war is inevitable.

Aloisi in preliminary talks gave the impression that Mussolini intends to establish Italian political influence in Ethiopia by force if necessary.

Tecla Hawariat, Ethiopian minister to Paris, while accepting the possibility of the cooperation of other powers for Ethiopia's economic development," again rejected any idea of a mandate and reiterated Ethiopia's intentions of maintaining "complete liberty."

VETERANS WILL STAGE PICNIC

V. F. W. To Entertain Auxiliary, Sunday At Soldiers' Club House.

Plans are completed for the first annual V. F. W. picnic to be held at the Soldiers' and Sailors' clubhouse at the lake Sunday, Aug. 18. Dr. the group will open at 1:00 p. m. Johnson-Messner post of Hibbing is entertaining the auxiliary and the children.

The Island Farm Creamery, Fitger and Peoples' have contributed the refreshments.

"Chuckle" Hill is general chairman. Every veteran and his family is invited to bring along their own basket lunch.

Arthur Gabardy, state vice commander, has been asked to deliver an address. In addition to the regular program of sports, there will be a ball game between the V. P. W. and the D. A. V. Cliff Rue and Chas. Smith will be the V. F. W. battery while the D. A. V. has made arrangements for an imported battery from the "House of David" team.

Any veteran or his family who has no way of getting out to the picnic is urged to notify "Chuckle" Hill, phone 87. Transportation will be arranged for.

In the evening there will be dancing.

NATION MOURNS DEATH OF POST AND W. ROGERS

Capital Leaders Express Their Grief.

(By The Associated Press)

WASHINGTON, Aug. 16.—Usually jolly Jack Garner had his head bowed today. His real friend, Will Rogers, was dead. "Awful bad" was almost all he could say on hearing of the Alaska crash.

Intimates of both knew how much this companionship of vice president and humorist meant for each. The annual Garner dinner to President Roosevelt never can be the same again without droll Will Rogers in his "old blue serge" to "lambaste everybody."

For Jack Garner—his fellow-hater of dress suits—Will was in his finest fettle at the January dinner each year. On Jan. 20, 1934, and Jan. 17, 1935, to enjoy Rogers the more, President Roosevelt each time lingered far past the hour he was supposed to go home, and Garner—famed for retiring early—stayed up until three in the morning.

The capital grieved to hear of his death.

Speaker Byrns incredulous at first,

(Continued on page 2, column 1.)

Northern Part of Minnesota Would End 'Bear Scare'

Do More Damage Than Wolves

(By The Associated Press)

ST. PAUL, Aug. 16.—Northern Minnesota's animal kingdom felt the weight today of the state's official sympathy and distaste.

Bad bears and an employing cupboard for the deer population provided for demands upon the state conservation commission to take a hand.

Marauding bears described as "worse than the wolves" brought instructions to the game and fish division to investigate depredations and request danger to human life in Koochiching county.

Farmers appealing for aid through L. J. Melrose of the state farm bureau federation asked an open season on the bears to forestall further fright to women and children and the slaying of sheep.

The game and fish officials will instruct members to look into the facts and, if necessary, aid farmers in trapping and shooting the bears despite a closed season.

So many deer roam the northern forests, the commission also was informed, that a food scarcity threatens with a possibility many may die from starvation this winter, particularly in Scott and Itasca state parks.

The commission decided to ask for legal advice about opening the season if reports warrant. A state law under this winter a closed season.

LIFE'S CROSS SECTIONS

Brought into Court. Calgary Has Cold Wave.

(By The Associated Press)

CHICAGO—Edward Swiruki was brought to court on complaint of two relief workers, who charged he kept them in his home more than two hours for a lecture against their insistence that his 2-year-old son needed a special diet including spaghetti. Swiruki told Judge Frank Padden, "it's a terrible situation, judge. Under the constitution I think I have a right to bring up my son to be something better than a spaghetti eater."

ABERDEEN, S. D.—While Aberdeen was sweltering in the season's highest temperature—107 degrees—yesterday a summer cold wave moved across the Canadian border. Aberdeen reported mercury dived to from 4 to 10 degrees below the freezing point in the High River district of southern Alberta.

Death Ends Aerial Vacation of Noted Humorist and Flier

Plane Crashes 15 Miles South of Barrow in Arctic Alaska Last Night; Word of Tragedy Received by United States Signal Corps

SHIP UP ONLY 50 FEET WHEN IT CRASHES

Had Landed Previously Because of Fog on River Bank; Had to Tear Away Wreckage of Plane to Find Body of Post

(By The Associated Press)

Staff Sergeant Morgan, only army man at small Point Barrow settlement, wirelessed today the plane crashed from only 50 feet in the air after taking off from a small river about 5 o'clock last night. Morgan wirelessed:

"Navy runner reported plane crashed 15 miles south of Barrow.

"Immediately hired fast launch proceeded to scene found plane complete wreck, partially submerged two feet water.

"Recovered body of Rogers then necessary tear plane apart extract body of Post from water.

"Brought bodies to Barrow turned over to Dr. Greist, also salvaged personal effects which I am holding.

"Natives camping small river 15 miles south here claim Post and Rogers landed, asked way to Barrow.

"Taking off engine misfired on right bank while only fifty feet over fierce engine back through back of plane.

"Both apparently killed instantly.

"Post's body scalded stopped 8:15 p. m."

(Copyright 1935, Associated Press)

SEATTLE, Aug. 16.—Death ended the aerial vacation of Will Rogers, famed actor-humorist, and Wiley Post, noted round-the-world flier, when Post's plane crashed 15 miles south of Barrow in Arctic Alaska last night.

Word of the tragedy was received today by the United States Signal Corps from Sgt. Stanley R. Morgan, operator at Barrow.

Sergeant Morgan said the accident occurred at 5 p. m. Alaska time (9 p. m. C.S.T.) last night.

"Post and Rogers crashed 15 miles south of here at five o'clock last night," Morgan reported to the signal corps.

"Have recovered bodies and placed them in care Dr. Greist.

"Standing by to Anchorage hourly."

No details of the crash was received in first reports.

Post and Rogers left Fairbanks, in the interior of Alaska, yesterday in their pontoon equipped monoplane but set down on Harding lake, 50 miles away, to await better weather.

Dense fog, low clouds and rain were reported at Barrow at the time. Post and his party had received his news yesterday of whenever conditions at Barrow were fair, but fogs are frequent at this season when the warm sun has melted off year around snow and ice to their lowest point.

Post's plane was a new one, built in Burbank, Calif., for the flight to Siberia. It was similar to the ship used by Col. and Mrs. Charles A. Lindbergh on their flight to Japan in 1931.

Flown to Seattle as a land plane, the ship was fitted with pontoons here.

Was Delayed

Post arrived from the south Aug. accompanied by Mrs. Post, who had planned to make a Siberian trip with her husband. At San Francisco he had been delayed several days obtaining passport permission to enter Russia.

He said then he planned to go to Moscow, after hopping layers in Siberia.

Rogers, freed from his moving picture work for a time, then flew north and joined them here Aug. 5. He left Los Angeles under an "assumed name" but his identity was soon discovered and he was welcomed here.

The plane party left here with plans for a slow vacation flight to Point Barrow. Rogers also flights in Post's plane. Rogers also found time for a polo workout with polo players here. He was their guest that evening and told them, among other things, he was going to "get a polo team going on to Matanuska project," as that was about the "ugly thing the democrats haven't done for the colony."

That evening, friends disclosed later, Rogers "kidded" Mrs. Post about the hunting and fishing they planned on isolated Alaskan lakes, saying it was "no place for a lady," "kidding," to which Post joined.

LOSS TO CLAREMORE

(By Associated Press)

CLAREMORE, Okla., Aug. 16.—This Oklahoma resort town, made famous by its first citizen, Will Rogers, suspended business today when word of the death of the humorist was received.

"It is the biggest loss this country could have had," said A. B. Robinson, whose wife was Rogers' cousin. "Every one in Claremore feels like he had lost his best friend."

When first told of the tragedy, finally convinced Mrs. Post to make the trip.

Consequently, the next morning, Aug. 7, when the two hopped from the Renton airport of Lake Washington, south of here, Mrs. Post was left behind. She said the trip might be "too strenuous."

She remained here only a few days and then flew south in a private plane to San Francisco.

Post and Rogers made a leisurely flight of eight hours, 15 minutes, that day to Juneau.

Gov. John W. Troy, of Alaska, and Joe Crosson, a hunting companion last year of Post's, welcomed the two on their arrival at Juneau.

Governor's Guest.

They were the governor's guests that night at the territorial mansion. The next day, it was still raining and their flight, which had become a "vacation trip," was delayed. Rogers bought robbers, two raincoats and other equipment saying humorously "with this weather, I'll need lots of them."

Within a few days, they hopped again over into the historic Klondike gold territory, at Dawson, Y. T., and even there found themselves the objects of much attention. Miners and prospectors came miles to see them.

Within two days they took off again, their destination unannounced as usual, and they turned up at Aklavik, N. W. T., at the mouth of the MacKenzie river, on the Arctic. Rogers commented in one of his dispatches that Eskimos there were "thicker than rich men at a save-the-constitution convention." He also found it cold. It was 40 above zero.

Their stay there was short.

A flight back to interior Alaska, to Fairbanks, followed, and then in a commercial plane they flew south to Anchorage and over the Matanuska project.

"Pioneering for spinach is different than prospecting for gold," said Rogers, but his next comment was favorable. "I didn't see any mosquitos there," he said.

Thy returned to Fairbanks, where their plane had been serviced, and they followed their tragic flight north to Point Barrow, ending in death.

(Continued on Page 2: Column 2.)

> I didn't leave home because of my curiosity
> to see what was going on elsewhere.
> I just wanted to get away. Yeah, get away.

It's a long way home from the movies. The marquee of the Lybba Theater was dark as the plump, sandy-haired boy walked into the merciless cold. First Avenue was even colder by contrast with the heat of the Texas plains he'd felt from the screen inside. Even James Byron Dean couldn't have been a hero on First Avenue. He'd have frozen in his tracks. Texas was rugged, Minnesota was impossible.

Across the street was the sign of the *Hibbing Daily Tribune*—stately Olde Englishe in flaming red neon. Out of First Avenue were fainter neon signs, in Moderne American, offering quick credit to the miners and quick drinks to help them forget their instant debt. The boy glanced toward the pool hall, hesitated, then decided against the small talk that would have accompanied a game. *Giant* was still in his head, with the stinging disbelief that James Dean was really dead, more than a year now.

The boy turned onto Howard Street. He stood "at one end of Hibbing on the main drag and saw clear past the city limits on the other end." There were red iron-ore mining dumps at nearly every fringe of town. "The richest village in the world" wasn't so rich any more. They'd cut down the trees and dug the good ore out of the earth. He walked by storefronts, well-stocked and confident, and others that had run empty when confidence and money gave out.

The stores of Hibbing, 1956—Montgomery Ward, J. C. Penney, Woolworth— patterned small-town America. Would there be the same shopfronts down in Macon, Georgia, where Little Richard was born? At least Georgia didn't have skin temperatures of twenty below. The boy stepped into the doorway of Chet Crippa's Music Store. He scanned the record display. No Little Richard, no Hank Williams, no Buddy Holly. Bing Crosby was still dreaming about a white Christmas.

In front of the New Haven Lounge, he could hear a sputtering little band. Some band! The wind from Lake Superior and the Canadian plains knew more

songs, but who else listened, as the boy did, "when I first heard the ore train sing," as he wrote in the liner notes to *Joan Baez in Concert, Part 2*.

No songs that night, as he approached Fifth and Howard, where the brick solidity of the Androy Hotel exuded permanence and prosperity for traveling salesmen and local Rotarians. A few hundred yards away, the Zimmerman Furniture and Appliance Company reposed in chrome and Formica: "A kitchen range for the Iron Range." As Howard tapered off toward the bush, the boy turned right onto Seventh Avenue. The darkness of the side street created a vacuum, which he filled with wide-screen Technicolor.

"James Dean, who was killed in a sportscar crash two weeks after his last scene was shot, clearly shows ... a streak of genius," reported *Time*

magazine in October 1956. "He has caught the Texas accent to nasal perfection, and has mastered the lock-hipped, high-heeled stagger of the wrangler, and the wry little jerks and smirks, tics and twitches, grunts and giggles that make up most of the language of a man who talks to himself a good deal more than he does to anyone else."

The fifteen-year-old moviegoer, who talked to himself a good deal more than he did to anyone else, filled Seventh Avenue with his own Actors' Studio. He pursed his lips, tried a line of dialogue, locked his hips, shambled like a wrangler, contorted his face to erase the North Country twang in his voice. As young Bob Dylan passed Hibbing High School, he halted his monologue-pantomime. The sprawling four-story pseudo-North Italian turreted castle brought him

ABOVE LEFT

James Dean, *Rebel Without a Cause* (1965), a key influence for Dylan, and not someone of whom his parents, Abe and Beatty Zimmerman, approved.

ABOVE RIGHT

Abe and Beatty Zimmerman in 1934, five years after their marriage.

back abruptly from Texas. The last few blocks, to 2425 East Seventh Avenue, were so familiar that in the dark Bob's feet led him past memorized breaks in the sidewalk. The corner house was ablaze with lights. Back to family life in a dying town.

He tiptoed through the back door into the kitchen, wishing he could get to his room without being seen. "Bobby, is that you?" His mother's voice, taut with tension. He reported to the parlor. "I've told you a hundred times, if I've told you once, how do you expect to grow up strong and healthy if you don't get your rest? What are the people in this neighborhood going to think of any boy of mine who's always out roaming the streets at night?" Why did she talk so fast, leaving no room for answers?

"Your mother is absolutely right, Robert," his father broke in, his voice low and controlled. Bob tried to explain: it was a special James Dean movie that ran late. His voice began to rise with anger. "Robert, stop that shouting," his father said. "You know we don't tolerate shouting in this house."

The argument spilled out of bounds and out of the room. It wasn't just this lateness, his father told me in 1968. It was Bob's "attitude." One night he was late, the next he neglected his schoolwork. He didn't show up at the store when they expected him. And soon it was going to be smashed-up cars and motorbikes, "that girl," and those "friends." "Robert, you come back here," his father said. But he was gone, through the kitchen, downstairs to the basement. His father followed, hurling recriminations: "We've given you a good home. We buy you the best of everything. What more do you want? I never had it so soft when I was your age."

In the basement den, Bob tried to explain that he had stayed to see part of the movie over again. He talked about Dean, waving his hand toward the walls covered with photographs of the dead actor. "James Dean, James Dean," his father repeated. He pulled a photograph off the wall. "*Don't do that*," Bob yelled. His father tore the picture in half and threw the pieces to the floor. "Don't raise your voice around here," he said with finality, stamping upstairs.

> *Hibbing's a good ol' town*
> *I ran away from it when I was 10, 12, 13, 15, 15½, 17*
>   *an' 18*
> *I been caught an' brought back all but once …*

Dylan didn't actually run away from "good ol' Hibbing" at all, except in his mind, and there he kept running for years. He spoke about Hibbing rarely, wrote about it fragmentarily. He had trouble coming to grips with his growing-up days, vacillating between nostalgia and repulsion. Hibbing was small-town Minnesota, home of provincialism, isolation, backwater conservatism. Dylan could say "Hibbing's got nothing to do with what I am, what I became" and yet sometimes reveal that his flight from small-town philistinism had shaped him to a degree he was usually unwilling to admit.

"North Country Blues," written in 1963, is an understated folk-epic encapsulating its history. Dylan's notes to *Joan Baez in Concert, Part 2* dwell upon his early attitudes toward beauty in life and nature. On his third album, the second of his "11 Outlined Epitaphs" paints a dark portrait of his hometown's hollow death and decay. That had set him running, made him a refugee.

Prior to my two visits to Hibbing, in 1966 and 1968, Dylan told me: "I didn't leave home because of my curiosity to see what was going on elsewhere. I just wanted to get away. Yeah, get away. Hibbing was a vacuum. I just kept going because I was bored. There's no lines where I come from. There never was. As far as I knew, where I lived, nobody had anything that anybody else didn't have, really. All the people I knew had the same things. I've thought about it some, but Hibbing really has nothing to do with what I am today, with that I became. Really nothing!"

He meant it when he said it. For Dylan, reality is a prism, not a plate-glass window. Through that prism he would look back on Hibbing and his formative years there sometimes with anger, frequently with remorse, sometimes with love, and warmth. "My family?" Dylan repeated while he chose his response. "I never really had that much contact with them." That's not quite the way his family remembered it.

Hibbing was built mainly by Europeans. While urban bankers and financiers made big money, immigrant hands did hard labor. Rich in iron ore, the Iron Range was a melting pot as diverse as any city. The loggers were mostly Scandinavian, Finns primarily. Others arrived to dig the pits: Yugoslavs, Poles, Bohemians, Czechs, Italians, even a handful of Eastern European Jews. While Hibbing was

digging itself into a golden hole, a pair of local drillers tapped another source of wealth. Andrew G. Anderson, a former blacksmith who came to be known as Bus Andy, and Carl Eric Wickham, a young Swedish immigrant, decided to use Andy's old Hupmobile car to transport passengers between neighboring Alice and Hibbing. In spring 1914, regular runs began. During the mine boom of World War I, the bus service expanded, and by 1916, the Mesabi Transportation Company had five buses. In the twenties, following more mergers and purchases that added links to small companies as far away as California, the Greyhound Bus Company was formed. Fatter with war profits, Hibbing boomed in the twenties. Residential additions were tacked on, schools built, Howard Street constructed.

While Dylan was later taunted for "having invented his own Depression" out of Woody Guthrie, he had only to listen to a few town elders to know what the slump was like. During the thirties, mining dropped off and the village fathers issued scrip money for local transactions. Thanks to the Works Projects Administration and World War II, prosperity returned; the Korean War gave the local mines another short-term boost. By 1953, the best iron ore had been eaten out of the canyon. The taconite process, in which huge magnets and sifters separate out commercially usable ore, had been developed. But it did not bring economic stability to the Range until the sixties. By the mid-fifties, the local Depression couldn't be ignored by anyone in Hibbing. Dylan mined that vein for "North Country Blues," which tells of the erosion of hope in a miner's family. The Iron Age along the Mesabi was over. Miners' children began to drift away—"for there ain't nothing here now to hold them."

Much as veterans rarely speak of combat, Dylan's family rarely spoke of its refugee past. Feelings of persecution and landless insecurity do not disappear quickly. The fears of those who escaped the czars' tyrannies persisted. The link to a young American-born musician becomes clearer if we consider that the life of Russian Empire Jews was not much better than that of black American slaves. Both societies were oppressive, both cultures

forced underground. Dylan's natural affinity with the descendants of black slaves was an extension of his background.

After hearing about Iron Range prosperity, Dylan's maternal grandfather, Ben D. Stone, made the trip to Hibbing from Superior, Wisconsin. In 1913, he opened a general store at Stevenson Location, a village twelve miles west of South Hibbing. From the handful of Jewish families in the area, he chose a wife, Florence Edelstein, whose family operated a chain of Iron Range movie houses. Movies came to Hibbing in 1906, and by the twenties Julius Edelstein, Bob's great-grandfather's brother, was part owner of the Lyric Theater. Julius and B. H. Edelstein, Bob's great-grandfather, prospered and took over the Garden Theater in 1925. They renamed

it the Gopher and in 1928 sold out to a larger chain. In 1947, the brothers built the Lybba Theater, named after Bob's great-grandmother. This family film link engendered Bob's early awareness of show business, a connection—however tenuous—to Hollywood and the glamour of the performing world.

Ben and Florence had four children—Lewis, Vernon, Beatrice, and Irene. Beatrice, born in 1915, was Dylan's mother, a bubbly woman, blond, headstrong, nervous, volatile, and warm. She felt locked in the small Hibbing Jewish community and longed to get away. Some of Beatty's restlessness was assuaged by her father's magnificent four-door Essex, when her father offered her driving lessons when she was fourteen. "You don't have to," Beatty replied. She had watched him drive often enough.

LEFT

The Andrews Sisters' close harmonies
were a much-needed balm for the war-
time generation, but rock 'n' roll was
a clarion call to baby boomers amid
the dull gray of the Eisenhower years.
Bill Haley: *Blackboard Jungle* (1956) and
"Rock Around the Clock" was a key
moment for Dylan's generation.

To her father's astonishment, she got behind the wheel and drove off. "Bobby is very much like I am," she said years later. "You either do or you don't."

For Beatty, the car meant access to Duluth and its more sophisticated social life. She sought status, solidity, and the right marriage to a nice Jewish boy. To that end, she dressed impeccably and kept the Essex highly polished. Beatty's dream of getting away from home began to be realized at a New Year's Eve party in Duluth at the start of 1932, a dark winter of the Depression. She was a popular girl, but one man she met had something beyond a sense of humor, quiet intelligence, and good looks. Abram Zimmerman had a job.

Born in Duluth in 1911, Abe Zimmerman had, in fact, had some sort of a job since he was seven. His father, Zigman, had run a substantial shoe factory in Odessa, Minnesota, but in 1907 he traded it for a peddler's cart in Duluth. He then sent for his wife, Anna, along with Abe's older brother and sister. Every member of what became a family of eight pitched in. Abe shined shoes and sold papers, and also became a semi-professional ballplayer. Although Duluth had its Jewish ghetto "up on the hill," the Zimmermans grew up in a neighborhood with many Scandinavians. Abe took long walks to play ball with his fellow Jewish boys. He spoke Yiddish to his family, but English otherwise.

By the time Abe was sixteen, the Zimmermans had moved to a nine-room house, and he was hired as a Standard Oil messenger boy for sixty dollars a month. He saved part, and contributed the rest to the family. "You wanted to do something for your parents *then*. You don't see parents working and suffering as hard as they did in those days."

> "People would laugh with delight at hearing him sing. He was, I would say, a very lovable, a very unusual child."
>
> ABE ZIMMERMAN

Abe also wanted to do some things for himself, and when he sighted the vivacious Beatty Stone at that party, he made a mental note to see her again. They were married in 1934, and Beatty escaped Hibbing for Duluth. By then, Abe was earning a hundred dollars a month and they feathered their first nest at 519 Third Avenue East, on the top floor of the two-family Overman frame house. Abe knew Standard Oil was no place for him to make a fortune, but it was secure. He rose through the seventy-five-employee office to junior supervisor.

One evening in mid-May 1941, Abe and Beatty were listening to the radio. Abe scanned the newspapers. The Nazis were on the rampage throughout Europe. Jews were being hunted again. The Battle of Britain had been won, but elsewhere Axis armies were triumphing. Roosevelt was in the White House. Minneapolis's own Andrews Sisters had sold their eight-millionth record. Beatty had a news bulletin of her own. "Abe, I feel it! I think the baby is coming." It was premature, but by 9 p.m. on Saturday, May 24, she went into forced labor at St. Mary's Hospital, and delivered a hefty ten-pound boy. Even the neighbors had to admit that Bobby Allen was a beautiful child. He had a golden head of hair, and Beatty would say to him: "You should have been a girl, you're so beautiful." A picture at fifteen months showed a cherubic child, apple-cheeked and smiling, with that burst of golden blond hair. His father continued at Standard Oil, an essential job that exempted him from military service.

In the late thirties, when the powerful John L. Lewis was organizing, Standard Oil had formed the Tri-State Petroleum Union, a company union to head off the demands of the militant Congress of Industrial Organizations. With around three hundred members signed up at a dollar a head, all the new union needed was a leader. They elected Abe. The company union was soon banned by the Wagner Act, and the Duluth drivers entered the tough-talking Teamsters Union. Standard Oil survived, and so did Abe.

When he was three years old, Bobby Allen gave his first public performances, perched atop his father's desk, talking and singing into a dictaphone. In 1946, there was a Mother's Day celebration in Duluth, where Bobby was taken with his grandmother, Anna. "It was the talk of Duluth. In fact, they still talk about it," Bob's mother recalled. "Everyone was getting up to perform, but nobody else but Bobby was listening to what was going on. They talked. Bobby just sat there and watched and listened. Then they called on him. This little four-year-old codger gets up with his tousled, curly hair and goes to the stage. He stamped his foot and commanded attention. Bobby said: 'If everybody in this room will keep quiet, I will sing for my grandmother. I'm going to sing "Some Sunday Morning."' Well, he sang it, and they tore the place apart. They clapped so hard that he sang his other big number, 'Accentuate the Positive.' He didn't know much more than those two songs. Our phone never stopped ringing with people congratulating me."

Within two weeks, Bob had another gig. Beatty's sister, Irene, had a lavish wedding reception at the Covenant Club. Bob's mother decked him out in a white Palm Beach suit—in 1968, she still kept the collarless, three-button outfit handy in a closet. A fan club of relatives sponsored Bob's first paid performance. Proffering a handful of bills, an uncle said "Bobby, you've got to sing." He refused. The pleading increased, and Bob turned to his father. "I told him that he should sing, because all those people had come to hear him. I told him that if he would sing we wouldn't pester him to sing publicly anymore." So he sang, and again the audience cheered, and Bobby walked over to his uncle and took the twenty-five dollars. He approached his mother with his first gate receipts. "Mummy," he told her, "I'm going to give the money back." He returned to his uncle and handed him the money, the hero of the day. His father remembered: "People would laugh with delight at hearing him sing. He was, I would say, a very lovable, a very unusual child. People would go out of their way to handle him, to talk with him. I think we were the only ones who would *not* agree that he was going to be a very famous person some day."

The end of World War II triggered a great migration. Everybody who could afford it moved house. Abe and Beatty considered moving to

Hibbing, but Abe had lost his job at Standard Oil. Bobby was by then attending kindergarten at Duluth's Nettleton School. Another son, David, arrived in February 1946. Bob was scrappy, but the brothers generally got along well, later trading *Classics Illustrated* comic books, rough-housing, and going to Dad's store to play with a portable disk-recording machine.

Then Abe was stricken in the 1946 polio epidemic. Always one to keep tight rein on his emotions, he took the illness with Spartan toughness, remaining in hospital for only a week because it was short of help and equipment. "I'll never forget coming home—I had to crawl up the front steps like an ape." He remained home for six months and the ordeal left him with one limp leg and weak muscles in the other. While Abe recovered, the Zimmermans moved in with Beatty's parents and Abe joined his brothers Paul and Maurice in a furniture and appliance business. They had prospects: consumer goods were rolling off assembly lines and everyone who could afford it was getting their home applianced.

Before grandfather Ben's death in 1952, Beatty and Abe had already found their own home, a spacious corner house on Seventh Avenue in the Fairview Addition. Three floors and nine rooms gave the boys plenty of space to explore and play, even after their widowed grandmother came to live with them. Their neighborhood was an uncrowded middle-class section of some six houses, containing fifteen children. The Zimmermans were the only Jewish family but everyone got on.

"No artist can accept reality," Nietzsche said, and the same could be said of "no Zimmerman." Middle-class, small-town propriety impelled Beatty not only to say, but also to believe, her own version of reality. Abe freely admitted, with appropriate rising gestures of his hands, "I've got pride up to here and ego up to there." For the parents, their home life and their son's early years were a placid paradise of parental permissiveness and sagacity. For Bob, the Hibbing years were so limiting that he came to accept no limits. As their son's career developed, the parents occasionally made light of his self-images, but their own image-making was nearly as prodigious. Abe wanted to

impress the town Rotarians, and Beatty wanted to impress the "old lady judges," as Bob would call them, of her family and community. Bob wanted to impress the world with a romantic flight to somewhere else. None of them were liars. All of them were compelled, like Pirandello, to find their own realities.

Abe was a short man with an appealing smile that revealed irregular teeth. Behind his strong glasses, his eyes were a soft boyish blue, until they hardened. His wavy black hair was flecked with gray. He dressed in sport shirts, slacks, and sweaters that suggested California more than Minnesota. He frequently sported a thick cigar. Abe's speech was slow and deliberate, in contrast to Beatty's torrential flow. He peppered his talk with double negatives, yet he didn't sound unschooled. On his home turf, he was a big man in commercial and community circles, and he wanted to be in charge.

Abe and Beatty were the social pivots of their large family and proud to have retained many Duluth friends. Beatty was warm, effusive, and outgoing. The neighborhood kids called her Beatty, without concern for formalities. She ran a house "on love, warmth and laughter." There were rules, of course, and Bob followed them where he could before he escaped them and tore up the rule book with a rip heard around the world. Abe was an organization man. He had belonged to the Golden Circle at Standard Oil, was active in various lodges of B'nai B'rith, a Jewish fraternal order, and he had designed basketball suits for one lodge's team. A loyal member of the Hibbing Rotary, Abe was delighted to have edged Bob into the Boy Scouts. "He got the uniform and I was glad he joined, but I didn't ask him if he liked it or not." Bob's membership was brief.

Around the early fifties, Bob began to spend an increasing amount of time in his upstairs room. Beatty will never forget her rapture when on one Mother's Day she saw his first poem. Written on notebook paper, it was carefully rhymed in twelve stanzas of four or five lines each. The sentimental words told how his mother's face shone in the light, and described his fears that without her love he would be "six feet under." Beatty recalled: "I had

OPPOSITE
Johnnie Ray,
"The first singer
whose voice and
style I totally fell
in love with."

to read it to the women. I must have had about twenty of them just crying their eyes out. … We were going to frame some of those other poems, but I just kept them in a drawer. One of them I read over so often that the wording was nearly rubbed off the paper." By June 1951, Bob had another poem to show, this time for his father.

The poems Bob wrote at ten or eleven were a chance to "make something"; he was not especially interested in crafts or model-building. He wrote a great deal. "We thought he would get it out of his system, but he never did," his mother told me. For a time, the writing was eclipsed by an exciting diversion. In 1952, the family acquired the first TV set in Hibbing. The new gadget delighted the boys and, after several moves, it reposed upstairs, in the room the brothers shared. Bob liked music and variety shows, and western adventure series. He loved the bravado of badman and lawman alike, and the names of the TV frontiersmen rang with earthy American directness. He could imagine himself as Wyatt Earp. Or, even more heroically, as the greatest frontiersman since Daniel Boone, that lean, laconic, fearless man of justice from Dodge City named Matt Dillon.

The boy called Bobby Zennerman and Zimbo by his playmates before he called himself Bob Dillon, sought assimilation. But before he drew his own maps, he followed by rote his parents' traditions, which reached a culmination when Bob turned thirteen. The bar mitzvah that Abe and Beatty arranged for their eldest son was lavishly American: five hundred were invited, four hundred attended. "This is only a small town," Beatty noted with pride.

To prepare, Bob studied Hebrew with Rabbi Reuben Maier, of Hibbing's Agudath Achim Synagogue, the only one on the Iron Range. Confirmation day arrived, and Bob stood on the synagogue rostrum with his rabbi, his prayer book, and five thousand years of prophets and pogroms behind him. He was dressed in white, a raised silken hat on his head and an ornate fringed shawl around his shoulders. He delivered the Hebrew scripture in a form of chanting known as cantillation. Having attained manhood, having confirmed his belief in the God of his fathers, Bobby was ready to start living by no commandments but his own.

Although Abe never called himself a great music-lover, music was important to him. He trooped Beatty off to a lodge dance at the drop of an invitation. A Gulbransen spinet piano arrived at much the same time as the TV, and was set in the front room for all to admire. Abe couldn't read a note, but he loved to fake a few chords. A cousin, Harriet Rutstein, gave piano lessons. David followed instructions, but Bob endured only one lesson. "I'm going to play the piano the way I want to," he declared impatiently. For a while he simply ignored the piano. But when he was about fourteen, music surged into his life, though he never learned to read it.

At Hibbing Junior High School, everyone who counted was playing in the school band. Bob started frequent visits to a Howard Street music store, which offered instruments on ten-dollar three-month rental/purchase plans. He first took home a trumpet, announcing he would master it soon. To general relief it was returned in favor of a saxophone. Defeated again, he tried another brass instrument, then another reed. Finally, amid fears that he had worn

OPPOSITE

Hank Williams,
"the hillbilly
Shakespeare."
Williams was
the poet,
Little Richard
the pulse.

out his welcome, Bob rented a cheap guitar, which he caressed like a Spanish heirloom. For hours he sat with the guitar cradled in his hands, experimenting and exploring. *Manoloff's Basic Spanish Guitar Manual* gave him some clues, but his own ears and fingers soon took the lead.

The guitar became his cane, weapon, security blanket, and swagger stick. Around Hibbing, some remember him walking up and down the streets with his guitar slung over his shoulder on a leather strap. As Dylan grew up, he grew inward, communicating less with family friends and schoolmates. He lavished attention on the friend he could trust without reservation, his guitar. "I didn't go hunting, I didn't go fishing, I didn't play on the basketball team," Dylan said later. "I just played the guitar and sang my songs. That was enough for me. My friends were like me—people who couldn't make it as the football halfback, the Junior Chamber of Commerce leader, the fraternity booster, the truck driver working his way through college. I couldn't do any of those things either. All I did was write and sing, paint little pictures on paper, dissolve myself into situations where I was invisible."

Bob started to want both personal privacy and public approval. A true Gemini, the introvert grappled with the extrovert, the shy boy turned brash, the kind lad became hostile, the studious boy went bad. There was a duality in his speech. From Abe he inherited a slow and considered pattern of dealing out words, while from Beatty he inherited a constant flow of volatile emotions, a tongue that sometimes could not move as fast as the feelings he wanted to articulate. From adolescence onward, Dylan's swings of attitude were always extreme. "I hate to do the predictable," he told me, and he began to be unpredictable in his mid-teens. There he was, the introvert setting his high school on its ear with wild rock 'n' roll; the homebody turned motorcycle cowboy; the courteous youngster acting as truculent as he could; the anti-sentimentalist falling in and out of love; the son of the middle class spending most of his time with poor folk; the white boy studying black jargon.

"Where I lived," Dylan told me, "was really hillbilly country. The radio stations I used to listen to weren't local, but those on a direct route from Louisiana, right up the Mississippi River." Hibbing's station, WMFG, was square before and after Bob's cousin, Les Rutstein, became its general manager in 1958. Bob often chided Les for not programming rock 'n' roll or rhythm and blues. Bill Haley and His Comets? Not on Hibbing radio!

Until eclipsed by Elvis Presley, Haley was the most successful white rock 'n' roll musician. His work, especially "Rock Around the Clock," became known around the world through the soundtrack of the 1955 film *Blackboard Jungle*. The rock tide had been rising since 1951, when DJ Alan Freed had begun to push the new music on Cleveland radio. By 1954, rock 'n' roll had spread to major Coast stations, but WMFG ignored it. Dylan had to turn his radio on to a thin line that linked him with the farmers of Louisiana and the truck drivers of Tennessee. "'Henrietta' was the first rock 'n' roll record I heard," Dylan said. He also calls Johnnie Ray "the first singer whose voice and style I totally fell in love with."

Bob took most of his journeys down the Mississippi late at night, when the air was clearer. He often placed his radio under the covers, to keep from

> I didn't go hunting, I didn't go fishing, I didn't play on the basketball team, I just played the guitar and sang my songs. That was enough for me.

waking anyone with sounds he caught from
Shreveport or Little Rock. Gatemouth Page, a
voluble southern DJ, alternated country music
with R&B. While Haley was syncretizing the
two musics, Dylan's radio fed him both. In 1954,
McCall's Magazine editorialized about togetherness,
an idyllic portrait of American family life updating
Saturday Evening Post covers by Norman Rockwell.
For Bob, togetherness was a midnight radio show
from the South that said white and black music
got along very well. In liner notes for Joan Baez
he would write:

> *... I learned t' choose my idols well*
> *T' be my voice an' tell my tale*
> *An' my first idol was Hank Williams ...*

Hiram "Hank" Williams was "the hillbilly
Shakespeare" to millions of farmers, truck drivers,
and factory workers. Born in an Alabama log
cabin, he took his only musical instruction from
Tee-tot, a black street singer. Williams, making his
sad songs sadder, died on New Year's Day 1953,
aged just twenty-nine. If Hank Williams was the
poet, Little Richard was the pulse, a rhythm and
blues John Henry. Richard Penniman, born in
1932 in Georgia, started to sing at the age of ten
in churches and on the street. His music, and life,
swung from sacred to secular, from tabernacles to
juke joints. In the mid-fifties, Dylan enrolled as a
student of Little Richard in the radio university,
heeding his raunchy sermon: "My music is the
healing music that makes the dumb and deaf hear
and talk." Dylan, who had not met Little Richard,

Barbara Yeshe: not for long—F.N.A. 3, 4; F.H.A. 2, 3; F.B.L.A. 4; Schubert Chorus 2; Pep Club 2.

Robert Zimmerman: to join "Little Richard"— Latin Club 2; Social Studies Club 4.

Shirley Zubich: not least, but usually last— F.N.A. 3, 4; F.B.L.A. 3, 4; Masquers 3, 4; Social Studies Club 4; Pep Club 4; Girls' League 3; Jr.-Sr. Prom Committee 3; "Stag Line" production 3.

assimilated his style seven years before the Beatles did. In his 1959 high school yearbook, he listed his ambition: "To join the band of Little Richard."

Grateful for these early musical influences but impatient with himself for not having understood more, Dylan once told me: "It was just like an adolescent, you know. When you need somebody to latch on to, you find somebody to latch onto. I did it with so many people, that's why I went through so many changes. I wrote a lot of stuff like Hank Williams, but I never grasped why his songs were so catchy or so classic. As for Presley, I don't know anybody my age that did not sing like him, at one time or another. Or Buddy Holly."

Soon after Dylan had learned his way around his first guitar, he wanted a bigger, flashier instrument. He saw it in a Sears, Roebuck catalog and saved toward the twenty-dollar down payment, and nineteen dollars more to pay it off. Fearing his father's annoyance, Bob hid the new guitar until he'd paid for it. He bought as many records as he could afford without a weekly allowance. His first collection was of Hank Williams 78s. He went on to the new 45s by Little Richard, Buddy Holly and Hank Thompson. Bob gyrated from record player to guitar to the family piano, where he aped Little Richard. Now, all he needed was a band.

In 1968, Le Roy Hoikkala, a shy, slight electronics technician, told me: "I met Bob downtown one day and we got to talking about music. We were in eighth grade, and I was very much involved in playing drums. Monte Edwardson was guitar player, and the three of us got together, around 1955, in Bob's garage for some sessions. Monte played lead, Bob played rhythm and sang. We figured we had the makings of a band, and we decided to call ourselves the Golden Chords. Nobody was the leader. Bob really idolized Little Richard then. He could chord quite well on the piano. We started to get some jobs. … Whenever there was a talent contest, we would show up."

The Golden Chords played some country songs but Bob soon led the trio toward Little Richard's extroversion. Le Roy was impressed: "He would write a song right at the piano. Just chord it, and improvise on it. I remember that he sang one song about a train in R&B style. He could make sense with a song

ABOVE

"To join Little Richard:" the 1959 Hibbing High School Yearbook.

> Bob was upstairs quietly becoming a writer for twelve years. He read every book there was.
> BEATTY ZIMMERMAN

in an instant." Sunday afternoons, Bob slipped out to jam sessions at Van Feldt's little snack bar and barbecue, at Fourth Avenue and 19th Street. For months, kids filled the place, making it "the scene" in Hibbing. The Golden Chords held public rehearsals, which the young people treated as a show. Dylan's other Hibbing bands were called the Shadow Blasters, and Elston Gunn and the Rock Boppers.

Bob's parents did not overtly discourage his music-making, but they certainly couldn't share his passion. Only in hindsight did Abe and Beatty realize that, from fourteen on, Bob was inexorably drifting away from all they held dear. Abe still thought that, inevitably, Bob would complete his schooling and join the family business. "He was never detached from family or friends, but he dreamt a lot," his mother told me in 1966. "He would go upstairs and dream that he would be very famous. He was going to do something very different. How often that boy told his grandmother: 'Grandma, someday I'm going to be very famous. You are never going to have to worry about anything.' He told her he would make a lot of money and that she would never have to want for anything." On both visits to Hibbing, I repeatedly pressed Dylan's parents on the genesis of his writings.

Mother: "Bob was upstairs quietly becoming a writer for twelve years. He read every book there was. He bought only comics that had some meaning, like *Classics Illustrated*. He was in the library a lot. I don't know what authors he liked, we hardly ever discussed writers. We would just be laughing and talking. Bobby could write and he could draw. He was an artist. ... I tried to push architecture. I figured at least he could make a living. ... In my day, a poet was unemployed and had no ambition. Here we would be at the back of him with a pitchfork. 'Bobby, you have to eat.' He still doesn't eat enough. He eats to live." I asked if he ever called himself a poet: "No!" they chorused emphatically. Mother: "I never called him a poet. Sometimes, when he was planning to go to college, I would say: 'Bobby, why don't you take something useful?' He said: 'I'll take something in science, literature, and art for a year and then I will see

what I want to do.' I told him: 'Don't keep writing poetry, please don't. Go to school and do something constructive. Get a degree'."

Beatty and Abe couldn't understand why they had not then shared their son's success, even though he often sent them money. They were mystified at his saying that he ran away from their happy home. For a while they blamed his manager, Albert Grossman, for keeping them out of the picture. Beatty: "Did Albert really think that people all over the world thought Bob was an orphan?" Abe: "I told Albert: 'This can't go on forever, our hiding from the world.' I told Albert we have something to be proud of. We gave Robert his start, the encouragement he needed from the beginning."

The Golden Chords fell into disharmony as Bob became increasingly interested in black R&B. Soon he was the key figure in another nameless band featuring Chuck Nara on drums, Bill Marinec on bass, and Larry Fabbro on electric guitar, with Bob on piano, guitar, and lead vocals. In autumn 1955, the four jammed often, exchanged recordings, and listened to Bob's plans for a life in music.

After about a year, Bob and his no-name band appeared at Hibbing High's Jacket Jamboree Talent Festival. Bob was such a quiet loner that no one was prepared for the sonic onslaught, though the mountain of equipment might have prepared them. Bob had also heightened the shock by insisting that his sidemen tell no one what they were going to do. Bob wore his hair in mounds above his forehead, Little Richard style. The band worked with amplifiers at full roar, and when Bob began to sing, in a hoarse, insistent, screaming wail, "it brought as much laughter as it did applause," Fabbro told me. "The songs were drawn from the repertoire of Little Richard and Elvis, and the one title that sticks out in everyone's memory was 'Rock 'n' Roll Is Here to Stay'." Not at Hibbing High, it wasn't! K. L. Pedersen, the principal, was guiding around some education officials. The combined force of the house mics with the band's amplification was too much, and he ran backstage and cut the microphones. Bob seethed, but kept pounding his piano.

Another student eyewitness was John Bucklen: "My first impression was embarrassment.

Our little community was unaccustomed to such a performance. I think a lot of people were embarrassed too. I realize now, of course [in 1969], that there was the young Bob Dylan in his very early form. He was a little bit ahead of everyone, but he didn't seem to mind. Because he had such a fantastic confidence in his talent, he didn't care. He just said: 'Here I am. Either you like it or you don't. I know that what I've got is great'." Bucklen, one year younger than Bob, became a smooth-voiced DJ in Fond du Lac, Wisconsin. He was soon to become Bob's best friend, shadow to his light, Sancho Panza to his Quixote. "If a musical opportunity came along, Bob wouldn't hesitate to go to the right person and say what he wanted. He had an unusual way of winning people over."

Tales of the talent contest rocked the school. Charlie Miller, who taught Bob social studies, remembered him as "different, from the viewpoint that he had a mind. He certainly showed he had talent. When I later heard 'Blowin' in the Wind', I was reminded of the social compassion he had shown in our classes."

Before Elvis donned black leather, the idols of many young Americans had nothing to do with music. A few idolized the genial general who moved into the White House in 1953, but a small circle of Iron Range youths found their models in the Actors' Studio, by way of the movies. Brando's *The Wild One* and Dean's *East of Eden, Giant,* and, especially, *Rebel Without a Cause* stunned these isolated provincials. Brando and Dean forged characters who eclipsed the western hero. The new folk heroes drove a motorcycle through the stoplight of acceptable behavior. In a decade of soft American affluence with no visible frontier to challenge, nothing was better than a bike—unless it was a guitar—to symbolize the young man's dream of sexual potency, to defy his father in his "safe" car. Harley and Davidson were the Lewis and Clark of the fifties.

The best biker in town was Dale Boutang, a cowboy on wheels. He drove a Harley 74. Bob bought a Harley 45, the next smallest model. "You can't be *bad*, man, *really* bad, unless you have a motorcycle and a leather jacket," Bob used to tell his friends.

Bob wasn't content to ride, posture, and think like Dean, Brando, and Presley; he wanted to be photographed like them. He enlisted his brother with the family Polaroid. In their room upstairs, between the ages of fifteen and seventeen, Bob learned how to pose, practicing the art of concealing art. For action shots, Bob roared around the street corner on his Harley, bearing down hard toward his brother on the curb. As Bob swerved past, he yelled back: "Did you get it?"

At sixteen Bob used to tell John Bucklen, "You are my main man"—high praise in fifties patois. Bucklen's family was working-class, mainstream American. John also had that sense of being "*bad, man, bad.*" The more relaxed atmosphere around Bucklen's home appealed. Beatty insisted on a 9:30 p.m. curfew on school nights. John's family seemed grittier. John and his mother, a seamstress, had known privation. His father, a railway man, had lost a leg in a rail accident, and was a semi-invalid until he died when John was fifteen. Bucklen told me that he was a born follower, while Bob was increasingly brash and aggressive. Music bound their friendship together. John often taped Bob at the piano: "Those tapes don't have any aesthetic value at all," Bucklen told me in 1969, "but they do have nostalgic value." They loved to ad-lib on tape. "We'd get a guitar and sing verses we made up as we went along. It came out strange and weird. We thought we'd send them in somewhere, but we never did."

They had some fine times with John's sister Ruth at her house out on Highway 165, which John hears echoes of in Dylan's "115th Dream." Everyone talked of getting out of Hibbing, but Bob's hungers were insatiable. A restless quest for new people and ideas led Bob and John to Jim Dandy, a black DJ in his mid-twenties who lived in Virginia, a neighboring town. With so much cheap European immigrant labor, there were few blacks along the Iron Range. Bucklen: "We visited Jim Dandy so often because he was a refreshing change. He was a Negro, involved with the blues. He had a lot of records we liked." Jim Dandy and his wife and kids were the only blacks among Virginia's 12,000 residents. Bob heard him broadcast on station WHLB in the summer

of 1957, and searched for the man behind the voice. He and John were startled, but pleased, to discover that the DJ was black. Seeing he was with simpatico lads, Jim dropped his radio "white voice" for hip black slang. They spent hours playing old blues and R&B disks. The meetings went on sporadically for months, Bob discovering a new Iron Range that his family scarcely knew.

"One thing that always surprised me was that Bobby ever had anything to do with me, because I was from the other side of the tracks. He was a nice Hibbing boy and I was from out of town. He was rich folk and we were poor folk. He was Jewish and we were German, Swedish, Russian, and Irish, all mixed together." Echo Helstrom smoothed down a cascade of whitish blond hair with one well-manicured hand, took a long, calming puff of her cigarette, and settled into the sofa of her Minneapolis apartment. It was spring of 1968, eleven years after she had met Dylan, but to her it remained a vibrant reality from the most exciting, most tortured year of her life. "What harm will it do to get my name in a book?" she asked, rhetorically. "Perhaps I can help you understand what he was like then."

The day before, in a shack near Hibbing, Echo's mother, Martha Helstrom, a genial, matronly woman who resembled Ma Joad, had said to me: "Well, it's about time someone gave my Echo a little credit for what she did for Bob. She was hurt by the whole thing, but she loved Bob well enough to let him go. We always gave Bob the feeling he was welcome here and that Echo and I believed in him. He was restless and impatient. He didn't have enough time to get everything done. He was like a man in a hurry." David referred to Echo as a nameless girl with whom Bob had been quite involved, but whom his parents did their best to persuade Bob to drop. "She was not Jewish and she wasn't from the right side of the tracks," he said, adding, "Bobby always went with the daughters of miners, farmers, and workers in Hibbing. He just found them a lot more interesting." In 1961, Bob said: "I dedicated my first song to Brigitte Bardot." Echo looked like a Minnesota Bardot, with a touch of Pat Neal. She had full lips, pouting round cheeks. The Helstroms

named her Echo because she was born exactly fourteen years after her brother.

"It was really funny how we met. I was in the L&B Cafe on Howard Street. Bob had been playing upstairs at the Moose Lodge and he and John Bucklen came downstairs. Bob started to talk to me. Right there in the street, he began to play his guitar and sing for me." Bob wanted to show her what he could do on piano, but the lodge was locked. "Bob slid a knife in the door and broke right in to play the piano. I was probably the only girl in Hibbing who could have known what Bob was talking about. I had always been very interested in music. … I had a record player at home, but my father wouldn't let me play it. I always listened to radio. I will never forget the first time I heard Chuck Berry's 'Maybelline' on the car radio. I got all excited, but my father turned the radio off. I had to go into one of the other little shacks behind our house to listen to the radio. Sometimes I stayed up to five o'clock in the morning listening to announcers like Gatemouth Page from Shreveport. In 1957, who had ever heard of rhythm 'n' blues in Hibbing? They were still playing *waltzes*! So when Bob started talking about rhythm 'n' blues, I knew what he was talking about. I was very happy when Bob said to me: 'Why don't you come over to my house and listen to some records?'"

The Zimmermans were courteous to Echo, but kept telling Bob she wasn't good enough for him. Echo's mother was warm toward Bob, but her father, Matt Helstrom, an ailing, embittered painter and welder and a keen hunter and woodsman, didn't approve. In the afternoon, if Matt Helstrom was away, Echo and Bob would laze in front of the shack. Bob crouched on the wooden stairs with a guitar, while his golden-haired girl sat in a little wooden swing, gently keeping time with a pendulum motion. Bob improvised verses. "The songs he sang to me," recalled Echo, "were mostly rhythm 'n' blues or talking blues. He didn't repeat the lyrics the way most singers did. His phrases were always different and they almost always told a story." By 1968, the swing was rusted and weather-beaten, but it still swayed in the breeze from Maple Hill. I felt the

> ## You can't be bad, man, really bad, unless you have a motorcycle and a leather jacket.

swing was "Rosebud," the reporter's long-sought clue to lost childhood in *Citizen Kane.*

"John and Bob used to do a lot of talking blues. Sometimes they did a hillbilly take-off of a song like 'Somewhere Over the Rainbow.' They were always trying to teach and learn from each other. I believed in him when nobody else did. When he was singing to me alone, you could see the talent, but whenever he would go out to perform, the amplifiers would be up so high that you couldn't hear him." Echo followed him from one performance to another. Did he tell her that he would spend his life in music? "That was the whole plan. He didn't tell that to anybody else because he didn't have anyone but John and me to talk to. He had casual friends, but he was always secretive like that. I remember when he decided what his name was going to be. It was 1958, and he was just a junior. He came over with John Bucklen one day and said: 'I know what I'm going to call myself. I've got this great name—Bob Dillon.'"

He didn't change his name legally until 1962, and didn't even begin to use it regularly until 1959. Ethel Merman, also saddled with the ungainly luggage of "Zimmerman," simply lopped off the first syllable, remarking: "Can you imagine the name Zimmerman in bright lights? It would burn you to death!"

Bob's new name probably had two sources. Matt Dillon was the fictional invention of television writer John Meaton and producer Norman Macdonnel for the western series *Gunsmoke.* Closer to Dylan's home was a pioneer Hibbing family named Dillion; James Dillion was the town's first drayman. Although Bob registered at the University of Minnesota as Robert Zimmerman, students and friends there knew him as Dillon. He told a few friends that Dillon was his mother's maiden name. Others heard that Dillon was a town in Oklahoma. Only after he had achieved some early recognition in New York did Minneapolis friends learn that Bob was spelling his name Dylan. In the interim, he had become acquainted with the life and work of Dylan Thomas.

Echo saw why Bob distanced himself from his family: "His family was trying too hard to form him and he wasn't about to be formed in any manner. I remember how much Bob hated having to sweep up in his dad's shop. I know Bob was afraid of his father, although he never said he hit him. His parents couldn't understand his making a pile of dough with his poetry. I don't think his father gave him all that much money. I think I had more money than he had. Sure, he had all the necessities, but no spending money. That is why I had to buy him all those hot dogs." Echo had no more affection for Hibbing than Bob did.

The three friends sympathized with working-class people. Mrs. Helstrom remembered: "Bob seemed much more humble than his family. Both Echo and Bob seemed so sorry for the working people." She and Echo recalled how interested Bob was in John Steinbeck. In 1968, Echo kept his books on a shelf. "We used to talk a lot about Steinbeck. Bob was always reading something by him—*Grapes of Wrath, Cannery Row. Grapes of Wrath* gave him his strong feelings for the Depression Okies."

For the junior prom at Hibbing High, Echo bought a pale-blue floor-length gown. She kept the corsage Bob brought her until the flowers turned dry and crumbling. In the 1958 Hibbing High yearbook, Bob declared: "Let me tell

you that your beauty is second to none, but I think I told you that before. …
Love to the most beautiful girl in school." They went to the prom, outsiders
passing through the mainstream. Echo: "We were so different, we shouldn't
have even been there. We really couldn't dance. Bob was a poor leader, and I
am a poor follower. … After the prom we didn't go to any of the parties. We
just sat in Bob's car and fell asleep. We weren't like the other people at school
in any way. I just couldn't stand being like other girls. I had to be different."

By summer 1958, they had moved in opposite directions emotionally. Echo
wanted to marry; Bob wanted to travel and pursue his music, to date other
girls. Echo became increasingly possessive; Bob was restless. John, a secret
admirer of Echo, suffered divided loyalties. She spent the summer reliving
their moments together. She walked up to Maple Hill, but the view didn't
look the same alone. She sat on that swing, remembering his voice, singing.
A decade later, Mrs. Helstrom said: "When Echo plays Bob's records, she feels
she is still talking with him." John Sebastian, formerly of the Lovin' Spoonful,
once told me: "You can't get too close to Dylan. He burns with such a bright
flame you can get burned." Echo Helstrom was the first of many people who
got too close.

She saw Bob briefly in Minneapolis in autumn 1959, hoping they might
revive their romance. When the Hibbing High School class of 1959 held its
tenth reunion, two unexpected classmates appeared separately—Echo, and
Dylan, who was there with his wife. Dylan had returned for a moment of
quiet triumph, the school's most notable graduate since Francis Bellamy, who
wrote the Pledge of Allegiance to the American flag. Bob was besieged by old
friends demanding autographs. He signed one for Echo, too.

Bob was keen to begin his last year of school because he was keen to get
out. "It won't be long now," he told John Bucklen. He slid off the honor roll
three times. He experimented with drinking and smoking. During his senior
year, Bob's career plans were crystallizing. He joined a cousin's little band, the
Satin Tones, a rough-edged group that played one number on a TV station in
Superior, Wisconsin, one dance at Hibbing Armory, and one tape on Hibbing
radio. A new and lasting musical role model emerged—Buddy Holly. Bob
began to imitate Holly's sweet, naive, almost childlike voice.

Dylan and his mates could identify easily with Holly—another small-
town boy; young, slight, vulnerable. Imagine the excitement on January 31,
1959, when Holly and musician Link Wray appeared at the Duluth Armory.
Hank Williams and Dean were dead, Little Richard and Brando never came
anywhere near Hibbing, but here was Buddy Holly right up in the North
Country! Rockabilly, Tex-Mex, Little Richard songs, everything!

Only three days after Dylan had seen him, Buddy Holly too was dead. The
aircraft flying him and fellow stars Ritchie Valens and the Big Bopper crashed
in a snowstorm, heading for a gig in Fargo, North Dakota. The shock was
brutal. The death of Holly had a traumatic effect on Bob. He was no longer a
boy brimming with life as much as a young man haunted by death. He acted
like his time was limited. All the car and motorcycle accidents pointed to it.
"I was burned with death around me," Dylan said in 1965. Gretel Whitaker,
a friend from the University of Minnesota, said: "We never really expected

Marlon Brando in *The Wild One* (1953): Dylan
aped his poses, getting his brother to capture
the moment on the family Polaroid.

Bobby to live past twenty-one." By the time Bob was nineteen, he had written a mournful blues, "One Eyed Jacks," passed on to me by Minneapolis friends:

> The queen of his diamonds
> And the jack his knave
> Won't you dig my grave
> With a silver spade?
> And forget my name.
> I'm twenty years old.
> That's twenty years gone.
> Can't you see my crying,
> Can't you see my dying,
> I'll never reach twenty-one.

There was a curious footnote to Holly's death. The Fargo concert manager desperately searched for a fill-in act and found two brothers, Sidney and Bill Velline, in nearby Moorhead, Minnesota. The 2,500 kids who turned out to hear Buddy Holly heard the Velline brothers' band. The Vellines let their kid brother, Bobby, sit in. Bobby Velline told the concert manager the band was called the Shadows—a name the high school sophomore had just invented. Bobby Velline, his name shortened to Bobby Vee, soon became the bandleader. With five hundred dollars saved up from a few dances, the Shadows cut four sides for the Soma label in Minneapolis. One of those sides, "Suzy Baby," featured Bobby Vee, singing like Holly. The Shadows later searched around Fargo for a piano player. Someone suggested a kid who had spent the early summer of 1959 as a busboy at the Red Apple Cafe. "There were very few rock piano players around," Vee told me in London in 1969. "We gave Bob Zimmerman a chance to work with us, and he played great— in the key of C. His style was sort of like Jerry Lee Lewis. Bob worked two dances with us in Fargo. But we decided that we weren't really making enough money to cut in another member."

Abe and Beatty were radiant at their son's graduation. By early 1959, it had been agreed that Bob would go to the University of Minnesota, the only "acceptable" way to get out of town. Beatty reluctantly admitted there was really nothing much to keep him and gave the biggest graduation party. Arrangements moved along with only one hitch—the guest of honor wasn't coming. He was going out with the boys. His mother thought he should come for fifteen minutes, at least, because she wouldn't call off the party. "To make a long story short, he came home with us."

Were any of Bob's friends or fellow musicians invited? "No," Abe replied. "We had neighbors and family. During graduation, the kids have their own parties. All you expect the children to do is to make an appearance. Bob stayed around much longer than we expected. He didn't know half of the people who came to celebrate his graduation, but they knew him."

At midnight, Bob went out—supposedly to see some friends. In fact, he just walked the streets of Hibbing. At 2 a.m. he returned, as Beatty and a cleaning woman were straightening the house. "Wasn't it a nice party?" his

That afternoon with Bob and Leadbelly was my first real indication that Bobby Zimmerman was turning into Bob Dylan.

JOHN BUCKLEN

mother asked. He admitted it had been. The dining room table was heaped with gifts from strangers. Among them was a set of 78s of Leadbelly, who had died in 1949. The recordings of the forceful Louisiana singer, discovered in a southern jail by folk collectors John and Alan Lomax, were a revelation. With only his voice and his twelve-string guitar, Leadbelly filled Bob's head with "Rock Island Line," "Take This Hammer," and "Midnight Special." The words meant more than most pop lyrics. Bob reveled in the musical storytelling.

Bucklen: "Bob almost shouted over the phone: 'I've discovered something great! You got to come over here!'" They listened, and Bob was flabbergasted. "'This is the thing, this is the thing,' he repeated. Leadbelly was too simple for me in 1959. There was another example of Bob's being way ahead of us all. That afternoon with Bob and Leadbelly was my first real indication that Bobby Zimmerman was turning into Bob Dylan." Leadbelly led Bob to the roots of the first folk song revival of the late fifties. The attraction was brief, just long enough to open the door to folk music and whatever lay beyond.

After graduation, Bob headed down to Minneapolis to play university student. He returned perhaps a half-dozen times, on school holidays, or on trips from New York with some new triumph to report. In spring 1964, Bob made a brief appearance when David graduated from Hibbing High. The trips became more and more infrequent and, after 1964, he returned only twice, to my knowledge. There'd been postcards, and telephone calls at all hours from stray places on the road, but Bob had nearly washed Hibbing out of his mind. In 1963, Walter Eldot, Sunday features editor of the *Duluth News-Tribune*, quoted Abe: "My son is a corporation and his public image is strictly an act. … He wanted to be a folk singer, an entertainer. We couldn't see it, but we felt he was entitled to the chance. It's his life, after all, and we didn't want to stand in the way. So we made an agreement that he could have one year to do as he pleased, and if at the end of that year we were not satisfied with his progress, he'd go back to school." Later in 1963, Eldot was legman for

a *Newsweek* piece that drove Bob farther from his family, Dylan raging to his parents over the telephone about the two articles.

In the fall of 1967, Abe and Beatty visited Bob and his family in Woodstock, New York. Their famous son was no longer playing orphan. The fact that Bob had married and had a growing family was, by their standards, as much a success story as anything that had happened in the intervening years. Abe took me to dinner in New York a few days later, keen to let me know there had been a rapprochement in Woodstock. He had already begun to rewrite his own history when I first met him in 1966. No longer was he the square father who thought pop music was nonsense. Behind his shop counter, awaiting the next customer, he would study the latest copy of *Billboard*. By spring 1968, Abe was in much better spirits about Bob, but he still felt compelled to tell friends and neighbors that no one saw Bob because he flew his private jet into Hibbing late at night and took off early the next morning. The story saved the father's face and added to the son's mystique. The story of the night flights so took hold around Hibbing that some swore they had seen the plane.

In the context of late fifties parent-child relationships in a thousand Hibbings, Abe and Beatty were not exceptionally square, but their son's heightened sensibilities made them seem so. By the spring of 1968, Abe and Beatty were trying to put it all in context. Abe: "At the time, he was influencing some of the kids in a way he should not have been doing. I think he was a rebel with a cause. He wanted to do things for people, but in a speedy way. He could not seem to understand why these things, why these changes, take time." Bob had watched *Rebel Without a Cause* a dozen times. What was their reaction to the film? Abe: "I thought it was overdone. I didn't think kids were like this, to tell the truth. Either they were worse than that, or they were much better." Doesn't every kid rebel—didn't you rebel? Beatty: "We didn't rebel, we went along. We knew that our parents were doing the very best that they could for us." Abe: "We were sometimes disappointed by what our parents made us do. We complained or cried a little bit, but eventually we did what we were told."

Abe took me around the house. In the basement recreation room, where Bob's James Dean collection once lined the walls, the parents now had a gallery of their own young rebel. His parents played me old practice tapes of his various high-school bands. Bob's young, harsh voice belted out "Rock and Roll Is Here to Stay." Piles of moldering 78s and 45s stood in a corner, a cross section of the fifties. Abe steered me up to Bob's room, passing on the stairway a picture of puffy-cheeked Bob with a neat tie—his graduation picture. Abe drew out several albums of family pictures: "Here's a picture of Bobby playing bullfighter, holding a bathroom towel as a cape. He was about twelve here. These are priceless now. Here he is playing the bongo. Here is the medicine he used to take for his asthma. He doesn't have too much trouble with that now. Here's the room when it had the cowboy wallpaper. Bobby was fifteen when he posed with a cowboy hat on and a cigarette dangling out of his mouth. I sent the picture to him a while ago with his photo from the ad for *Dont Look Back* [*apostrophe intentionally omitted*]. It had exactly the same expression. Here we are at the Paul Bunyan site at the headwaters of the Mississippi. Yes, he liked those tall tales of Paul Bunyan."

Abe leafed through the memorabilia with a mixture of pride and sadness. "Here's a picture of Bobby as a Boy Scout."

"Do you think he will come back to Hibbing one day, or don't you know, Abe?" He went on leafing through the photographs. Three weeks later, Dylan went back to Hibbing for the first time in four years. Abe's son had returned to attend his father's funeral.

Abe suffered his first heart attack in summer 1966, shortly after Bob's motorcycle accident. It was a mild attack, but it forced him to cut down. However, no doctor could cure Abe of worry over his boys, of his public image as a father. In spring 1968, he had a new family problem: David's impending marriage to a Catholic. "When my boys make mistakes, they make big ones," Abe told me a few weeks before he died. The wedding, scheduled for the last week in May, was postponed.

On the morning of June 5, Abe awoke feeling weak and "strange." He stayed home, taking it easy. He was not feeling any better by the time

Beatty returned from work. A little after 5 p.m., Abe suffered a fatal heart attack, collapsing on the living room sofa as Beatty summoned their neighboring doctor. At first, Bob was reluctant to appear at Abe's funeral, lest it charge the atmosphere. He flew in alone the next day on a commercial flight. David met him at the Hibbing-Chisholm airport in drizzling rain. Bob had on the round black hat he wore on the cover of *John Wesley Harding*. He and David found the house filled with relatives and neighbors. Within minutes, Bob steered his mother and brother into a corner: "This isn't a garden party. Let's get these people out of here." Beatty explained that this was the mourning tradition. Bob insisted the family be by themselves.

David was struck by Bob's demeanor. His older brother seemed to have quietude, firmness, and serenity befitting "a fifty-year-old man." When the two discussed the funeral, David was startled by Bob's familiarity with Jewish ritual. Early on Friday morning, David and Bob went to the Dougherty Funeral Home on First Avenue. Upon seeing his father's body, Bob, previously restrained, was deeply upset. He took the death harder than either Beatty or David, as if he were caught up by all the things he and his father had never been able to say. ("I never knew my father," Bob later told Woody Guthrie's former agent.) By the time the funeral home opened to the lines of mourners, Bob, again his controlled self, stood in one corner, taking it all in. At the synagogue service, Bob wore a gray double-breasted suit with jade cuff links, a white tie, and the traditional skull cap, a final concession to his mother. He had wanted to wear his *John Wesley Harding* hat, which could have passed for the black hat worn by some pious Jewish sects. The rabbi concluded the service and most of the mourners prepared for the long ride to the cemetery in Duluth. Beatty, David, and Bob were silent most of the trip.

That afternoon, David took Bob for a drive around Hibbing in the rain. Bob let the town pass before his eyes like a long, silent movie flashback. He passed the hill where some boys had once put up a small sign: HIBBING, MINNESOTA – HOMETOWN OF BOB DYLAN. Bob told David the town looked

ABOVE

Leadbelly, discovered in a southern jail by folk song collectors Alan and John Lomax. A set of Leadbelly 78s was among Dylan high school graduation presents and were "a revelation."

like a giant funeral parlor to him. Again, David was struck by his brother's serenity, "So calm, so reserved, so clean … almost so saintly!" That night, Bob asked to see a few of his old friends. Bonn Rolfsen and Father Michael Hayes of the Catholic Church up Seventh Avenue came by. The priest had been teaching Bob's songs, and their meaning, to his students. Echo, John Bucklen, and Monte Edwardson were gone. And so was Bobby Zimmerman. A stranger in his own house, he said "he no longer felt himself the same person he had been in Hibbing."

Beatty was pleased that Bob could stay on until the following Tuesday. He urged her to sell the house and think about doing something different to readjust. They talked about the early years, and Bob assured her that she and Abe had been good parents. To the outsider, Beatty and Abe *had* been good parents. Had they acted differently, had they not resisted him at crucial points, could they have been the diving board from which he sprang? Didn't they give him the impetus to run, the cause to rebel, the materials from which to build his own special personality? The "saintly" son who came home to bury Abe was proof that he and Beatty had not failed as parents. Beatty told Bob that all the family money was frozen until the estate was settled. Bob took out his checkbook and wrote her a five-figure check. Beatty and David were staggered. She insisted: "Bobby, I don't want to deny your children anything."

"I can always do a couple of concerts," he replied.

Over the weekend, Bob slept in his father's old bedroom, and spent hours poring over his childhood memorabilia Some people around Hibbing now found him amazingly like his father: he was somewhat stern with his children, careful then with his money, reserved and conservative in manner. Could he have become what he had so long opposed?

His wife was expecting another baby, and Bob had to be on hand. On his way to the airport, he took one final swing down Howard Street, passing the window of a drugstore, where, weeks earlier, a visitor to Hibbing had been startled by the juxtaposition of two paperback books. *Dont Look Back,* drawn from the film starring Dylan, was right next to a novel called *The Runaway.*

02

THE WRONG END OF THE MISSISSIPPI

30c   no. 8

THE LITTLE SANDY
REVIEW

A TRIBUTE TO
WOODY GUTHRIE
no. 5

THE LITTLE SANDY
REVIEW

30c   FOLKLORE CENTER
110 MAC DOUGAL ST.
N. Y. 12, N. Y.

> ## He is a great artist. Dylan is a genius, that's all there is to it. He is irksome and irritating, very much the Chekhov genius. He is not more complex than most people; he is simpler. HARRY WEBER

PREVIOUS PAGES

Jesse Fuller, whom Dylan met at the Exodus in Denver, copying his use of the harmonica neck brace.

OPPOSITE

The Little Sandy Review, launched in 1959 by Paul Nelson and Jon Pankake, an early folk song magazine. These issues show Jean Ritchie and Woody Guthrie. They bear the stamp of Izzy Young's Folklore Center.

The highway was a key Dylan used to unlock one of the doors to his future. He arrived at the University of Minnesota on Highway 61, took byways, blind alleys, and detours, and left the University of Dinkytown on Highway 12.

Sometime after his abortive encounter with Bobby Vee in Fargo, Dylan ended up in a reconstructed nineteenth-century gold-mining boom town high in the Rockies, singing in a sleazy striptease joint a thousand miles from home and college. Bob and his family told me he went to Denver and Central City, Colorado, before enrolling at Minnesota. Others have placed him in Colorado in summer 1960. Maybe he was there twice. I *know* he returned in early 1964, and I was with him there in March 1966 (see *One Foot on the Highway*), when he went back to Central City.

In 1959, Bob heard from one of the Golden Chords, Monte Edwardson, that there was a lively folk music scene around Denver. He decided to try his luck there, and plunged into the coffeehouse scene. The Exodus Gallery Bar at 1999 Lincoln Street was the focal point for local beats, artists, and poets, and a sprinkling of button-down college kids. Denver's trendies gravitated to the Exodus, and Dylan tiptoed around; it seemed like the big time. One Exodus singer offered to share his flat with Bob for a few weeks. Walt Conley, a large, gentle, black man from Nebraska, had learned folk songs in the late forties from Pete Seeger and composer Earl Robinson. From Walt, Bob reportedly picked up a topical song called "The Klan." Dylan and Walt fell out over a girl, and over the sudden disappearance of a bunch of Walt's favorite recordings. Dylan told me without remorse "Yeah, I was run out of Denver for robbing a cat's house."

Two Denver performers influenced Dylan. The sweetheart of the Exodus was nineteen-year-old Denverite Judy Collins, a classically trained musician beginning what would be a long career, becoming one of the first and best interpreters of Dylan songs. Two songs Judy was singing ended up on

Dylan's first album: "House of the Rising Sun" and "Maid of Constant Sorrow" (as "Man of Constant Sorrow.") Bob also met a rollicking old gamester, the late Jesse Fuller, who often played the Exodus. Born in Jonesboro, Georgia, in 1896, Fuller fused traditional songs, blues, rural ragtime, and just plain "good-time" sounds. Dylan watched the way one-man-band Fuller held his harmonica and kazoo in a metal neck brace that allowed him to alternate between singing and riffing on his mouth harp. Dylan quizzed Fuller and learned how to play the harmonica in its distinctive holder.

Bob conceded his few performances at the Exodus and other Colorado clubs were nothing memorable. Still, he was gaining experience and credits, if little money. Colorado also gave him anonymity and a chance to romanticize. He told his family that in Denver he had been wildly appreciated. His parents still thought, as they drove him to Minneapolis, that college would wash away this music compulsion.

In 1959, some 25,000 students were attending the University of Minnesota. It was the largest single college center in America, with students and faculty accounting for 10 percent of the city population. Dylan, a small-town boy, was somewhat overwhelmed at the impersonality of his new world.

A cousin, a law student, belonged to Sigma Alpha Mu, and Bob lived briefly at the fraternity house. His first reaction to the group was negative, and he quit even before he was pledged. A counselor recalled that Bob was "hard to know, kept very odd hours, and moped a lot." The people he liked were the few folk-oriented intellectuals who lived around Dinkytown, the university business district and bohemia. One of these beatniks and dreamers was "Spider" John Koerner, a middle-class Huck Finn intensely involved in music.

"I first met Bob in the Ten O'Clock Scholar, a Dinkytown coffeehouse that later burned down," Koerner told me. "Bob just drifted in. … Bob and I both played the same sort of guitar things. He was writing some songs, but they were those folky spirituals that were popular, like 'Sinner Man.' He got very interested in those easy-rocking things of Odetta's. Dylan had a very sweet, pretty voice, much different from what it became. I don't remember Bob's talking about making it in show business. We were more interested in immediate things, in making up songs."

Campus people thought Spider John would be a star and that Dylan was the lesser talent. One of Koerner's roommates was Harry Weber, a PhD candidate in Latin literature and a ballad scholar. "When I arrived in

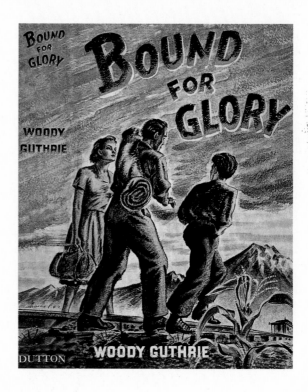

> He always went as Bob Dillon, not Dylan. … Everyone nearly flipped when he came out spelling it the way Dylan Thomas spelled his name.
>
> HARVEY ABRAMS

OPPOSITE

The Dutton
hardback edition
of Woody
Guthrie's *Bound
for Glory*. Dylan
allegedly read
the book at one
sitting and carried
it everywhere.

Minneapolis in 1955 with a guitar," Weber told me in 1966, "folk music was very much underground. The older people came from the Old Left. Their idea of folk music was a union song.

"I became friends with Koerner and later roomed with him. The first songwriter I ever heard around here was Dylan. Old Dave Morton was the earliest to write songs, but I never heard them. The first song of Dylan's I heard was 'Every Time I Hear the Spirit.' Bob didn't make much of a fuss about it. It was like the Negro spiritual he based it on, except it had a rockabilly beat. When Bob came down here in 1959, he looked pretty, fair-haired, absolutely beardless. His eyes were vaguely popping, and his cheeks were a little bit too full.

"When Dylan arrived he looked awfully small-town. He dressed in an almost finicky way. He acted very high-schoolish, very brash. He posed a lot, with his hand in his belt, his legs straddling the room. He wasn't big, of course, but he was heavy. … Almost from the start, there used to be inconsistencies in Bob's stories, but I don't think he's a liar—just a romantic.

"I met Dylan only about a month after he got here. He would come over to visit Koerner, but he would get interested in some song or technique I knew. We were living at 42 7th Street Southeast, a horrible place, sort of a three-man slum. There always seemed to be a lot of music going on. … Dylan never cared much about the battle here over tradition. Maybe he became as good as he did because that sort of thing doesn't bother him. He uses what he wants to use. In 1959, Dylan met folk singer Cynthia Gooding. After her concert we had a party, and Bob sang to her for half an hour. Cynthia was amazed. It was quite a sight, because she was somebody then."

Weber said he had "trouble with Dylan the person. It relieves my conscience to talk about Dylan the artist. He is a *great* artist. Dylan is a genius, that's all there is to it. He is irksome and irritating, very much the Chekhov genius. He is not more complex than most people; he is simpler. I was aware when I met him that he was very talented. I was not awed by him then. I am now. Awed with his ability. I don't think he was aware of his talent when he came to Minneapolis. But, wait a minute. I take that back. He walked around like a young Shelley. He was very self-confident."

Although Dylan enrolled at the liberal arts college of the University of Minnesota in September 1959, within a few months he was really at the University of Dinkytown. He was majoring in music with advanced seminars in coffeehouses, minoring in radical life-styles, doing seminars in scene-making, preparing for graduate work in Woody Guthrie. Bob's Minneapolis friends and foes formed a circle of exceptionally intelligent, colorful, talented, and perceptive characters. It mattered little what they did or where they stood on the social ladder. Take a student radical and folk song enthusiast named Harvey Abrams, whom I interviewed in spring 1966.

"Bob never really went to school, and he carried a notebook that never contained schoolwork. He was playing weekends at the Scholar, earning five dollars a night. Then, Bob Beull and I opened up a coffeehouse. We leased an old house near Oak and Washington Avenue and rebuilt it, and named it the Bastille.

"Dylan and I were pretty good friends by then. I lived in Melvin McCosh's boarding house, above his bookstore. Dave and Gretel Whitaker were also living there. Bob began to play at the Bastille weekends. I thought he was fantastic! He always went as Bob Dillon, not Dylan. The only time we saw it with the Dylan Thomas spelling was in your *New York Times* article. At school, he was registered as Bob Zimmerman, but all of his music billings here were spelled Bob Dillon. Everyone nearly flipped when he came out spelling it the way Dylan Thomas spelled his name."

Weber and Abrams emerged from the bohemian-beat-hippie scene as straight characters. Others were uncompromising, like the reigning Dinkytown guru Dave Morton, who moved to the West Coast around 1961. Morton radiated gentle, distilled wisdom, and was one of the best professors at Dylan's peripheral university. I caught up with Morton in Los Angeles in 1966. He had become a senior West Coast hipster, painting, editing *Regent*, an avant-garde literary magazine, studying the *I Ching*, and leading a folk-rock band, the New Improved Jukes Savages. "Back at

Minneapolis, I studied mathematics, but I didn't get far. Mostly, I was connected with the new All-American Gallery, at the Dinkytown firehouse building. I first met Bobby Dylan at a party there in the fall of 1959. Bob was pretty lively, funny, and nervous. His leg always bounced when he sat down."

Hugh Brown had been Morton's chum from high school in Portland, Oregon. Soft-spoken and humble, Hugh studied classics, wrote poetry, and later became a highway engineer. Brown: "I always liked Bob. At the time, I think I played guitar better than he did. We ended up living together, along with Dave and Max Uhler and several others. Living arrangements changed week to week. When we were living on Fifteenth Avenue Southeast, three blocks from Dinkytown, I would try to wake him when he had a special test, and it was always a struggle. One time he threatened to throw me down the stairs. Mostly, he played his guitar. Bob talked about taking off for New York, about going to see Guthrie. He also said he wanted to go to New York to strike it rich. At the Scholar most people liked him, even though he wasn't really very good then. He was on an Odetta kick, singing other people's songs. I don't know why Harvey Abrams says he spelled his name Dillon then, because as I recall, he spelled it Dylan here. Of course, he said a lot of things that proved to be untrue. He was trying to overcome being from Hibbing. … We all thought it was pretty funny he was going to New York to make his fame and fortune."

Two aficionados who helped put Minneapolis on the folk map were Paul Nelson and Jon Pankake. The pair started a lively, mimeographed shoestring publication, *Little Sandy Review*. While not anti-Left, it put musical ahead of social values. Sharp personal and critical arguments among Nelson, Pankake, and Dylan continued for years. *Little Sandy* was the first publication to reveal that Bob had "invented" his new personality and name.

Nelson, who went on to become an editor of *Sing Out!*, could document changes in his own perspectives through phases of Dylan's growth: "In 1959, Bob and Koerner were playing the standard repertoire, out of Josh White, Odetta, and [Harry]

Belafonte. There was no promise that Dylan or Koerner were at all exceptional—adequate guitarists and singers, but plenty of other kids were as good. Dylan seemed to learn so incredibly fast. If you didn't see him for two weeks, it would seem as if he'd made three years' progress. … He always seemed to have an unerring instinct for a great song."

Pankake, who thought Bob was "just beginning, still thinking about all his chord changes" was away from his flat for a weekend and, following campus custom, left his door unlocked. Returning, he discovered around twenty of his records missing. "My first suspect was Dylan because he had been expressing interest in my records. Tony Glover said he had been surprised to see certain records at Bob's, including some English recordings by Jack Elliott … Elizabeth Cotten, some Woody Guthrie stuff. He had very good taste. When I found out that Bob had them, Tony, Paul, and I burst in on Dylan, unannounced. I got him up against the wall, and slapped him a couple of times and let him know that I wasn't going to take this lightly. I was a pretty good actor playing a tough guy. I even had a cigar that I didn't take out of my teeth. He offered some of them to me immediately, and said he would bring the rest over the next day. Bob insisted I keep his guitar for security. … The next morning, Dylan brought the missing records back and exchanged them for his guitar. I think he apologized, but I'm not sure. He didn't come around to see me any more after that. The funny thing is that I didn't feel that there was anything malicious about his stealing the records. I think he believed that he needed them more than I did. But it expressed a certain amount of contempt for me personally, because you don't steal from people you respect."

Dylan had an unerring sense of what to take when he found his own idol, spiritual father, and musical model in Woody Guthrie. Bob would describe him in his "Epitaphs" as "the last idol/ because he was the first idol/ I'd ever met."

Guthrie was an Okie Walt Whitman, carrying his song of the open road down a modern highway, a farm-boy Carl Sandburg, a genuine hobo with dirt on his hands. Dylan's conversion

was a dramatic, explosive turning point. He swallowed Woody's early autobiography, *Bound for Glory*, as if he'd discovered the Bible. An amazing number of people are sure they told him "Bobby, you've got to read Woody." Dave Whitaker was probably the first. Gretel recalls: "After David turned Bob on to *Bound for Glory*, there was an awful lot of talk about Guthrie. … When he learned Guthrie was in hospital in New Jersey, he decided he had to go out and see him."

A few first editions of *Bound for Glory*, published by Dutton in 1943, were floating around Minneapolis: Bob borrowed Weber's copy. The last two hundred pages hadn't been cut. Bob took the book to the Scholar and proceeded to devour it. Some say he read the book at one sitting, cutting the pages with a kitchen knife. Few had seen Dylan read *anything* before.

Harvey Abrams: "The book came as a real shock. For the next two years he patterned his life after what he'd read. Bob started doing everything the way Guthrie did. For many months thereafter, everything Bob sang sounded like Guthrie. It was phenomenal. Even his speech patterns began to change. That Oklahoma twang, which became much more extreme after he left here, came into his voice. That incredibly harsh gravel sound in his voice became more and more a part of him. It really became much more than identification. He *was* the people he identified with, especially Guthrie. I don't know how, but he memorized the whole of Woody's 'Tom Joad' in just one day or two. He could really sing that ballad beautifully."

The role-playing began around summer 1960. To a few close friends, Dylan admitted that the changes grew out of a genuine need for a new identity. He simply wasn't pleased with his former bland, directionless self. Gretel: "He was very open about it. He explained that he was building a character." Tony Glover added: "He said it was an act, but only for about two days. He said: 'After that, it was *me*.'"

BELOW

Migrant Okies: Three related drought refugee families stalled on the highway near Lordsburg, New Mexico. They had left Claremore, Oklahoma to become migrant workers in California and Arizona, and were trying to get to Roswell, New Mexico for work chopping cotton. "Would go back to Oklahoma but can't get along there. Can't feed the kids on what they give you [relief] and ain't made a crop there you might say for five years. Only other work there is fifty cents a day wages and the farmers can't pay it anyways."

Bob started doing everything the way Guthrie did.
HARVEY ABRAMS

Bob wanted to contact Woody, slowly dying of Huntington's chorea.

Who was this "hero with a thousand faces"? Woody Guthrie was the archetypal American troubadour, a singer, tale-teller, poet, union man, traveler, journalist, hitchhiker, migrant worker, refugee. He was a footloose rebel, an early dropout. He became the voice of the disinherited Okies and Arkies, blown off their land by the droughts and dust storms of the thirties. He was the bard of the Depression, a walking, singing, cussing, drinking, father of the beats of the fifties, the hippies of the sixties, and some of the political activists of the seventies. Woody was compounded of equal parts of Whitman, Sandburg, Will Rogers, and Jimmie Rodgers. Guthrie was his own man, an individualist who may have used his art to serve himself, but who also served music and literature and his own people.

The Guthrie of *Bound for Glory* and on recordings was a vibrantly healthy young man. Woody was really too short to be a giant, too lean and delicate-faced to pose for heroic statues, too ungrammatical to be a poet. His voice was too flat and shaky to be a great singer. Yet, he was all of those things: a giant humanist, a heroic American culture figure, a major poet, still largely undiscovered, and a singer and composer of some of our greatest songs. Woody symbolized the strongest fibers in American folk culture—empathy with the downtrodden, dislike for sham, joy in music. This wispy hobo and self-educated ballad-maker sang, like Whitman, of himself, but his self was a type, a cross-section, a multitude. His intoxicating vision was of an America of breadth and variety, promise, and character, and he was angered when that promise "got busted" by the banks and the cranks and the phonies, by those who would rob you "with a fountain pen," as he wrote in "Pretty Boy Floyd."

Dylan identified passionately with Guthrie's rugged independence, the richness of his language, the soulful and playful ballad-making, the flood of personal creativity, the harmonica, guitar and scratchy voice. At last, he had a model after which to shape himself. At last he could say goodbye to the Hibbing middle-class. At last, he had the big

brother and spiritual father he'd longed for. Woody was Dylan's first Tambourine Man and even after he outgrew his specific image, Guthrie remained an indelible stamp upon Dylan's personality. Guthrie provided a way of looking at the world.

Woodrow Wilson Guthrie was born in 1912 in Okemah, Oklahoma, oil-boom country. A few days after his father had built a six-room house, the place burned down. A little later, Woody's fourteen-year-old sister was burned to death in a kerosene fire explosion. His mother died from Huntington's chorea. Then his father died in a fire, perhaps a suicide. Woody was farmed out to foster families. By seventeen, he was off for Galveston and the Gulf of Mexico. He joined the westward migrations of rural Okies, Arkies, and Texans. In California, some fruit ranchers paid these "Dust Bowl refugees" a dollar a ton for picking peaches. Woody was soon singing for them and doing a daily radio show for a dollar a day on Los Angeles's WKVD. Like Steinbeck's Tom Joad, hero of *Grapes of Wrath*, Guthrie was of the disenfranchised, impoverished migrants.

When Woody came east in 1939, he met and traveled with Pete Seeger, a Harvard dropout hell-bent on experience in music and in building unions. In 1940, Woody, twenty-eight, went down to the Library of Congress's Archive of Folk Culture to record his songs and life story for Alan Lomax. By the time he hit New York, Woody was the darling of the Left. It was Seeger who encouraged Woody to start *Bound for Glory*, published at the height of World War II. Guthrie also wrote at least one thousand songs, including the folk national anthem, "This Land is Your Land." Dylan's work finally brought Woody to a large contemporary audience.

When journalists stumbled on Echo Helstrom, they were convinced they'd found Dylan's "Girl of the North Country." A much likelier candidate was Bonny Jean Beecher. A sophisticate from a well-to-do family, Bonny was a rebel before she met Bob at a party in early 1960, as anxious to adventure from her WASP background as Bob was to assimilate into the mainstream. As friends tell it, Bob fell deeply in love, but for her the relationship wasn't as important. They drifted apart. When there was some triumph in New York, he'd call or write her.

> **I stood on the highway during a blizzard snowstorm believing in the mercy of the world and headed east, didn't have nothing but my guitar and suitcase.**

One Dinkytown friendship, with Dave (Tony) Glover, outlasted others. In 1963, Bob described Glover as "a friend to everything I am. Dave Glover, who I really love. Dave Glover, who feels and thinks and walks and talks just like I do." Glover helped me reconstruct Dylan's early days in Dinkytown. Glover also saw Bob at Newport, visited him at Woodstock, and attended some of his New York recording sessions. Tony was tough and taciturn, yet gentle, cool as a bluesman, and passionate about his music and friends. "Bob is not an ordinary kind of human being. There are two people, the cat I know and knew here and the one who's 'on' in public. Both of us were on the edges of the scene here, accepted, but outside because of some need or difference of our own. I guess that's the real basis of our friendship then, a feeling that there was more, something else, somewhere else." Glover, who became a music journalist and novelist, was perhaps the first musician friend who dared to criticize and advise Bob. Because it was constructive, Bob apparently took it well.

Of all the trips back to Dinkytown, perhaps the most poignant was that in July 1963, when Dylan was about to break out nationally. He told the old crowd about his travels to London, called his manager, Albert Grossman, "a beautiful guy, a genius." Then he became unabashedly sentimental about how far he had traveled: "I left this town on the highway, I think it was Highway 12. I wasn't even thinking—it was the first of my non-thinking. I never cared in the three-and-a-half or four years since I left this town about anything. Time and chance. Man, that's why I'm there now. There are a million me's, all over the United States. They are all hung up, but they can't split from where they are." He was being self-deprecating, speaking as a figurehead for song, poetry, and leadership.

Dylan's leave-taking of Minneapolis is difficult to document. Dylan often made Guthriesque exits, setting out to hitchhike, but then someone would see him a few hours later at the bus terminal. Dave Whitaker told me that right after one of those phone calls to Guthrie's hospital, Bob took off. Bob's final lines to Whitaker: "I'm leaving for New York! I'm going to see Woody!" Whitaker: "He just up and left. There was a driving blizzard in Minneapolis, but he set off for Chicago." Jerry Connors, one of the local scene-makers, distinctly recalls sitting in the Scholar at a table adjoining Dylan's and hearing Bob say: "I'm going to New York and I'm going to be somebody!" Connors says Bob left that very day. Whether he traveled along Highway 61, as he celebrated in song, doesn't much matter; Highway 61 is as much a metaphor as a highway, for it links Duluth to Minneapolis, then runs down into blues country at the *right* end of the Mississippi.

Dinkytown chums had some warning that Dylan was going. Landlords and his parents certainly didn't. Abe and Beatty went to look for Bob at his last known address. In a stark, little-furnished room, they found only a few scraps of paper. They pulled open bureau drawers, searched empty closets. He was gone, really gone, this time. Dylan said: "I stood on the highway during a blizzard snowstorm believing in the mercy of the world and headed east, didn't have nothing but my guitar and suitcase."

03

TALKING GREENWICH VILLAGE BLUES

> ## The American public is like Sleeping Beauty waiting to be kissed awake by the prince of folk music. ALBERT GROSSMAN

Dylan pulled himself out of college and, with his own hands, got a tenuous grasp on show business. Actually, he used mostly his thumbs. He thumbed his nose at formal education, thumbed his way through *Bound for Glory*, thumbed his way (metaphorically at least) to New York to see Guthrie, and thumbed through a roster of influential people in folk music and got to know them.

Intoxicated with the romanticism of Guthrie's hard traveling, he made a precipitate exit from university and from Dinkytown. Some saw him heading for the open road out of Minneapolis, other say they saw him a few hours later at the bus depot, buying his ticket east. In any event, Dylan arrived in New York in January 1961, on a cold, inhospitable day. Slush filled the streets but the heat of his mission kept him aglow. He has told of his first attack on New York in several ways. The most entertaining version is in "Talkin' New York," written in May 1961 at a truck stop west of New York.

No community better represented personal and artistic freedom than Greenwich Village. Within the Village, no scenes were livelier than off-Broadway theater and the new upsurge of folk music. The folk boom arrived just as the first thrust of rock 'n' roll had run its course. Steeped in the traditions of musical dissent, folk seemed a "purer" alternative to the overt commercialism of rock.

Albert B. Grossman, who would become Dylan's manager, once remarked ruefully that some "pure" folk singers "act as if money were heroin." Grossman, who denied that there was anything addictive about the acquisition of wealth, did a lot to convince others that they could get rich with integrity. "The American public," he told me in 1959 at the first Newport Folk Festival, which he and George Wein co-produced, "is like Sleeping Beauty waiting to be kissed awake by the prince of folk music." Grossman was one of the first businessmen not only to kiss Sleeping Beauty but also to climb right into bed with her.

Dylan had come east to meet Guthrie, but was determined to carve his own niche. His ambition was tempered by the style of the folk revival around him, a movement where the individual contributed to the whole, and "making it" also meant making a contribution. Dylan recaptured those early years of folk togetherness in a prose-poem written for the album jacket of Peter, Paul and Mary's *In the Wind* in 1963:

> *Snow was piled up the stairs an onto the street that first*
> *   winter when I laid around New York City*
> *It was a different street then—*
> *It was a different village—*
> *Nobody had nothin—*
> *There was nothin t get—*
> *Instead a bein drawn for money you were drawn*
> *   for other people—*
> *Everybody used t hang around a heat pipe poundin*
> *   subterranean coffeehouse called the Gaslight—*
> *It was at that time buried beneath the middle a*
> *   MacDougal Street …*

Dylan got off the subway in the Village in a furiously ambitious mood. He looked much as he did when he left Minneapolis, slight and spare in denim, sheepskin, and suede. Village folk virtually adopted him. He looked in need of love and attention and brought out the brother, sister, lover, or parent in everyone he met. Dylan was up to his earlobes in folk music, and soon his boots were deep into Beat poetry. Hugh Romney, the poet-comic-fantasist (later aka Wavy Gravy), was big then on MacDougal Street. Dylan arrived with little Beat vocabulary; six months later he was talking and digging everything like Romney. "Dig yuhself" became Dylan's shibboleth as it had been Romney's. The Beat poets were working alongside the folk-guitar pickers. Both were cheap labor. Dylan was artistically reborn to dual parentage. Where the romanticism of Whitman, Guthrie, Kerouac, and Ginsberg left off, the new romanticism of the city folk singers took over.

Dylan pounded his way through endless doors in 1961: the Commons, the Gaslight, the Café Wha? and the Folklore Center all faced MacDougal, a bustling main drag that made Dinkytown look provincial. Dylan acquired people with stunning speed. And no one seemed to challenge his stories of country-wide travel and friendships with legendary bluesmen.

ABOVE

Hugh Romney, who read poetry at the Gaslight and became the club's entertainment director, gave Dylan his Beat vocabulary.

Dylan's first performance in the Village that anyone recalls was at the Commons coffeehouse, a sprawling club on the west side of MacDougal. He wrote to Tony Glover about this milestone, sending a postcard of Woody Guthrie and rhapsodizing about having met Woody ("The greatest, holiest, Godliest one in the world") and Jack Elliott. When Dylan entered the coffeehouse circuit, an army of folk musicians was struggling for recognition. Folk music was tracking its country boots through Manhattan's nightlife, from the grimiest Village espresso joint up to midtown's Waldorf Astoria Hotel. Concert audiences, meanwhile, were paying attention to a sensitive young folk singer named Joan Baez. Joan, Pete Seeger, and the Kingston Trio were really uptown folk singers then—professionals with recordings, managers, and concert circuits. The Village crew that Dylan joined were unknowns trying to break through. Like at the Thirdside, a 3rd Street coffeehouse where "passing the basket" was the only way to get paid.

The Village Vanguard, under Max Gordon and Herbert Jacoby, had long fostered talent. The Weavers began at the Vanguard in 1948 and the club gave Harry Belafonte his major launch. Another nightspot dating back to the earliest days of folk's arrival in New York was One Sheridan Square. This basement club, situated at Washington Place and West 4th Street, had been Café Society Downtown. During World War II, under Barney Josephson, it had been a folk hangout, with Josh White a regular attraction. By 1960, White was reappearing in the club, revamped and renamed by Kelsey Marechal and Martin Lorin. Other regulars included Carolyn Hester and a group of Irish folkniks, the Clancy Brothers, and Tommy Makem. Since its 1958 opening, the Village Gate, run by Art D'Lugoff and his brother, Dr Burt D'Lugoff, had been heavily identified with folk music. Among those who had New York debuts there were Leon Bibb, Theodore Bikel, the Limeliters, and Odetta.

For a time, the hottest scene was in the Café Wha?, a basement boîte where manager Manny Roth was always offering jobs to young musicians who drifted in. There, one night in early 1961,

Dylan took his harmonica onstage to accompany the gifted white blues singer-songwriter Fred Neil, who attained recognition in 1969, when his song "Everybody's Talkin'" was the theme for the film *Midnight Cowboy*. (Dylan told *Rolling Stone* in 1969: "There's a movie out now called *Midnight Cowboy*. You know the song … 'Lay, Lady, Lay'? Well, I wrote it for that movie. These producers wanted some music for the movie last summer. By the time I came up with it, though, it was too late.")

Dylan has said that several MacDougal Street coffeehouses could qualify for the dubious distinction of saying he sounded like a hillbilly. The Commons and the Café Wha? seem the likeliest candidates. (Some collectors maintain that Dylan's first recorded onstage words in New York were at the Wha?: "Just got here from the west. Name's Bob Dylan. I'd like to do a few songs. Can I?") The two folk clubs that gave Dylan his real start in New York were the Gaslight and Gerde's Folk City.

At 11 West 4th Street, a few blocks east of MacDougal, just a verse or two between the old bohemia of the West Village and the emerging hippie East Village, stood a dingy six-story brownstone built in 1889, once a spray-gun factory. On the ground floor was a neighborhood saloon named Gerde's, after its prosperous nineteenth-century owner. Since 1958, it had been run by Mike Porco, a gentle Calabrian with a thin moustache, thick glasses, and a thicker accent. He was just about making ends meet at Gerde's, and had experimented a few times with bongo players and avant-garde jazz pianist-poet Cecil Taylor.

Late in 1959, Tom Prendergast, a New England businessman, and Israel G. Young, proprietor of the Folklore Center, a music shop at 110 MacDougal, were looking for somewhere to stage folk music. They agreed to run the show at Gerde's for a cut of admissions. Tom and Izzy decided to call the club the Fifth Peg, after the drone device on a banjo and, in January 1960, it opened as "New York's center of folk music." But Young and Prendergast's inexperience as producers forced them to quit the Fifth Peg after three months; they had brought in quality performers, such as the Clancys, Brownie McGee, and Sonny Terry, but lost money while Mike

> ## "The biggest excitement in popular music was coming from folk music, a revival that was to set the tempo for the early sixties.
>
> ROBERT SHELTON "

Porco, who scarcely knew a ballad from a bologna sausage, raked in profits on drinks.

In February 1960, Mike moved in on the Fifth Peg's closed Mondays with what he first called an "amateur night." I suggested he call the free-for-all a "hootenanny," a word he could barely pronounce. When Prendergast and Young pulled out, Porco assumed management and renamed the club Gerde's Folk City. After a distinguished start with Cisco Houston and the Reverend Gary Davis, a famous blind "holy blues" man, Gerde's continued a policy of booking serious folk talent.

Mike used his "hoots" as public auditions, often listening not to the music, only to the applause. One female folk singer auditioned while he was cutting sandwiches in the kitchen. "You didn't even hear me sing," she complained. "I heard the clapping," Mike said. "We can put you in for a couple of weeks." Not the least of Porco's charms was the fact that he never mastered English. He called his new club "a-Folk a-City," and once telephoned an ad to the *Village Voice* that ran for two weeks billing Anita Sheer as a "flamingo singer" rather than a flamenco singer. Another performer, who sang in several languages, was advertised as "a linguistical folk singer."

If Mike always watered down his English, occasionally his whiskey, and frequently his payments to musicians, he was usually receptive to new talent. "Give them a chance" was his working motto, while "the newer the cheaper" was his fiscal policy. When, in March 1961, one of his regular customers, Mel Bailey, urged him to give Bobby Dylan a chance, Mike showed interest. He liked Bobby, but was afraid he was too young, but a Dylan "concert" for the NYU folk club on April 5 made a persuasive "credit." Finally, Mike had a two-week opening for Bob beginning April 11 on a bill with John Lee Hooker, a Mississippi bluesman who had been working in Detroit for years. It was Dylan's first real job in New York, and he was ecstatic.

Mike gave Bob some of his kids' old clothes and then took him to the American Federation of Musicians to get a union card—he had to join to play. "The secretary, Max Aarons, gave Bobby an application, and I put up the money for his initiation. … They asked how old he was and at the time he was only nineteen, I think. The union man says if you are not twenty-one you should bring your father in to sign the papers. Bob said his father and mother were not around. So the union man looks at me and asks: 'Well, what are we going to do?' I understood that his mother and father were in a different state, and also I had the feeling that he had run away. So I signed the papers as Bobby's guardian, the first contract he had. Bobby held on to that book with the membership like it was the Bible. On the way out, I said to him: "Bobby, now you have to go for the cabaret permit." He had to have some pictures taken. We went into one of those Sixth Avenue subway photo machines. His hair was kinda messy, so I asked him if he wanted to comb his hair. Bob said: 'I don't ever comb it.' So, I gave him my comb, but he looked in the mirror and hesitated. … I think that even then he was thinking about his image. He combed it a little bit, anyhow, for the picture, and I gave him two dollars to get the cabaret card. He came back to the place and he was as happy as if he had won the sweepstakes. 'Mike,' he said, 'I've got the card!' Was he happy! He was a good-natured kid."

Mike said he paid Bobby a little more than the union scale of ninety dollars a week, plus the old clothes, sandwiches and drinks. Bob thought only about having his name on a New York bill with John Lee Hooker, one of the great bluesmen. His elation soured as he sang for noisy drunks and heard the carping of jealous musicians, but his coterie of friends and fans kept growing. Bob sensed how much more he had to learn about performing, how much harder he would have to develop his songs. Not a single official recording surfaced. He was stung that I, then the *New York Times* reviewer, had been so busy listening to Hooker and interviewing him that I never heard his own sets.

For most of the summer of 1961, Dylan was everywhere in the Village, impatient to be seen, to impress important people, to learn. He moved through New York and Boston folk circles absorbing everything he heard and saw, spying for his ambitious masterplan. While Folk City didn't

immediately lead to jobs or a recording contract, he could more easily step on to Village stages to accompany featured singers. He became a sought-after backing harmonica player and guitarist. In mid-1961, he was a fixture at the Folk City hoots, developing amusing stage tricks.

The two musicians who most attracted Bob were Dave Van Ronk and Jack Elliott, arguably the best Village folk singers. Elliott was the living, breathing reincarnation of Woody, a citybilly of whom Guthrie once remarked: "Jack Elliott sounds more like me than I do." Van Ronk was a white urban intellectual who masterfully interpreted black songs and blues. Their impact on Dylan was enormous, a bridge to the past.

Van Ronk was the musical mayor of MacDougal Street, a tall, garrulous, hairy man of three-quarters,

or, more accurately, three-fifths Irish descent. Topped by a cascade of light-brownish hair and a leonine beard, he resembled an unmade bed strewn with books, record jackets, pipes, empty whiskey bottles, lines from obscure poets, finger picks, and broken guitar strings. He was Bob's first New York guru, a walking museum of the blues.

Dylan outgrew the friendship with Dave and his wife, Terri Thal, but still returned to see them. At times Van Ronk was cynical, because Dylan had taken so much of what he had taught him and made a fortune with it. But he was more often philosophical: "The part of Dylan that was the sponge could function on all eight cylinders. He gets what he can and then discards it. This is why Terri and I are not Bob's best friends anymore. He got whatever he could absorb here, and he moved

ABOVE

Izzy Young, owner of the Folklore Center, leads a rally in Washington Square Park on April 9, 1961, protesting Parks Commissioner Newbold Morris's banning of folk music in the Park.

much a product of the Beat generation," Van Ronk replied. "Dylan really does belong in a rack with Kerouac. You are not going to see any more like him. Bobby came into beat poetry just at the very tail end. He towers above all of them, except perhaps Ginsberg. But Bob was a latecomer and will have no successors, just as his namesake had no successors."

Did Dylan ever say he admired Dylan Thomas? "He assiduously avoided it. I think the reasons are obvious. I did come on to Bob about François Villon. I also told him about Rimbaud and Apollinaire. I once asked Bobby: 'Have you ever heard about Rimbaud?' He said: 'Who?' I repeated: 'Rimbaud - R-I-M-B-A-U-D. He's a French poet. You really ought to read him,' I said. Bobby kind of twitched a little; he seemed to be thinking about it. He just said: 'Yeah, yeah.' I raised Rimbaud with him a couple of times after that. Much later, I was up at his place. I always look at people's books. On his shelf I discovered a book of translations of French symbolist poets that had obviously been thumbed through over a period of years! I think he probably knew Rimbaud backward and forward before I even mentioned him. I didn't mention Rimbaud to him again until I heard his 'A Hard Rain's a-Gonna Fall,' his first symbolist venture. I said to Bob: 'You know that song of yours is heavy in symbolism, don't you?' He said: 'Huh?'"

One Sunday, probably in early February 1961, Bob came face to face with Woody Guthrie, then ravaged by Huntington's chorea. Woody had written eloquently in *Born to Win* of the way the illness had affected his mother. By November 1954, Guthrie was writing from Brooklyn State Hospital about his own ailment, and by May 1956 he had been moved to the New Jersey state hospital in Greystone Park for better treatment. His condition deteriorated, but he could still have outings to the Village. On Sunday, July 26, 1959, folk musicians, headed by Ralph Rinzler, John Cohen, and Lionel Milberg, gathered some two dozen friends and fans to greet Woody at Washington Square Park. Surrounded by young singers, Woody stretched out on a balding patch of grass fifty yards from the fountain and called out for some of his own songs

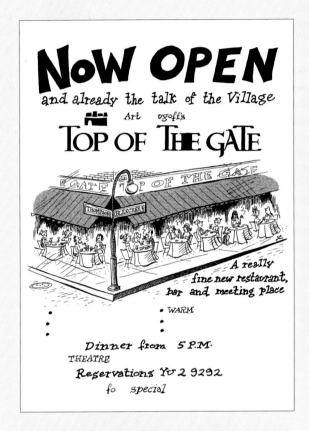

NOW OPEN
and already the talk of the Village
Art D'Lugoff's
TOP OF THE GATE

A really fine new restaurant, bar and meeting place

• WARM
•
•
•

Dinner from 5 P.M.
THEATRE
Reservations YU 2 9292
fo special

ABOVE RIGHT
The Village Gate, on the corner of Thompson and Bleecker Streets, was opened by Art D'Lugoff in 1958. *Jacques Brel Is Alive and Well and Living in Paris* opened there in 1968—the sign is still outside.

on. He did the same thing with Joanie [Baez], but there was an element of professional opportunism there too."

Dave was less jarred than most watching Dylan catapult to fame. The Van Ronks had their own lives. Dylan could be relatively free with them. Dave and Terri spent a lot of time with Bob when they lived on 15th Street and after their move to Waverly Place, across the street from me. Terri became his first business manager, arranging most of his bookings for about eight months.

On topical songs, Dave continued: "He was always a very good barometer, very sensitive to mood. But when it comes to analyzing the content of moods, he simply never had the patience. He doesn't care." How can so intellectual a writer as Dylan be so anti-intellectual? "Bobby is very

OPPOSITE

The Café Wha?
on MacDougal
Street where
some believe Bob
Dylan made his
New York debut.

and others he loved. Woody—gaunt-cheeked, gray circlets of hair tumbling over his creased forehead—indicated how much he enjoyed hearing his own music from young musicians. To me and others there, he was already sick beyond hope.

In summer 1960, folksingers Logan English, the Clancy Brothers and Tommy Makem, Molly Scott, and Martin Lorin held a special day for Woody at One Sheridan Square. On October 23, 1960, when his son Arlo Davy was marking his thirteenth birthday, Woody was brought to a Second Avenue dance studio. I tried to talk to Woody, but could not get through to him. At each outing we could see Woody failing. Soon he could no longer travel, even into Manhattan. A pair of middle-aged folk enthusiasts, Robert and Sidsel Gleason, who lived in East Orange, not far from Greystone Park, started Sunday gatherings for Woody.

At one, Dylan, who frequently stayed with the Gleasons, finally met his first and last idol. He found the writer who was once "bound for glory" now a suffering shell. Guthrie's hands quivered, his shoulders shook involuntarily, and he spoke only in thin, unintelligible rasps. He could show appreciation, summon a tentative smile, indicate slightly that he had heard what was being said to him.

There was another dying man in the room. Cisco Houston, Guthrie's longtime sidekick, was making his final visit to Woody. For nearly two years, Cisco had been living with inoperable cancer and, by early 1961, he had to stop working. Cisco had been a fixture at Folk City and Mike Porco had done his best to make him feel he could always get a free drink to ease his pain. That day, Woody sat propped up with pillows on the sofa as Cisco tried to tell him that they had both neared the end of their hard traveling. Jack Elliott tried to keep sadness from overcoming everyone, so he and the Gleasons focused on the youngest person in the room, "that nice kid," Dylan. Whether awed by the company or depressed by the "smell of death," Dylan held back. As Elliott described it to me: "Whenever I was around Woody in those days, Bob was there. Funny, Bobby sort of hung back in the shadows, just watching everything, just listening. Bob was shy then, you know. He still

is. But, right off, I could see that Bob was very much influenced by everything about Woody. Bob probably felt he could get through more than I could, but I knew Woody so well that we would talk to each other without words. But it was the same with Bob. He told me he had the 'feeling' of talking with Woody that went beyond words. I knew then what he meant. Those were the days, when Bob was sort of commuting between East Orange and various New York sofas." Jack played and sang for Woody, and Bob played a tune or two. He wrote "Song to Woody" right after that first Sunday visit.

Did Jack resent Bob's success? Elliott munched on that awhile. "He had a tremendous energetic drive for success that I've never had. If he was tramping on anyone's toes to get where he was going, he could have tramped on mine, but he didn't. I suppose I could have made it," said Jack, looking over my shoulder. "It doesn't make me jealous, it just makes me hate myself. It's funny, you know, but for a while Bob Dylan was often known as 'the son of Jack Elliott.' Sometimes I would introduce 'Don't Think Twice' or some other song to the crowd: 'Here's a song by my son, Bob Dylan.' I suppose I taught Bobby a few of my songs. … But I also remember when Bob sang some of the grooviest hobo songs in the style of Jimmie Rodgers, like 'The Baggage Coach Ahead.' There was some of that sad spirit in Bob's song about Hibbing, you know, 'North Country Blues.' He hummed it to me once in a taxi. I just thought it was about a deserted mining town; I didn't realize till later that it was about Hibbing."

Jack was proud that Dylan had sat in on his first recording on Vanguard, adding a touch of bronchial harp on the old gospel tune, "Will the Circle Be Unbroken?" Bob used one of his recording pseudonyms, Tedham Porterhouse. One of the ironies of their relationship was that Bob didn't immediately realize that Jack was a citybilly. Around March 1961, Dylan was in the Figaro coffeehouse with musician-publisher Barry Kornfeld and Van Ronk. When they referred to Elliott's being a Jewish cowboy from Brooklyn, Van Ronk said, "Bobby nearly fell off his chair laughing. It seemed to strike him much funnier than it did

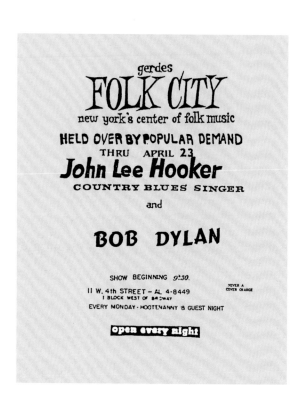

Club 47, and acquired fans and friends. Betsy Siggins, the 47's hard-driving talent coordinator, was the den mother of the Boston folk clan, and she readily adopted Dylan. He befriended the bearded, uncommonly warm Eric Von Schmidt, a commercial artist as passionately interested in folk song as were the careerists, as smitten with the blues as Van Ronk, and almost as gravelly voiced but considerably less didactic.

One Boston couple helped Bob land his first recording contract. Carolyn Hester and her then husband, Richard Fariña had moved to Boston because they found it less rancorous than New York. I had introduced Fariña to Carolyn at the White Horse Tavern in the Village and, after a whirlwind thirteen-day courtship, they married. They got to know each other afterward around Boston, and in Europe and North Africa. Later, when Dylan was involved with Joan Baez, he and Fariña met again after Richard married Joan's sister, Mimi. He and Carolyn loved Bob's harmonica playing. In September, when Carolyn cut her first recording for Columbia, she asked Bob to join her sessions. Because Dylan showed up in the right moment, he too won a recording contract.

With Boston on side, Dylan returned to New York for more intensive electioneering. He oscillated between the Gaslight, Folk City, the Commons, the Folklore Center, the bar of the Mills Hotel, the Kettle of Fish, and the White Horse. Sometimes he joined me at McGowan's after the Horse closed. He always carved out hours for practicing, listening to records, and writing songs, but mostly he was a street person, hanging out. His New York friendships multiplied. John Herald, lead singer of bluegrass group the Greenbriar Boys found Bob easy to be with. John Hammond Jr., a gifted young white blues re-creator, also became a pal. He occasionally briefed his producer-father on promising talent. Len Chandler and Dylan became close around this time. Len was not one bit reticent or repressed. Even when things were tough for him, as a black musician, and they were for years, Len had dash and bravado, and he loved a put-on as much as Dylan did. He and Len walked around a cityful of blocks for many a smoke.

us, because we never assumed anything else about Jack but that he'd been a self-styled cowboy. It was then, two years before *Newsweek* revealed Bob's own background, that I knew that Bobby too was an actor. He never said anything—he just laughed till I thought he would burst."

Van Ronk, Guthrie, and Elliott were only three faces from a crowd. By autumn 1961, Dylan knew so many people you'd think he'd been on the East Coast five years.

Having lined up the New York electorate, Dylan attacked the vital precinct of Boston and neighboring Cambridge, the hub of northeastern college life. This was Newport Folk Festival turf, where Baez had started. Music dominated the less frenetic scene along the Charles River. In June 1961, Dylan got a three-day job at Cambridge's

> ## "
> **Hi, I'm Bob Dylan. You said I should call you if I got a job. Well, I got a job. I'm at the Gaslight for a week.**
> "

COVER CHARGE
MON. — THURS. —
FRI., SAT., SUN.—

GASLIGHT CAFE

World Famous For Best Entertainment in The Village

The Gaslight Cafe

" . . . THE GASLIGHT CAFE HAS SPAWNED MORE GENUINE FOLK MUSIC, BLUES, AND SCENE-DISSECTING HUMOUR THAN ANY OTHER PLACE IN NEW YORK . . . "

J. R. GODDARD
THE VILLAGE VOICE

THE HIGHWAYMEN SPEAK OUT

We are often accused of being "commercial", and, to the extent that nearly everything that "sells" is commercial, we freely admit it.

However, here at the Gaslight, which has nurtured so many of America's finest folk performers, we have found a sympathetic and understanding atmosphere in which to continue our own particular quest.

Why?

Because at the Gaslight, the management and patrons (those patrons include some rather formidable personalities as well as "regulars" and off-the-street pleasure seekers) seem to become infected with the genius of the Gaslight:

A WILLINGNESS TO LISTEN TO WHAT ONE HAS TO SAY HONESTLY AND TO JUDGE HIM ON HIS OWN TERMS.

We consider the Gaslight our New York Home.

AND THE-GASLIGHT

In a recent article in the Village Voice I wrote

" . . . The Gaslight Cafe has spawned more genuine folk music, blues and scene-dissecting humor than any other place in New York . . ." That statement still stands. Of course the Gaslight's history far predates me, going back to the Roaring Twenties when it was a speakeasy, and when famous Bohemians like Maxwell Bodenheim and Jake Spencer were among its constant patrons. My time came much later — February of 1959 to be exact — when a great new Gaslight era began.

Jack Kerouac, Allen Ginsberg, Gregory Corse— those were the talents who began reading poetry in the Gaslight that winter, to establish a whole new coffee house trend on MacDougal Street. The names of the performers who came after them make an impressive list. On the folk music side there's Tom Paxton, Dave Van Ronk, Len Chandler, Noel Stookey of Peter, Paul, and Mary — while Peter Seeger, Bobby Dylan, Jack Elliot, Ian and Sylvia and others have sung there on regular gigs or guest sets. Then come the poets like John Brent, Hugh Romney, Steve Tropp— or the great comics like Bill Cosby or Adam Keefe — and then the list swells beyond belief. In fact the Gaslight seems to have no entertainment limits. Famed for molding new talent, never afraid to try out the new or controversial, its legend will continue to grow with the coming exciting years.

J. R. GODDARD

For Reservations call: YU 9-3759

ABOVE

An early sixties Gaslight handbill featuring a potted history of the club.

I first encountered Dylan at a Monday night hoot at Folk City in June 1961. Bob was doing his musical shaggy-dog story, "Talkin' Bear Mountain," inspired by routines that Noel (Paul) Stookey, later of Peter, Paul and Mary, was doing at the Gaslight. Bob looked like a European street singer or tumbler. He bobbed and swayed, played with his black corduroy Huck Finn cap, made faces, winced, and joked his way through the ridiculous narrative. I walked over to Pat Clancy, the Irish folk singer, and said: "Hey, Pat, you have to catch this kid!"

Pat turned from his Jameson's to watch Bob. "Well, what have we here?" he exclaimed, half-curious and half joyful. When the enthusiastic audience released Bob from the stage, I told him how much I liked his work. He appreciated my appreciation. I told him when he had his next job to call me and I'd try to review him in the *Times*. "I sure will, I sure will," he replied. "I think you missed me when I was here last April."

A week or two later, my phone rang and a thin, nasal voice said: "Hi, I'm Bob Dylan. You said I should call you if I got a job. Well, I got a job. I'm at the Gaslight for a week." Several days later, I arrived at the Gaslight to see the regulars listening to Van Ronk and Dylan. At his usual table in the rear was Albert B. Grossman, who often held court in coffeehouses. He usually smoked a king-size cigarette the way an oil sheik would hold a hookah, making a circle of his thumb and forefinger, slightly crooking his little finger, and blowing the smoke out slowly through his hand. I told Dylan the gig was too short to write up, but

I introduced him to Albert, saying I thought this kid was going to be the next sensation. Grossman, as usual, said nothing. After Dylan left our table, Grossman asked what I thought of Van Ronk. I was enthusiastic but I predicted that Dylan would go further. Grossman smiled, a Cheshire cat in untouched acres of field mice.

The Gaslight was then owned by a wild-looking bohemian, John Mitchell, who had fought many legal battles against police and fire authorities who had cracked down on the MacDougal Street coffeehouses. Mitchell found Dylan especially droll. Although Dylan was frequently nostalgic about the Gaslight, he also made fun of his first job there. His Gaslight stint ended inconclusively. Grossman said nothing. I hadn't written a word about him. Bob kept working at his music, at his western speech. Sometimes his mangled dialect made words virtually indistinguishable. He started to mumble about "ramblin' and tumblin' with his coat collar turned up high."

Dylan rambled and tumbled into his first New York concert appearance and radio broadcast on Saturday, July 29, 1961. The marathon was run by a new FM station, WRVR, operated by the Riverside Church. To inaugurate the station's live-music project, Izzy Young and Bob Yellin mobilized folk musicians. In those days, at a call for folk talent, youngsters like Tom Paxton and Molly Scott, and old-timers like the Reverend Gary Davis and blues singer Victoria Spivey, would rush to perform, even without pay. The studio audience was as restless and partisan as a high school assembly.

There were workshops on the blues, an Eastern Mediterranean segment organized by Jack Goddard of the *Village Voice*, and showcases for various banjo styles. No big-name stars, but the show was an impressive display of available talent around town. Midway through the afternoon, a slight musician who sang, looked, and twanged like Woody Guthrie made his way to the microphone. Dylan, with his harmonica in a holder improvised from a metal coat hanger, was on for five quick songs, joined on some by Elliott and bluesman Danny Kalb. In the *Times*, I briefly described Dylan's style as a "curiously arresting, mumbling, country-steeped manner." Dylan's little stint received warm applause, his circle making enough noise to simulate a crowd.

After he left the stage, he was introduced to a seventeen-year-old, wide-eyed, long-haired beauty named Suze Rotolo, and began two years of an ecstatic, erratic romance. Dylan's reputation was growing as another Jack Elliott or Woody Guthrie, yet recording seemed the only doorway to national recognition. In late summer, a bright pair of Village girls, Sybil Weinberger, who worked in TV production, and Suze's older sister, Carla Rotolo, then personal assistant to Alan Lomax, suggested a demo-tape of upcoming Village folk singers.

Because of the urgings of the Dylan coterie in general, Carla in particular, and my all but guaranteeing that I would review the show, Mike Porco booked Bob into Folk City again for two weeks: SEPTEMBER 25 THRU OCTOBER 8: GREENBRIAR BOYS, PICKING & SINGING THRU BLUEGRASS WITH THE SENSATIONAL BOB DYLAN. The Greenbriar Boys (Ralph Rinzler, Herald, and Yellin) were city

bluegrass wizards. They were not an easy act to follow, but Dylan followed superbly.

During those two weeks, he alternated between three costumes, each seedier than the next. His Gibson guitar had a song-sequence sheet pasted on its upper curve, and his harmonica holder hung around his neck. He looked studiously unkempt and very slight and frail—until he began to sing. His pinched, constricted voice seemed to be fighting its way out of his throat like a captive breaking jail. It was a rusty voice, suggesting Guthrie's old recordings. It was

etched in gravel, like Van Ronk's. It sometimes crooned a bit, like Elliott's. Yet it was also a voice quite unlike anyone else's. You didn't think of it as something beautiful or sinuous, but as something that roiled up from the heart. He didn't sound a bit citified, but more like an old farmhand folk singer. Most of the audience liked Dylan those two weeks, regarding him as a masterly ethnic singer, but some thought he was just a bad joke.

In the background were the usual Folk City distractions. Bartenders clinked and poured as if starring in TV commercials. The cash register rang. At the bar a few drunks were gabbing while others tried to silence them. Dylan was all concentration. The audience responded more to Dylan's wit than to his slow, serious, intense material. Audience reaction led him to play Chaplinesque clown. He closed with his own "Song to Woody," suspensefully built to keep attention focused on each new line. After his set, we went back to the Folk City kitchen for his first press interview. The answers came fast, but I had a feeling that he was improvising and concealing.

Bob went on for another set. I told Carla that it had been a good interview and that I really loved his work and manner. But, I told her, I had the strange feeling he was putting me on. I told Carla to tell Bob there was a difference between kidding around with a Village guy and talking for publication. Minutes after Dylan's set Carla huddled with Bobby, and then we continued the interview at a table in between songs by the Greenbriar Boys.

"Listen," Bob told me, "I'm giving it to you straight. I wouldn't tell you anything that isn't true." Did he want me to call him Bobby Dylan or Bob Dylan? He thought that one out, as if he were about to sign a contract. Half aloud, he repeated the two names to himself: "Bob Dylan, Bobby Dylan, Bob Dylan, Bobby Dylan. … Make it Bob Dylan! That's what I'm really known as," he declared confidently. I wrote the review, which appeared in the *Times* on Friday, September 29, 1961. It said in part:

> A bright new face in folk music is appearing at Gerde's Folk City. Although only twenty years old, Bob Dylan is one of the most distinctive stylists to play in a Manhattan cabaret in months. … Mr. Dylan's highly personalized approach toward folk song is still evolving. He has been sopping up influences like a sponge. At times, the drama he aims at is off-target melodrama and his stylization threatens to topple over as a mannered excess. But if not for every taste, his music-making has the mark of originality and inspiration, all the more noteworthy for his youth. Mr. Dylan is vague about his antecedents and birthplace, but it matters less where he has been than where he is going, and that would seem to be straight up.

This was followed by four laudatory paragraphs about the Greenbriar Boys. As good as they were, Dylan seemed to be the news. By chance, the entertainment section had a canyon at the top of one review page. Across three columns ran the headline: BOB DYLAN: A DISTINCTIVE STYLIST. A rough photo of Dylan with his hat, his tie, and his big guitar got three inches of space. The layout, the picture, and the headline, trumpeted Dylan even louder than my story.

Reactions couldn't have varied more. Very few musicians were pleased. Elliott read the notice aloud in his best Dylanesque voice to a few drinkers at the Dugout on Bleecker Street. Van Ronk, cool but gulping hard, told me I had done "a very,

LEFT

Carolyn Hester's third album, but her first for Columbia. It was recorded as Dylan was fulfilling the Gerde's residency that would launch his career. He played on the album, which was produced by John Hammond and featured Bruce Langhorne, with whom he would also work.

OPPOSITE

Dylan in the Columbia Studios during the sessions for his debut album in November 1961. Suze Rotolo was with him.

very fine thing." Pat Clancy and his brother, Tom, said, "Bobby has a lot of talent. He deserves to go places." Izzy Young said he had discovered Dylan months earlier than anyone. Much of the Village music coterie reacted with jealousy, contempt, and ridicule. To a man, the Greenbriar Boys were hurt that this "kid" had eclipsed them. Fred Hellerman, a songwriter and arranger, formerly of the Weavers, was openly derisive: "He can't sing, and he can barely play, and he doesn't know much about music at all. I think you've gone off the deep end!" Manny Greenhill, Baez's kindly manager, said my review was "talking about Bobby in a year or two, not now." Most enthusiastic, however, were Carolyn and Richard Fariña. They liked Bob, personally and musically, and he was scheduled to play on Carolyn's upcoming recording. The non-musician fans—the MacKenzies, the Gleasons, Carla, Sybil, Suze—were all delighted.

Dylan showed up at Folk City that Friday night stunned and shaken. There was a very big turnout. Bob looked uncertain that he could deliver, now that the order had been placed. And at the fourth night of his gig, Bob had an even more engrossed audience.

During that evening, Dylan steered me to a quiet corner and said: "I don't want you to tell anybody about this, but I saw John Hammond, Sr this afternoon and he offered me a five-year contract with Columbia! But, please, man, keep it quiet because it won't be definite until Monday. I met him at Carolyn's session today. I shook his hand with my right hand and I gave him your review with my left hand. He offered to sign me without even hearing me sing! But don't tell anyone, not one single soul! It could get messed up by someone at the top of Columbia, but I think it is really going to happen. Five years on Columbia! How do you like that?"

Each participant in Dylan's meeting with Hammond told it differently. A synthesis indicates that Hammond acted on instinct and reputation more than any objective proof of Dylan's talent. Yet Hammond had the experience to trust his instincts. Carolyn Hester's first recording for Columbia was a step forward for the young Texan singer, but proved an even bigger break for Dylan, who was just a walk-on with a mouth harp.

Dylan's version was simply that he handed Hammond the *Times* review and went around the room doing his harmonica business. By the end of the session, at which Bob had not sung one note, Hammond said that he had heard a great many good things about Dylan from his son and others and wanted to sign him to Columbia for a "standard" contract—one album—with options to do four more LPs for the next four years. Fariña generally substantiated this account, although he told me that he had huddled with Hammond during the session to say that Dylan was a first-rate singer and songwriter.

Hammond was one of the great jazz producers, the man who discovered Billie Holiday and was a close associate of Benny Goodman in the thirties. He had also been closely identified with Count Basie, Teddy Wilson, Benny Carter and the kings of boogie-woogie piano, Meade "Lux" Lewis, Albert Ammons, and Pete Johnson. A wealthy Ivy Leaguer devoted to jazz and black musicians, he'd organized the "Spirituals to Swing" concerts at Carnegie Hall in 1938 and 1939; they were a preview, by thirty years, of all the elements that would cross-fertilize rock. He was always uneasy about Dylan's assertion that he offered to sign him without first hearing him sing.

Hammond met Dylan at a rehearsal at a West 10th Street apartment the Fariñas were borrowing. "I felt Bob was a poet, somebody who could communicate with his generation," he said. "I remember the first album cost something like $402 because he was the only guy on it, no arranging costs, no musicians to pay. While he was doing his second album for us, he came up to me and asked

> ## He can't sing, and he can barely play, and he doesn't know much about music at all. I think you've gone off the deep end!
>
> FRED HELLERMAN

ABOVE

Dylan playing
the harmonica
as Karen Dalton
and Fred Neil
duet, Café Wha?,
February 1961.

their relationship was tempestuous, clouded by her mother's efforts to split them up. Many of the songs were clearly for her, and the changes he made in traditional lyrics showed how strongly he wished to express himself to and about her. Dylan remained outwardly cool, putting down most of his songs in less than five takes. Hammond was delighted to be working with a kid who knew so much about the blues. Dylan told me the next day that while he was taping "Fixing to Die," an old black janitor who was cleaning up the hall stepped into the studio to listen. The tragic old lament froze him in his tracks, and the janitor leant on his broom, watching and listening. Bob never forgot it, for it impressed him more than anything Hammond said. Bob knew then that he could get a lot more people to listen.

Despite what Hammond said later about the limits of Bob's guitar, harmonica, or mic technique, at the time he was openly rapturous about the album. Dylan's guitar work was strong for a twenty-year-old's debut album. His harmonica work may not have been virtuoso, but it gave the album some of its flavor and texture, weaving the fabric of voice and guitar together. It helped stimulate the resurgence of interest in blues harmonica in the early sixties. Dylan's understanding of black blues remains the dominant impression of the album.

Hammond sent me the test pressings so that I could write the liner notes under the pseudonym of Stacey Williams, a name I pulled out of a hat. There was an unwritten rule, constantly broken, that members of the *Times'* music department should have nothing to do with the production of recordings they might review. When I told Dylan about the ruse he was delighted, but continued his far larger game of concealing his Hibbing background. We agreed that if anyone should ask who Stacey Williams was, Bob would "just mumble something about some old jazz and blues guy who wrote things for Columbia Records."

To prepare his official story, Dylan came to my pad one afternoon in December 1961 and spoke volubly and quickly, never giving any indication of manipulation of facts. He was keen to praise his sources and influences.

Turning to his official biography, Dylan was

me about Albert Grossman, who wanted to sign him. I said we'd been on the board of the Newport Festival together and I thought I could work with him. I found out later I couldn't."

Once he began to do well, Dylan the performer was the object of both instant love and instant aversion. With each new success, followers and detractors grew in number. There were converts, of course; some who had laughed at him went on to idolize him. Envy even reverberated back from Minneapolis, where folk circles were aghast at both his *Times* review and his Columbia contract. The pressures that later nearly destroyed him began that last week in September 1961. Could he live up to public praise? Could he ride out jealousy? He developed so quickly that by the end of his two-week stand at Folk City he was a stronger, more secure performer. Very few people felt lukewarm about Dylan; they either loved or hated him.

The first album, simply entitled *Bob Dylan*, was recorded at three sessions in November 1961. After a brief run-through, Bob and Hammond were ready to move into Columbia Studio A on Seventh Avenue. For Hammond, this was almost effortless. All he needed was his singer-instrumentalist, an engineer, and himself. Dylan brought his talent, and the girl with the long brown hair.

Suze sat at the sessions in quiet admiration yet

still not prepared to go far in discussing his early days. He said he had graduated from high school in Hibbing, "way up by the Canadian border." For a spell before graduating, he went on, he lived in Sioux Falls, South Dakota, and Gallup, New Mexico. "I went to the University of Minnesota on a scholarship, but I left after six months. I didn't agree with school. I flunked out. I read a lot, but not the required readings." Of his pilgrimage east, Bob said: "I headed for Greystone Hospital to see Woody. I talked with Woody, and it was an experience I'll never forget. Now, when I get depressed, I visit Woody in Brooklyn and then I get to feel better. I've visited Woody many, many times, but I would never want to be another Woody Guthrie."

Did he anticipate stardom? Dylan looked as modest as a hobo with a nickel in his pocket. "I never thought I would shoot lightning through the sky in the entertainment field." He sketched his influences: "I started to sing and play the guitar at the age of ten. Hank Williams had just died and I first liked country music—people like Jimmie Rodgers. Then I got interested in old blues, and people like Jelly Roll Morton. I remember Leadbelly and 'See See (C. C.) Rider,' but I also liked the country songs of Jack Guthrie. I really couldn't decide which I liked best, country or blues. So I suppose I ended by becoming a mixture of Hank Williams and Woody Guthrie."

What about his fascination with Charlie Chaplin? "He influences me, even in the way I sing. His films really sank in. I like to see the humor in the world. There is so little of it around. I guess I'm always conscious of the Chaplin tramp." Then what about death songs? "Well, I feel a closeness to songs like 'See That My Grave is Kept Clean.' I'm representing myself and a whole lot of people who sing in that manner." He was anxious to be in the very best company, song-swapping with Van Ronk and Elliott. He was a great fan of old rock 'n' roll—Presley, Little Richard, and rockabilly singer Carl Perkins.

He linked his harmonica work to Jesse Fuller, "Little Walter" Jacobs, and Sonny Terry. "Now I am 'blowing out' more in my own style." What did the future look like? "I would just like to keep on singing like I am. I just want to get along. I don't think

about making a million dollars." He summarized his approach to songwriting: "Either the song comes fast, or it won't come at all." Some songs marinate for a long time. "I just jot down little phrases and things I overhear."

A gap between recording and release is customary, but the album was not released until March 19, 1962, a long delay, caused by bureaucracy, that annoyed Dylan very much. He felt he was moving with such momentum that to have the record in limbo for five months was a cruel anticlimax. By the time the album was released, he was embarrassed, regarding it as early work best left in a bottom drawer. It was the last will and testament of one Dylan and the birth of a new Dylan.

Don Hunstein's cover photograph of the callow boy barely matches the performance by the old man within. Dylan looks almost delicate and tentative, yet the singing and playing are packed with bold assertion. But the photograph did show Dylan much as he looked in those days, the hat making him appear even younger than he was. The unsmiling, pudgy face reflected a mixture of shyness and aloofness. His pseudo-western gear was standard 1961 hippie dress. The absence of a smile was also characteristic, for by then Dylan wasn't finding too much to smile about.

The recording received several very fine reviews but, as they say in the record business, "nothing happened." Not until two years later did this creditable first recording begin to sell in quantity. Around Columbia, they began to call Bob Dylan "Hammond's folly." Only a handful of people thought Dylan had much promise. Suze did, but almost from the beginning she feared Bob's death-hauntedness. By November 1961, love was a four-letter word to Dylan, and so was Suze. Bob felt the romance was doomed—enough to make any twenty-year-old sing an old man's song and think that life might be over.

04

POSITIVELY 161 WEST FOURTH STREET

THE FOLKLORE CENTER

Presents

BOB DYLAN

IN HIS FIRST NEW YORK CONCERT

∽∽∽∽∽∽∽∽∽∽∽

SAT. NOV. 4, 1961   **8:40pm**

CARNEGIE CHAPTER HALL

154 WEST 57th STREET • NEW YORK CITY

All seats $2.00

Tickets available at: The Folklore Center
                            110 MacDougal Street
GR 7 - 5987   New York City 12, New York

                            or at door

> ## "He would sit at a table in some cheesy little luncheonette and write. He would write in his little spiral notebook while drinking coffee. SUZE ROTOLO

Within two weeks of taping his first album, Dylan found his way to Carnegie Hall—not the main Carnegie, but its neighboring debut room, Carnegie Chapter Hall. For his first important solo concert, on Saturday, November 4, 1961, fifty-three people turned out, mostly the Village gang. Dylan performed with assurance and pointed professionalism. As much as his sad songs could touch, it was still the comic routines, the talking blues, to which the audience responded most warmly. The concert was sponsored by Izzy Young of the Folklore Center. Charging two dollars a ticket, Izzy had pulled off another of his aesthetic coups and financial flops.

Around Christmas, Dylan did a small concert at Rutgers University in New Jersey. He went over very well, but again the comic eclipsed the musician. In February 1962, he went upstate to a small coffeehouse, the Caffé Lena, in Saratoga Springs, where he played a gig arranged by Terri Van Ronk. He did very little other stage work during 1962. He had played at a Toronto coffeehouse and a benefit concert at City College in Manhattan for the Congress on Racial Equality (CORE). From April 24 to May 6, he returned to Folk City, where he could always be sure of a warm reception.

Right after the Columbia taping, Harry Belafonte was looking for a harmonica player, and Dylan was asked to play on Belafonte's RCA sessions for the album *Midnight Special*. Following its release, some radio jocks, like Bob Fass of WBAI, played the track, not saying "That was Harry Belafonte singing 'Midnight Special,'" but "That was Bob Dylan playing the harmonica."

Dylan's diary as an artist, from late 1961 through most of 1962, was dominated by his seeking out established performers, his songwriting, his contact with *Broadside* and the civil rights movement, and his managerial affiliations. Above all, his long, stormy love affair with Suze Rotolo affected much of what he did throughout 1962.

Returning from Minneapolis in early summer 1961, convinced that Bonny Jean Beecher and he had no future, Dylan pinned his expansive hopes on Suze.

Her manner was shy, tentative, gentle. Her eyes and ears caught everything, although she was often curiously inarticulate. She was creative, whether sketching and drawing, planning a stage production, or helping to run *Streets* magazine.

From mid-1961 through the spring of 1964, whether living with Dylan or running away from him, whether in Greenwich Village, Woodstock, or Italy, whether trying to get closer than he would allow or farther than he wanted, Suze (pronounced "Suzy") was a central figure in one of Dylan's most quickening periods. He probably wrote more than a dozen songs for or about her, and she inspired countless more. She was only seventeen when they met. She was a New Yorker from an urbane Italian-American family of readers, political activists, and socially concerned people. Bob wrote most directly of her in an "Outlined Epitaph":

> *the true fortune-teller of my soul*
> *I think perhaps the only one*

Although I spent dozens of evenings with Suze and Bob, I had difficulty grasping her spirit. She tended to be overshadowed by Dylan when she was with him. Although I sensed her keen artistic perception, she was generally unassertive in those early years. Dylan must have been a handful to live with. I knew only that she had a power over Bob, and, in those pre-feminist days, to her chagrin, I often urged her to put his needs above hers. I couldn't see then that she was right from her side too, grasping for her own identity in the whirlpool of his urgent needs. Before the end of 1961, he was talking about marriage, sometimes flippantly, sometimes in dead earnest, planning the ceremony in detail.

Suze's mother had other ideas. Mary Rotolo was a volatile, strong-headed, intelligent woman in her early forties, whose factory-worker husband had recently died. She was a translator for a medical journal and was planning to marry a New Jersey teacher. Suze was too young to become involved with anyone she felt, let alone that scruffy beatnik. Mrs. Rotolo didn't approve of Bobby at all, although both her daughters, Suze and twenty-year-old Carla, thought so highly of him. "My

mother was the only one at that point who disliked Dylan heartily," said Carla (whom Dylan often called "Carla-in-law"). "Yet, when Bob was sick, she put him up at her flat." Suze knew little of Bob's background until *Newsweek* broke the story of his parents and Hibbing in 1963. But Carla told me: "In fall 1961, my mother knew who he was. She felt he was taking advantage of everyone around to get ahead. She called him a sponge to his face. Dylan could fight anybody's mother, but the fact that she saw through him, which no one else did, scared him. He paid court to her, he did everything he could over the years to win her over, and it never worked. The ultimate thing was that 'Ballad in Plain D'."

At seventeen, Suze was tortured by her mother's dislike of Dylan. Carla became increasingly negative toward the relationship. Dylan's intensity,

ABOVE

Broadside, Sis Cunningham and Gordon Friesen's topical songwriting magazine. Dylan was contributing editor. Impromptu performances were taped. A 1972 compilation features four Dylan contributions—he is listed as "Blind Boy Grunt."

restlessness, and darkness also frightened Suze. Although she tried repeatedly to break away, she was ineluctably drawn to him. Especially in their early days, Bob and Suze seemed to us magic lovers closely bound in a hostile world. I, for one, was surprised at their first split-up—but I was seeing through Bob's eyes, not hers.

In summer 1961, Mary Rotolo was living in the penthouse of One Sheridan Square, atop the old Café Society Downtown, which was in the basement. On the fourth floor lived a folk den mother, Miki Isaacson, who ran a kibbutz for strays. Miki didn't like to be alone and she only felt useful if surrounded. At first, the contingent in her large, triangular living room consisted of Jack Elliott, Greg Levasseur, Greenbriar Boy John Herald, and, soon, Dylan. Toward the end of the summer, Jean Redpath, a Scottish singer, joined the family-style commune, sloppy but not hippie. Nearly everyone picked or sang until three in the morning, then dropped off to sleep on the sofa. Redpath recalled, "I nearly blew a gasket blowing up so many of those rubber mattresses." Dylan glided into this permissive family, pleased to be sleeping under the same roof as Suze.

Suze graduated from Bryant High School in Queens, spent part of 1961 at the New School, and held part-time office jobs. She was interested in drawing, theater, design, and poetry, and worked as an usher in off-Broadway theaters. When she first met Dylan at the Riverside Radio all-day hoot, she thought he was a joke, she told me in 1966, through her sunburst smile. "A nice joke, but a joke. … I don't think I ever saw him sober for a while. Half of that was put-on drinking, though. … I guess I was always aware that he would be big one day. Especially after you wrote that he was a sponge that absorbs everything. Once I got to know him, I knew that quality. I soon discovered that he wasn't a joke at all. When you got to know him separately you knew just how frighteningly sharp he was. … He could be sitting in a room filled with people and be absorbing rays from everyone, from everywhere."

Was it difficult to live with a genius? "I guess it was hard," Suze replied. "Their heads are going all the time. But you can't treat them as being so extraordinary. They are just human beings." Did he communicate well to her? "Yes, definitely. But he certainly can express himself better in what he writes than in what he says. Those first few months at Gerde's and at the first recording session, I was very awed. I didn't realize this was such a big phenomenon, and I still don't. When I see his pictures everywhere and see him quoted, I still think it's a joke. You see, to me, it's still old Bobby."

Suze was in Italy from May until December, 1962. "When I came back, it was to the stardom of Dylan. That's when he was really getting big. A lot of things were going on, and I became more aware of his public image. Even though he wrote me often and called me all the time in Italy, he would only talk about us, and would never talk about what he was doing." Dylan was in England in late 1962 when Suze returned, and she was greeted not by the man but by his songs. Hearing "letters" written to her on a jukebox was "very strange. I was torn. It became very flattering to sit back and hear a song like 'Don't Think Twice' or 'Tomorrow Is a Long Time' on the radio. It was especially strange to hear them being sung by other people."

Suze recalled Bob at work in early 1962: "He would just say to me: 'I'm going to do some writing tonight,' and would sit down at the typewriter, or would play with his guitar. I never minded that all that much. The apartment on 4th Street was a very small place to have someone constantly playing chords over and over again. He was very fast about his writing. He also liked to go out to write. He would sit at a table in some cheesy little luncheonette and write. He would write in his little spiral notebook while drinking coffee."

In spring 1962, before she left for Italy, "he was especially close-mouthed. The funny thing about our relationship was that it started small but kept getting bigger and bigger all the time. The thing that struck me about Bobby was his despair, that deathlike quality about him. I sensed, long after we

> ## "He knew exactly where he was going and how big he was going to be."
>
> CARLA ROTOLO

ABOVE

Outside Izzy
Young's Folklore
Center in May
1962. It was
one of Dylan's
first stops in
the Village and
ground zero
for artists and
fans alike.

had gone our separate ways, a lack of excitement
to him. People live with hope for green trees and
beautiful flowers as far as I'm concerned, but Dylan
seems to lack that sort of simple hope, at least he did
from 1964 to 1966. This darkness wasn't new to me.
It became stronger as the years passed by—or else,
I was just becoming more aware of it. He hasn't
turned against anything, but he sees something and
just wipes it out. It's a philosophy of despair, so to
speak. But he has got a lot of life in him, so it's all
very contradictory." I told Suze how Bob had once
talked to me at length about suicide, and the next
day had said that if I thought he was pessimistic,
then I didn't understand him at all. "He's like—he
just won't accept anybody's point of view about
himself. That's his way."

Suze's sister grew more hostile to the relationship.

Carla was fantastically enthusiastic about Dylan
and yet often competitive with her sister. As "big
sister," she always seemed to know what was best,
and that didn't always mean Dylan. At first, Carla
big-sistered him as well. When she was living at 129
Perry Street in autumn 1961, Bob stayed. Carla:
"Bobby was still in his dirty period then. But he
was very fussy about his clothes. His concern about
his image started then. He would always ask if
he looked right, jiggling with his dungarees: 'Are
they tight enough? Is the shirt OK?' I would go to
work in the morning and Bobby would be asleep
on my living room couch. He spent most of his
time listening to my records, days and nights." He
read voraciously. "My library was quite eclectic,"
Carla recalled, "and he read whatever he found.
He started with our poetry books. I think he met

François Villon through us. He was borrowing from anyone who had a large book collection." While still giving the public impression of being neither reader nor student, Dylan jumped headlong into the best folk-music collections, by the Lomaxes, Sharp, Child, and as much poetry as he could absorb. Bob read Suze's European and American poetry books, and bought her more, which they read together. All the time he scribbled notes. Whatever dormant energy remained from university was unleashed in the Village.

Carla sensed that the kid she was mothering needed very little protection. "Bobby was still at my flat, and his record was in the planning stages. I'm not sure just when I asked him to move out. What had started as a two-week stay stretched from September into November. We were all concerned about what songs Dylan was going to do. I clearly remember talking about it. Suddenly, I realized Bobby knew what he was going to do and how he was going to go about it. He *knew* exactly where he was going and how big he was going to be. This is a very important point. Up to then he had just been a bumbling kid, and everybody was helping him with money, clothes, and everything. Then, suddenly, I remember feeling *this isn't a kid!* Although we were the same age, I always thought of him as being much younger than me, in the sense of emotional maturity.

"Bobby certainly is a classic Gemini," Carla continued. "I've known other Geminis in Italy, just like him—schizy. The classic Gemini definition really fits Bobby—split, flashes of brilliance, contradictions, and the inability to stay in one place.

I'll never forget that day when I got that feeling that he didn't need me or *anyone*. None of us had seen it, because he was so good at masking it, with the kid stuff, with the indifferent, lost attitude. Even musically, he knew every step he was taking. … Here was a man who instinctively knew which way to go. The only mistake he made was being caught up in the vortex of being 'the messiah.'

"We were all used, not necessarily as a sounding board. We were all quite necessary to Bobby, but how foolish we were all in that time, when he was laughing through his teeth at us, and yet he needed us just the same. He may still have been the shambling, bumbling, angelic one with the cap on, on the surface, but he wasn't that underneath, to me. It was a time to pull off the masks. The bumbling child covered over the ambition and the carefully thought-out plan. He didn't need anyone's help or advice. From then on, I made no reference about his recording or how he should do it. My mother was the only one who disliked Dylan. I still liked him very much, and may have even admired him more after I saw how smart he was."

Early in 1962, Bob found a two-room apartment of his own at 161 West 4th Street. The building rose four flights over Bruno's spaghetti parlor, and Dylan rented the first floor rear for around sixty dollars a month. There was a tiny bedroom and a kitchenette/dining/living area. He built a table with space for meals, the TV in the middle, and a niche for his typewriter. The portable nearly always stood ready with a piece of yellow copy paper in it, a few lines of a song-in-progress peeking out. The apartment was decorated with dust, a hard wooden chair, instruments of all sorts, a few Mexican belts, guitar straps, and a ceramic bull. There was barely room for one person. When Suze moved in, there was scarcely room for anyone.

Within months, Suze fell under heavy pressures to go to Italy. Her mother and stepfather wanted her to study, so she decided to take a summer course at the University of Perugia, then study art at the Accademia. Through the spring, Dylan was miserable and Suze was ambivalent, wanting to stay and wanting to be on her own. She seriously considered marrying him. "Maybe you should marry him," Carla told Suze, equivocating that if

the relationship were good it would be just as good after six months. At the end of May, Suze prepared to leave from Hoboken. At the boat, both Bob and Suze were distraught. During nine months of separation, Bob spun chaotically in a great whirlpool of personal loss but artistic gain. Acutely lonely, he turned to his New York friends—the MacDougal Street hippies—me, Sybil Weinberger, Gil Turner, and, increasingly, to various southern civil rights activists.

Another Rotolo friend was a drawling Louisianian actor, Quinton Raines, who had been working on *Brecht on Brecht*, a musical. Suze wanted to bring Bob into her theater world; Quinton seemed the ideal bridge. An experimental meeting with Quinton, at Jack Delaney's restaurant, lasted five hours. *Brecht on Brecht* opened new doors of perception for Dylan. Brechtian ideas, language, and style coursed through Dylan's politicized period of 1962–63. Brecht's theme that Hitler's Germany was caused by sheepish belief in leaders was echoed in one of Dylan's cardinal tenets: "Don't follow leaders." In the seventies, a gifted Yugoslav-born London-based singer, Bettina Jonic, performed and recorded twenty-two works by Brecht and Dylan. Jonic saw the two writers reflecting Germany of the twenties and America of the sixties: "To relate Brecht with Dylan was natural. Their simplicity of style and use of language were so alike; yet they were two unique voices speaking with enormous force and directness. A black boy killed out of bigotry [Dylan] or a girl killed for sleeping with a Jew [Brecht] becomes that timeless voice speaking out against atrocity. Following this pattern leaves one with a sense of the poet's range, despair, his need to speak and hold up to life a bitter mirror."

Criticizing the American way of life then was not only unfashionable, but downright dangerous. The cold war against Leftists, dissenters, or even independent liberals in the arts had been slowly putting a glacial crust over the landscape. The fifteen gray years that followed World War II, instead of being a liberated era in which the defeat of tyranny was savored, became instead a witch hunt. Every radical American was perceived as a Soviet agent. Systematically, the steamroller of repression crushed hundreds of careers.

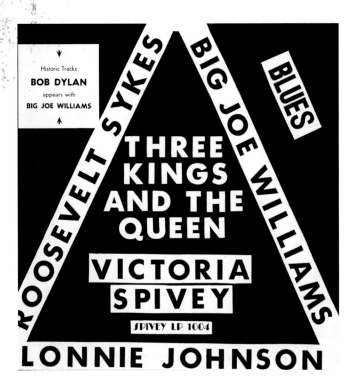

Historic Tracks
BOB DYLAN
appears with
BIG JOE WILLIAMS

ROOSEVELT SYKES
BIG JOE WILLIAMS
BLUES
THREE KINGS AND THE QUEEN
VICTORIA SPIVEY
SPIVEY LP 1004
LONNIE JOHNSON

In folk music, there were successive smears against the organizations People's Artists and People's Songs, outgrowths of the war-time radical folk-song movement. For a time, the witch hunt managed to silence the Weavers, who enjoyed hits in the early fifties. Being a dissenter, with or without a guitar, was a risky business. Postwar Americans seemed more interested in security than sanity; more anxious to hail the status quo than to expose the status woe.

Dissenters included new satirical comics like Lenny Bruce, Lord Buckley, Mort Sahl, and Dick Gregory, who found the repressive fifties grimly laughable. Another form of dissent came from the beat poets and writers—Allen Ginsberg, Lawrence Ferlinghetti, Jack Kerouac, Gregory Corso, and others—who had different visions of America. The beats retreated from mainstream society, making dropping out hip. During Madison Avenue's fifties heyday, a precious few began hiking Kerouac's open road. Keeping the flickering light of protest glowing in music were Seeger, and People's Artists and People's Songs, mostly through *Sing Out!* magazine. Nothing that could be done against Seeger stopped him using his lanky, country-booted personality to talk and sing of a better world. Seeger devotees included Guy Carawan, who helped spur the "freedom song" movement among Southern integrationists, and Peter Yarrow and Mary Travers who with Paul Stookey became Peter, Paul and Mary.

Another tireless protégé was Gil Turner from Bridgeport, Connecticut. Gil had been a Baptist preacher who left the church when he discovered Seeger's wider pastorate. His attachment to Pete was like Dylan's and Elliott's to Guthrie. He had a large, warm baritone, played guitar and banjo, and was a wizard chorus master. In autumn 1961, he became Folk City's MC, and met all the singer-songwriters passing through. None struck him more forcefully than Dylan.

Several times a week, after Gerde's closed around midnight, Gil, Bob, and I walked over to the White Horse near the docks, or to Jim and Bertha McGowan's off-Broadway bar on Greenwich Avenue. The Horse was a storied English-style pub, a hangout of Dylan Thomas's during his declining days. Richard Burton used to come by and, in the late fifties, Irish folksingers the Clancy Brothers were regulars. Writer-habitués (like Mike Harrington and James Baldwin), salty longshoremen, painters, talkers, and drunkards, kept the Horse galloping. McGowan's was quieter, but it stayed open until 4 a.m. It was decorated with theater playbills and stage pictures. A framed letter from Sean O'Casey to the McGowans hung on the wall. The McGowans loved Dylan and often subsidized his sandwiches and drinks. One night there, Gil told Bob about a new concept for a magazine, recruiting him into the *Broadside* experiment.

After Seeger had toured Britain in 1961, he returned excited about the burgeoning of topical songwriting there, and wanted something comparable in the States. Seeger longed to develop younger writers to carry on the work that he, Malvina Reynolds, and others had done. Pete was joined by his old friend Sis Cunningham, long in the Southern labor movement, a friend of Woody's from Oklahoma, and a member of the Almanac Singers.

At their first meeting, Pete, Sis, and Sis's husband Gordon Friesen launched a little mimeographed bulletin of topical songs called *Broadside*, named after Elizabethan song or news sheets, printed for rapid dissemination. Pete retained strong links with *Sing Out!*, but that magazine took a couple of months to publish and stressed traditional folk song. *Broadside* aimed to be small and easy to publish. Pete and Sis needed a sparkplug and found one in Gil Turner. Besides recruiting Dylan, Gil brought the liveliest young songwriters to the monthly meetings. Two young music journalists, Josh Dunson and Julius Lester, cut their teeth there.

Dylan was keen on *Broadside* from the start. It printed his new songs and made him part of a movement. He listened to song tapes from around the country, and even tried to improve some himself. He heeded Seeger and what Sis and Gordon could, with authority, interpret as "what Woody would think." *Broadside* clearly stimulated Dylan's writing in 1962 and 1963. Dunson described a typical, lighthearted meeting in *Broadside* 20: "*Broadside*'s home is a small little room. … Gil Turner took out his twelve-stringer, borrowed a flat-pick. Sis took

out the mic for the tape-recorder, and out came a talking blues Gil just wrote about the newspaper strike that had us all quietly laughing.

"Then, Gil took out his six-string Gibson, handed it over to Bob Dylan, saying how Bob's new song, 'Masters of War' was one of the best Bob had ever written. I kept on thinking he had written … some that had real lyric poetry, like 'Blowin' in the Wind' and 'Hard Rain's Gonna Fall' which makes you think right away of [Federico Garcia] Lorca, and I waited for the images of rain, and thunder, and lightning to come out in great spectacles. But no, this time there was a different kind of poetry, one of great anger, accusation, just saying who the masters of war are, without compromising one inch in its short sharp direct intensity … right after that, not waiting … to get two breaths, Bob came along with 'Playboys and Playgirls' a group song Pete said 'is going to be sung by a million people in the next year.' Its tune catches whole crowds easy, and the words come right along from the feeling."

In came Phil Ochs, and Happy Traum, another member of Turner's group, the New World Singers. Pete said: "You know, in the past five months I haven't heard as many good songs and as much good music as I've heard here tonight." Dylan was one of a half-dozen regulars at *Broadside* meetings in 1962 but Pete knew, and nearly all of the others came to know, that Bob was turning out topical songs of a quality unheard since Guthrie. Along with Paul Krassner's the *Realist*, and the *Village Voice*, *Broadside* probably pioneered the sixties underground press.

Seeger was the first established performer Dylan influenced. By the end of 1962, he was performing Dylan songs and singling him out as the most important new songwriter of the time. Dylan had his first song printed in *Broadside*, the lyrics to "Talkin' John Birch Paranoid Blues," in the first issue, February 1962. "Blowin' in the Wind" was on the cover of *Broadside* 6 in May 1962. For eighteen months, the first place one saw Dylan's songs, even before performance, was in *Broadside*, where Bob was listed as a contributing editor. By the time *Broadside* was a year old, issue 20 of February 1963, "Masters of War" was on page one with illustrations by Suze, "Playboys and Playgirls" was

on page two, and the issue included an early version of "Don't Think Twice." (The last, neither political nor topical, indicated *Broadside*'s flexibility.) Nearly every other 1963 issue had either a new Dylan song or some Dylanology. This continued throughout the sixties, although Dylan had drifted away from the magazine by 1964.

The *Broadside* experiment was seminal. By stressing songs relevant to the real world, by underscoring "songs that said something," *Broadside* succeeded, out of all proportion to its modest format, its readership of a few hundred. With *Broadside*'s encouragement, Dylan flowered before he was accepted by the public, and sharpened his craft. The roots of the revolution in popular music that Dylan led lie partly in those monthly meetings and the crudely mimeographed pages of *Broadside*.

Albert B. Grossman, known as "the bear," had a body and manner to match the sobriquet, and a face suggesting an owl forced into the light. A portly, prematurely gray man, he had large eyes slightly hidden by glasses that suggest Ben Franklin before *he* went electric. "When I first met Albert, I thought he was just a street bear," Dylan told me once of the man who was his personal manager from 1962 until the relationship was legally dissolved in June 1971. After Dylan's accident, dealings between Dylan and his "Dear Landlord" were never quite the same. Grossman, who actually lived in Bearsville, just outside Woodstock, was a teddy or a grizzly, depending on your point of view.

When Dylan met Albert, he was wary. Bob knew how pivotal the right manager would be, and how many would wave pens at him once he had a recording contract. Working informally with Terri Van Ronk, Bob was still in charge, and did not have to deal with the uptown business world. Albert, however, was always around the Village, chatting with musicians, sitting like Buddha contemplating (they hoped) their futures.

Bob and Albert's strange, often stormy, relationship was in some ways a true marriage of minds and temperaments, each man adopting the worst traits of the other. The striking difference was that Bob had appeared to be a relatively open person with considerable human compassion, while Albert had always been the chess player. At his worst,

Grossman was contemptuous; at his best, a tasteful talent manager who worked with a minimum of commercial vocabulary and tawdriness.

As soon as Dylan had his Columbia contract, music-business sharks smelled blood. Bob played a waiting game. Hammond suggested Harold Leventhal, who represented Seeger, Judy Collins, the Weavers, and, best of all, Guthrie. Dylan's relationship with Leventhal never jelled. Paul Stookey believes he was the first to tell Albert that Dylan was a talent to watch. Albert watched. Around the time of Bob's LP release, after months of cultivating Dylan's trust, Grossman made direct overtures. Bob told me then that Albert said he was not interested in working with any artist who couldn't make at least $50,000 a year, a figure which staggered Bob. Albert had built his reputation representing Odetta, whom Bob had admired since Dinkytown. The growing stature of Peter, Paul and Mary also impressed Dylan. I advised Bob to consider Grossman's bid seriously. I recalled that he had discovered Baez, though Joan had chosen to work with a gentler sort, Manny Greenhill of Boston. To many, Grossman was a sinister, relentlessly naysaying figure. "He just thinks he's God," said Tom Clancy. To others, he was a "beautiful cat," dedicated to the highest standards of performing integrity, not a hawker of talent, but a creative force. Even those whom Grossman represented vary in their opinions. And from 1960 onward, Albert changed a good deal.

He preferred to work in the shadows, seeking neither credit nor limelight, but he appreciated his growing reputation as a kingmaker. Enduring his charges' idiosyncrasies, he was confessor and psychiatrist to them

> "Albert is totally involved creatively. His ears are good. There would have been no Baez, no Dylan, and no Peter, Paul and Mary without Albert.
>
> PETER YARROW

all, including Janis Joplin. His chief reward was money, bags of it. His subsidiary reward was power, which he used judiciously at first, until he gradually became possessed by it. The performer-clients who most admire Albert describe him as a protector against the machinations of the music business. Peter Yarrow told me in 1970: "Albert is totally involved creatively. His ears are good. There would have been no Baez, no Dylan, and no Peter, Paul and Mary without Albert. He kept us insulated from the flesh-peddling aspect of show business. Next to Albert, Dylan was an amateur at cutting people down. Albert is an expert at destroying other people's sense of self. He readily admits it. Albert only attacks when others are playing a role. Albert basically doesn't trust the press. He is very shy, and cynical, because he has seen friends corrupted. He is also an idealist. Bobby was imitating everyone at one stage, and he naturally began to imitate and learn a lot of Albert's tricks. I think that Albert stimulated Bobby a great deal."

Paul Stookey answered me with a question: "If a plumber comes to your house and unplugs your drains, would you say he was helping your life, creatively? Albert was like that plumber. He would point out superfluous things we were doing or saying. When Albert says to do something, he's always right. When he says he thinks you shouldn't do something, he may not be right." Like Dylan, Mary Travers is a former admirer. In 1970–71, when I was seeing quite a bit of Mary in London, she clearly felt Grossman had taken advantage of her. When she discovered he had been earning more than she or Peter or Paul, she switched to Leventhal. Feeling she had been used, Mary described her once-respected manager in vituperative terms.

That Dylan and Grossman found each other was no surprise. Although Grossman was a good dozen years older, no other performer so influenced him. Dylan's taste prompted Grossman's signing of Paul Butterfield, John Lee Hooker, the Kweskin Jug Band, and the Band. Peter Yarrow maintained that Dylan found in Grossman the father he was looking for, and that, as their relationship deteriorated in 1965–71, Bob was symbolically destroying the father, the authority figure, to whom he was indebted. Grossman may have found a rebellious

son in Dylan. From 1964 to 1966, he put up with a great deal from Dylan. Grossman feigned modesty when I told him that some people maintained Dylan would never have made it without him: "That's ridiculous! He would have made it without anyone," Albert replied.

Working closely with Grossman was a former Tommy Dorsey Band road manager, a bright, aggressive executive, Artie Mogull, who was with the publishing house of M. Witmark & Sons, of Music Publishers Holding Corporation, later Warner Bros Music. In early summer 1962, Grossman and Silver brought Dylan to Mogull, who immediately he heard him wanted to sign him for Witmark, but discovered that Hammond had already arranged for Dylan to be published by Leeds/Duchess music. In a move vaguely reminiscent of the Russian sale of Alaska, Mogull got Dylan released for nothing; he then signed a three-year publishing contract with Witmark on July 13, 1962.

"I offered Dylan one thousand dollars to sign with Witmark," Mogull told me. "I had to fight to get that one thousand dollars, and now the songs have easily earned a million dollars and will continue to earn for years to come."

"In his three years with Witmark, Dylan gave them 237 copyrights. That was unheard of! He is amazingly prolific. Ordinarily, it would have been something to get twenty-five songs out of a writer in three years." (In his autobiography, *John Hammond on Record*, the producer said that Dylan used five hundred of Artie's thousand dollars to buy his way out of the Leeds/Duchess publishing contract.)

Mogull, the self-described "world's greatest talent scout," may have been instrumental in getting Grossman into the financial big time. For signing Peter, Paul and Mary, Warner Bros advanced $30,000, which Grossman parlayed into millions. Although not under Grossman's roof, Mogull was one of his key people. In 1965, when the Witmark contract ran out, Dylan and Grossman formed their own music-publishing company and hired as its manager—Artie Mogull.

My relationship with Grossman reached its low note in late 1965 when, one night at the Limelight

The Freewheelin' Bob Dylan, released in May 1963, established the younger singer-songwriter as a major talent. It featured five of his most recorded songs.

in the Village, I told him that some publishers had approached me about writing a Dylan book. "If you do that, I'll sue you, before the book comes out, or after it comes out, or both," Albert exploded. Mary Travers and Canadian singers Ian and Sylvia, who were also at our table, looked astonished. "Albert," I said, "someday we ought to have a talk about power and its abuse." When I saw him in his office a week later, he was not quite so litigious: "It's opportunism, it's premature. You can't report anything that hasn't been specifically stated for publication." How opportunistic was it for him, I asked, to use the press for publicity but not for documentation of what really goes on? "You're being Italianate," he said.

"Well," I concluded our chilly confrontation, "let's see what Bob says when he gets back from the Coast." Dylan showed immediate interest in my project, and told Albert to lay off.

Whatever differences Bob subsequently had with his record producer, in the early months John Hammond gave Dylan keen encouragement. Even though the first royalty check gave Bob barely enough to pay his electric bill, Hammond remained convinced that Dylan was a major talent. Columbia cynics continued to call him "Hammond's Folly."

Dylan's other chief advocate at Columbia was an uncommonly bright publicist named Billy James. He recalled: "Hammond called me and said: 'Billy, I have a marvelous boy in the studio right now. Do you have a moment to come up?' I knew that it was happening—right there! He had such an incredible blend of influences, and presented them with such conviction that my first exposure was very moving. Bobby came up and we spent about three hours talking about everything, but he was reluctant to talk about his past."

Billy set up Dylan's first magazine interview, in 1962, with Edwin Miller of *Seventeen*. Even at twenty-one, Dylan was eminently quotable. He told *16* magazine that "people should develop their own thoughts and feelings and not follow the herd. Everyone has a gift and they should be proud of it—whether it's cleaning the street, sewing a dress or singing a song."

Throughout 1962, while Suze was in Italy, Dylan continued making friends in New York. Jimmy Richmond, who ran the Music Inn record store a few doors west along West 4th Street, knew Dylan as a regular. He didn't buy but popped in several times a week to hear new tracks. He consolidated his friendships with musicians, learning and teaching, absorbing and sharing, influencing and being influenced. The music scene was a campus without walls. One of Dylan's favorite new friends was Paul Clayton, a gentle, lost, earnest folk singer, whose knowledge of balladry was wide. Through "Gentleman Jim" Kweskin, Bob was in touch with an ease and flash, onstage and off, that was rare among Village folkniks. Long before I had really tuned in to Clayton or Kweskin, Dylan was prodding me to write them up. "It's just not fair that they're unknown," he said.

"People should develop their own thoughts and feelings and not follow the herd. Everyone has a gift and they should be proud of it—whether it's cleaning the street, sewing a dress or singing a song."

RIGHT

The Singers Club, run by Ewan MacColl and Peggy Seeger, was at the Pindar of Wakefield pub in King's Cross in London. Dylan played its Christmas party.

In 1962, Dylan befriended some of the leaders of the "freedom song" civil rights movement. In the summer, on a survey for the *Times*, I had made my own discovery of the breadth of freedom songs in the South. In Atlanta, I met the articulate, militant James Forman, a leader in the Student Non-Violent Coordinating Committee. Although the SNCC was then close to the Southern Christian Leadership Council of the Reverend Martin Luther King Jr., the student group found its own directions. Music was a prime vehicle. Two young activists, Bernice Johnson and Cordell Reagon, were leading the long desegregation campaign in Albany, Georgia. They and Forman had spent time in jail and made their way north, where folkniks became working allies and friends. Dylan took warmly to the SNCC activists, and they to him. He began to think their topical songs were more relevant than *Broadside*. The New Yorkers embraced Johnson as a young Odetta. The first she heard of Dylan, he was singing "Hollis Brown" and "Hard Rain." Bernice, in tribute, mastered the complex "Hard Rain" lyrics and soon began to perform the song. In late 1962, she had her purse stolen and, with few friends in New York, called Dylan. He invited her to stay in his apartment, played her Robert Johnson records and talked with her about the music and civil rights struggle. "We all thought, those of us in the movement and those of us in the Freedom Singers, that Dylan was fantastic as a songwriter and as a person. … I've always just regarded Bob as a friend. He's never been a star to me, just a friend."

Dylan was also drawn to a sixty-year-old bluesman, Big Joe Williams and when Mike Porco considered booking Big Joe at Folk City in early 1962, Dylan hyped him: "He's the greatest old bluesman. You gotta put him in here." Mike did, for three weeks in February. Dylan showed up nearly every night, jamming with Big Joe several times. For Joe, who had worked the streets, this first job in New York was exciting. The chemistry between Big Joe and Little Bob was so good that Joe invited him on his session for an LP he was scheduled to cut with Victoria Spivey, a blues doyenne. Bob cut the session under the nom de blues of "Big Joe's Buddy." The album, *Three Kings and a Queen*, released in October 1964, featured two tracks with Dylan.

Two important concerts in autumn 1962 advanced Dylan. On Saturday, September 22, *Sing Out!* presented its annual Hootenanny at Carnegie Hall. Seeger introduced Dylan as an especially important writer. Bob did only three songs, then wandered offstage disappointed with his performance. The audience, however, was not. Two weeks later, on October 5, Dylan was top-billed in a Town Hall concert with Ian and Sylvia, John Lee Hooker and Judy Collins. Sponsored by the Folklore Center, the concert presented almost all Grossman clients or choices. Dylan, in much better form, was among the most enthusiastically received. He did his "Talking New York," "John Birch," "Hollis Brown," and finished with "Hard Rain." Those who doubted Dylan's poetic gifts began to see what all the fuss was about.

By this time, the *Sing Out!* issue featuring Dylan was published, its cover showing him dragging on a cigarette, eyes half-closed, à la Guthrie. Gil Turner's story called him "the most prolific young songwriter in America today." The article included two other photographs, the music and lyrics of "Blowin' in the Wind," "Letter to Woody," and "Ballad of Donald White," plus excerpts from other songs. *Sing Out!* never pushed a new songwriter so strongly. By 1962, Grossman had moves ready on his mental chess-board.

Almost the first management step Grossman took was to try to get Bob out of his Columbia contract. He saw all its flaws, from percentages to its "special publishing rate," under which Dylan's compositions earned more if recorded by others than if he recorded them. Hammond's version of the hassle: "By this time, Bob had written 'Blowin' in the Wind' and Peter, Paul and Mary were convinced this was a masterpiece, as I was. He'd gone over

> **Nobody told me to go electric. I didn't ask anybody. I asked not a soul, believe me, I didn't ask anybody.**

to Warner Brothers [Witmark, later acquired by Warners]. Grossman tried to take Dylan away from Columbia because his parents hadn't signed his contract also. Bobby had told me he didn't have any parents. The letter from the lawyer didn't mean anything, because Bobby by that time was twenty-one, and had been in the studio four times since he was twenty-one. I got Bobby to repudiate the letter, which got Grossman very uptight. We then decided that since Tom Wilson loved Bobby, this would be a very good marriage."

Wilson, a tall, handsome, affable man, was Columbia's first black producer. Although Hammond is listed as producer of Bob's second album, Wilson was the de facto producer of "Girl from the North Country," "Talkin' World War III Blues," "Bob Dylan's Dream," and "Masters of War." Dylan's first single, "Mixed Up Confusion," backed with "Corrina, Corrina," released on December 24, 1962, soon went out of print, but "Confusion" is historic. Had it been more widely known, it could have stemmed confusion that Dylan was only an acoustic performer. When

Dylan endured audience ferocity by switching to electric music in 1965, he was anxious to call attention to his first single and the deleted tracks from *Freewheelin'*. Here was folk-rock long before the Beatles, and long before anyone would be able to charge him with selling out to commercialism.

"Nobody told me to go electric. I didn't ask anybody. I asked not a soul, believe me, I didn't ask anybody," Dylan stressed later. According to Bob, *Freewheelin'*'s electric songs, including "Rocks and Gravel," were taken out to make room for his "Blowin' in the Wind," "Masters of War," and "Girl from the North Country." "John Birch" was removed because after the Columbia Broadcasting System censor had refused to allow the song on *The Ed Sullivan Show*, Columbia Records panicked, fearing the song was libelous.

Released just after the success of *Peter, Paul and Mary*, *Freewheelin'* did amazingly well, despite all the problems. Its cover shows Suze and Bobby reunited in a slushy Village street, Dylan shivering in suede and denim, a smiling Suze holding his arm.

05

NOT A PUPPET LAUREATE

> **Bob Dylan is the most important songwriter in the country today. He has his finger on the pulse of America's youth.** PETER YARROW

PREVIOUS PAGES

Keep a good head and always carry a bullwhip: Dylan on the tennis court of what was then the Newport Casino during the 1963 Newport Folk Festival.

OPPOSITE

Rehearsing for *The Ed Sullivan Show*, May 1963. When he was asked to sing something other than his "John Birch" song he walked off the set.

Timing is almost as crucial to star-making as talent and Grossman's timetable for launching Dylan was worked out in strategic detail. Dylan was not always aware of Grossman's moves, just as Grossman was not always aware of Dylan's, but in 1963 their schedules merged. Albert's master plan required a hit recording, strong word-of-mouth from stars, and crucially, a major publicity break, like the Newport Folk Festival. If Newport '59 could launch Baez, Newport '63 could launch Dylan.

One of Albert's deals had to proceed without Bob's knowledge, for nothing is so fragile as a young performer's ego. Applying economic theory, Grossman bought out Roy Silver's share of their partnership using OPM—Other People's Money. Not that Grossman wasn't enjoying a bumper year. Of the $10,000 that Albert paid to buy out Silver and get Dylan into his fold, half was put up by Peter, Paul and Mary. The deal was kept quiet mostly to give Dylan the feeling that he was achieving everything on his own.

From 1962 on, there were rumors that Peter, Paul and Mary had a part interest in Dylan's future, but the trio's constant denials tended to make the arrangement seem sinister. All it meant was that the trio was backing privately what they said publicly. Dylan didn't learn about the deal until sometime after "Blowin' in the Wind" became a Peter, Paul and Mary hit. After he knew, and after the events of 1963, Bob's recurring litany, for a while, was: "Albert's a genius, a real genius."

In late 1962, at the Gate of Horn in Chicago, Grossman had played Peter, Paul and Mary a Dylan tape of "Wind." Peter was enraptured, convinced it was the ideal sequel to their hit single of Seeger-Lee Hays's "If I Had a Hammer." Neither Paul nor Mary was quite that ecstatic. Nevertheless, they worked out their own arrangement featuring their distinctive harmonies. On June 18, 1963, Warner Bros. released the single. Within eight business days it had sold 320,000 copies. Mogull described it as Warner's fastest-moving single ever. Two key radio tastemakers, Bill Randle and Bill Gavin, began to call it "the record of the year." Some Cleveland, Washington, and Philadelphia stations were playing it hourly, and airplay and sales in the Deep South were surprisingly strong. As "Blowin' in the Wind" crested a million, American popular music was being redefined.

"Blowin' in the Wind" inspired a wave of northern freedom songs. Integration became a hot topic for folk and pop singers, *Variety* did a lead story on message songs, stressing the song's dual life as a pop standard *and* a civil rights anthem. Within a year nearly sixty other versions were recorded by artists as diverse as Duke Ellington, Lena Horne, and Marlene Dietrich. As the trio toured, Peter stressed repeatedly his belief that Dylan was sui generis: "Bob Dylan is the most important songwriter in the country today. He has his finger on the pulse of America's youth." A red carpet was being laid for Dylan's own grand entrance.

His return to Town Hall in a solo show on Friday, April 13, 1963, was a turning point. Forgetting his late 1961 appearance, Leventhal and Grossman billed Town Hall as Dylan's first solo concert. Now he had the material and experience to be a serious performer, as well as a witty one. It may have been the last Dylan concert that reminded listeners of his influences. From now on he could be compared only to himself. That night his hobo look evoked memories of Guthrie. Dylan resembled Holden Caulfield lost in the Dust Bowl. To round off the evening, he read his poem to Guthrie, which won an ovation.

In the balcony, Seeger and his wife, Toshi, glowed benevolently. Two rave reviews, mine in the *Times* and Barry Kittleson in *Billboard*, gave Grossman fuel. A paper dependent on record company advertising rarely offered quotable criticism, but Kittleson was an uncommon trade paper reviewer. Under the heading "A Legend Under Construction: Folk Poet Dylan Weaves a Spell," he wrote that Dylan was "the stuff of which legends are made … an absolute original … profound … poetry born of a painful awareness of the tragedy that underlies the contemporary human condition. … It is his primary purpose to speak, not to entertain. … The prediction here is that his talent will be around for a long, long time."

Afterward, there was an impromptu party, Yarrow volunteering his mother's Upper West Side apartment. Grossman's partner, John Court, gently shooed away the well-wishers and escorted Bob into a waiting taxi. About twenty-five people showed up. Mrs. Yarrow, a warm, volatile woman, didn't even realize that Dylan was the guest of honor. "Would you get some ice cubes for our guests, dear?" she asked him, assuming he was just another admirer of her son, the folk singer. Bob wasn't put off. After a few drinks, he asked her: "How'd yuh like to marry me? I mean it, you're a real groovy chick." The long-divorced Mrs. Yarrow was, for a rare moment, speechless.

Through Yarrow, Dylan first visited Woodstock, in early summer 1963. The gracious upstate New York art colony had long been Peter's retreat. His uncle owned a forty-year-old cabin, which Peter subsequently bought. The first summer, Bob and Suze shared the cabin. Suze was painting, Bob was writing, and the three shared household responsibilities. Since Bob's cooking was primitive, Peter and Suze prepared most meals. "Bob was never more at peace with himself than that first summer in Woodstock," Yarrow recalled.

"When Bobby and Suze went back to the Village, they were down. When they returned to Woodstock, their spirits inevitably rose. Albert wasn't anywhere near Woodstock then." During summer 1963, I saw Dylan when he bounced back to the Village from Woodstock, refreshed. New York summers made him furtive. He told me I should come up where "we stop the clouds, turn time back and inside out, make the sun turn on and off. It's the greatest, man, the greatest place."

Grossman booked Dylan on TV's prestigious *Ed Sullivan Show* on Sunday, May 12, 1963. It may have seemed an unscalable Everest for a singer identified with protest, but Sullivan based his format on popular taste. The booking became an ironic coup for Dylan. Because he was forced to walk off it, Dylan made national news.

Earlier in the week, Dylan had sung his "Talkin' John Birch Society Blues" to Sullivan and his producer, who liked both the singer and the song. But immediately after the dress rehearsal, the editor of CBS-TV program practices—a fancy title for a censor—said the song could not be used. He feared possible libel action because Dylan compared

the right-wing Birchites to Hitler. Sullivan was annoyed, Grossman irate, Dylan furious. Sullivan asked Dylan if he wanted to substitute another song. Without hesitating, Dylan whirled around and said: "If I can't sing that song, I won't sing *any* song." He stomped out of the studio and crashed around the Village that night in a blazing, raging temper cursing "those bastards!" "What a story that would make," I told him. It did.

Val Adams, the *Times* radio-TV reporter, went after the higher echelons of CBS. Did they stand behind their censor? "No comment." On Tuesday, May 14, Bob Williams of the *New York Post* gave Sullivan's views: "We told CBS: 'It's your network, but ... the decision is wrong and the policy behind it is wrong.'" Dylan, in a formal letter, asked the Federal Communications Commission for a public investigation. No hearing was held, but Dylan often retold the story at subsequent concerts.

Dylan next appeared on a freedom songs show on WNEW-TV, New York. The producer, Arthur Barron, hired me as a consultant, and I called Bob and described the civil rights content of the show. He agreed at once to do it and to "tell Albert," no matter what the money was. Odetta and the Freedom Singers rounded out the bill. Grossman groused during the taping, in July 1963, because he wasn't sure Dylan and Odetta were getting the treatment they deserved. Another annoyance was that Dylan had called Joan Baez to the studio. While cameras and lights were being prepared, Bob and Joan huddled in a corner. Bob played her a ragtimey dance tune, while Joan did an improvised clog dance. They were having their own party, despite audience and technicians milling around. Grossman, whose peripheral vision often matched his foresight, took in the scene. "Can you imagine the offspring of a union of those two?" he asked me.

When Mike Porco started his Monday night hootenanny, he had no idea that by 1963 it would become a household word. The hootenanny craze sprang from a TV series on ABC. Dylan never appeared on it, yet the show's influence on mass taste ultimately benefited him and other performers who shunned it. "Hootenanny" is a nonsense word, like "thingamajig" or "whatsit." In July 1940, according to Peter Tamony, a West Coast word detective, some Seattle Democrats launched fund-raising parties with folk songs. Someone suggested calling them hootenannies, a word remembered from youth in Indiana, and the title stuck. Two young singers at those Seattle hoots were Seeger and Guthrie, who brought the word and concept east. *Sing Out!* and the Old Left kept the word alive. Then an ABC producer, Richard Lewine, and his

BELOW

Program for the First Annual Monterey Folk Festival, which repeats a familiar early Dylan story: that he toured with a carnival at age fourteen.

talent coordinator, Fred Weintraub, tacked it on to a TV show set amid lively collegiate audiences. Their cardinal mistake was to blacklist Seeger and the Weavers.

A weekly audience of up to 11 million watched *Hootenanny*, and soon the word described or promoted sweatshirts, pinball machines, brogans, and vacations. New Jersey's Palisades Amusement Park even had a Miss Hootenanny contest. There was a *Hootenanny Hoot* feature film, a dance step called the hoot, and albums titled *Hootenanny for Orchestra*, *Hot-Rod Hootenanny*, and *Surfing Hootenanny*. There were two dreadful magazines called *Hootenanny*, including the late, unlamented monster I edited. The over-exploited hoot craze wore itself out. Dylan and Baez, among others, spoofed it at their concerts.

Before the Newport Folk Festival of July 1963,

when folk-song fever ran high, Dylan had four festival-like settings with different audiences—eastern collegiate, West Coast public, Mississippi political, and Puerto Rican commercial. Still only a rising star, his uphill effort demanded as much self-possession as Bob could muster. His increasing popularity could only impress Suze, even while each tour meant another separation. Ready to go almost anywhere, neither he nor Albert was saying no to any reasonable invitation.

On May 10, there was a folk festival at Brandeis University, outside Boston. Grossman made sure Dylan had the two best spots—before intermission and the finale. Brandeis hailed. Dylan. On May 18, Dylan was booked for the first Monterey Folk Festival, the program including the Weavers and roots folk singer Mance Lipscomb. Dylan was delighted to work in Steinbeck country and he was paid $1,500 for Saturday night. Audience reaction was quizzically appreciative. Monterey was Dylan's first real encounter with Joan Baez, who lived in nearby Carmel. Monterey affected her life and Dylan's, artistically and personally.

In early July 1963, the Student Non-violent Coordinating Committee (SNCC) had planned a voter-registration rally in Greenwood, Mississippi, a cotton center on the Yazoo River, where Highway 82 curls its way toward the Delta. Local activists had been trying to persuade blacks to register to vote. Seeger, Theodore Bikel, and Dylan flew down, at some personal risk, to play for a few hundred black farmers. Dylan was now emerging as spokesman and star, and Bikel, who told me he had paid Dylan's plane fare, treated him with deference.

Arriving at the Jackson, Mississippi, airport, Dylan saw water fountains and toilets marked WHITE and COLORED. He asked Theo what he thought would happen if he decided to drink from the COLORED ONLY fountain. They arrived, still thirsty, at Greenwood, where Pete, Bob, and Theo sang on the edge of a cotton patch. Around three hundred people attended, mostly local blacks, with a score of young white supporters, newsmen, and four TV men from New York.

By summer 1963, even Columbia Records began to realize Dylan's potential. In July, at the annual Columbia sales convention in Puerto Rico, Dylan was an honored guest, along with Aretha Franklin and Tony Bennett. Dylan flew to the Hotel Americana in San Juan with Albert, Suze, and Carla. He performed only once, at the salesmen's dinner, when he was applauded roundly, but he was expected to shake hands and banter with faceless regional distributors, sales managers, and field representatives. Except for a few private moments on the beach, he felt ill at ease.

Dylan arrived at the Newport Folk Festival of July 26–28 an underground conversation piece, and left a national star. Newport '63 was a dress rehearsal for Woodstock Nation. The weekend's total attendance was only 47,000, less than 10 percent of those who turned out, and on, at Woodstock '69. But Newport '63 was the cocoon of an alternative culture. The seventy performers and their audience

were high on the music, high on "their" civil rights revolution. Musicians and listeners felt they were saying something to the rest of the country about another way of living and thinking. The hootenanny craze and the music business only provided the vehicle for a mass expression of social purpose.

Newport '63 was a turning point for folk song as a new popular music, and for Dylan. With his raggedy clothes, biting songs, anti–show business posture, identification with black rights and peace, and shaking off of the outworn myths of history in "God on Our Side," Dylan became the Festival's emblem. His picture was everywhere—lean, gaunt face, frail shoulders covered in a faded khaki army shirt with wilted epaulets, blanched blue jeans. Most of the weekend he walked around with a long leather bullwhip wrapped tightly around one

ABOVE

July 1963, downtime at the Viking Hotel, home base for artists playing at the Newport Folk Festival.

shoulder. Reporters dogged his steps. It all looked as spontaneous as the group spirit of Newport itself. Yet Albert and Dylan had done considerable planning, insisting on the honored closing spot for Dylan at the first major concert. The pair also had timing on their side: Newport Nation was hungry for a new leader and Dylan was elected by acclamation.

Despite the board's disavowal of the star system, Seeger and other big names still dominated. The first step out of the incubator on Friday afternoon at the Newport Casino Tennis Club was quiet enough. About a hundred youngsters sat, barefoot or in sneakers, as Bikel told a panel discussion that the swelling interest in folk music was more than a fad: it represented a rebellion against canned recreation and a return to do-it-yourself culture. Seeger said TV and its power had to be watched so that it

"makes a place in the mass media for minority tastes. We all know folk music has mushroomed, and now we're beginning to worry about the fallout."

A few singers commented melodically. Baez was among the first. Her silken voice was joined by Bob's raspy, raw-edged voice. As the pair went through "With God on Our Side," listeners craned to see the stranger singing with Joan. In the weeks since Monterey, Joan had learned many Dylan songs. That workshop duet was the first time Joan and Bob sang together publicly. For the next two years, and intermittently until 1984, they appeared dozens of times on each other's programs.

For the major opening concert at Newport that Friday night, July 26, more than 13,000 people turned out, as many as at the entire 1959 Festival. Newport police rated it the city's biggest single

> **Bobby Dylan says what a lot of people my age feel but cannot say.**
>
> JOAN BAEZ

RIGHT

With Joan Baez, Woodstock 1963, between Newport and Baez's East Coast tour on which Dylan would appear as her special guest.

crowd. According to the *Newport Daily News*, Peter, Paul and Mary did best on "Wind," after Yarrow's standard homily to Dylan. The audience didn't want to let the trio off the stage. Of Dylan's solo set in the second half, the *Newport News* described him as "the voice of the oppressed in America and the champion of the little man." After his set, Dylan relaxed backstage on the grass with me and my girlfriend Shelden Ogilvy. "We've got a little surprise for you at the end of the show," he teased. Peter, Paul and Mary returned and sang "Wind" again, then brought on Dylan, Joan, the Freedom Singers, Seeger, and Bikel for a grand finale of "We Shall Overcome."

Dylan made two more stage appearances during the weekend. A workshop hosted by Seeger, on topical songs and new songwriters, drew the largest crowd. Sunday night, at Baez's main appearance, she brought Dylan, unscheduled, on to the stage, to join her in "With God on Our Side." Grossman was all smiles. The program ended with a mass grouping onstage for "This Land Is Your Land." The concept of a festival run by musicians had worked, and the civil rights commitment gave the event purpose and drive. Everyone seemed to agree that Dylan was the "find" of the festival. The weekly news magazines duly noted that Baez, the reigning queen of folk music, had named Dylan the crown prince. Dylan's apprenticeship was over. He left Newport a star.

Right after Newport, Baez had ten solo concerts in the east, her most rigorous schedule to date and everything pointed to Dylan as her next tour guest. Albert worked out details with Joan's manager, Manny Greenhill: Bob would do about a half-dozen songs at each gig, and would earn slightly more than Joan, who wasn't pleased but didn't make an issue about the pie slicing. She was always keen on some cause or other, some musician, and all that enthusiasm converged now on Dylan. For his part, Bob promised to bring Joan on his future shows.

The East Coast tour blossomed into a close personal relationship, an erratic friendship, a stormy on-again, off-again love affair. Bob's and Joan's fans were fascinated and mystified by their motivations. Rasped Dave Van Ronk: "I think the relationship was purely opportunistic on both sides. Certainly, Dylan the sponge was functioning on all eight cylinders. In 1963, he really needed Joanie and really wanted to make it. He wanted to be a rich man." Couldn't it have been opportune for Joan to want a new toy, a new enthusiasm? Didn't she drop him when she got tired of him? "No," Van Ronk snapped back, "Joan was burned and Dylan wasn't. She was expecting a new bright light to save the pacifist movement, and Bobby wasn't having any of that crap either."

Right after Newport, Joan visited Woodstock. Dylan came back to the Village happier than I'd seen him in months. Now, instead of the endless wrangles with Suze and her family, he'd found a girl whose own identity was established. He was clearly infatuated. That summer, Dylan somehow managed to juggle two women.

On August 17, the Baez-Dylan tour was due at the Forest Hills Stadium in Queens, their sixth concert since Newport. The morning of the concert, Dylan called me to join him for breakfast at the Gallery Delicatessen on Christopher Street. "She promised to set up a special room in her house in Carmel with a piano for me. Imagine me having my own piano out on the Coast!" He sounded like a struggling painter who had just found a beautiful patroness to buy him oils.

> I think the relationship was purely opportunistic on both sides. Certainly, Dylan the sponge was functioning on all eight cylinders.
>
> DAVE VAN RONK

Newport Folk
Festival, July 28,
1963: Dylan
arrived "an
underground
conversation
piece, and left
a national star.
Newport '63 was
a dress rehearsal
for Woodstock
Nation."

Dylan had periodically come up to my apartment
to listen to records, talk, and play the piano. Now he
had the prospect of a piano of his own, and the well-
tempered attentions of Baez along with it.

At Forest Hills, Joan introduced Dylan as an
unbilled "surprise" guest. Nearly half her program
was songs by or with him. "Bobby Dylan says what
a lot of people my age feel but cannot say," Joan
told nearly 15,000. Dylan's presence seemed to relax
Joan, who was obviously getting a lot from having
Dylan on her side. At the previous five concerts,
audiences reportedly had been restrained toward
Dylan. By the time the pair arrived in Queens, he
won as much applause as Joan.

Dylan's own natural senses told him to accept
Joan's invitation to stay with her in Carmel that
autumn. He probably still loved Suze, but she had

decided to move out of West 4th Street that summer.
Bob still thought he could balance things. I had
visited Joan, her sister Mimi, her brother-in-law
Dick Fariña, and her mother Joan in Carmel only a
few weeks before Dylan arrived. We had watched a
report on the August 28 march on Washington. Joan
was waiting for her new home to be built in Carmel
Valley, and was living in a modest, wood-beamed
cottage less than a mile from the Pacific. Glass walls
brought the countryside right into the spacious living
room, dotted with modern sculpture, benches, and
casual chairs. I had a preview of the serenity that
Dylan was to find there. Carmel and Big Sur was a
land of craggy coastlines and wind-twisted cypresses.
At Joan's place, in autumn 1963, as Dylan had his
first sojourn in peaceful country, he wrote his first
withdrawal song, "Lay Down Your Weary Tune,"

inspired by a recording of a Scottish ballad. "What good are fans?" Dylan asked me just before he headed west. "You can't eat applause for breakfast. You can't sleep with it," he said, after three months of stardom, ready for the simpler country life.

Carmel was the Bakersfield he had dreamed of. Not far north was Steinbeck's Cannery Row in Monterey. The district became Dylan's "East of Eden," perhaps even beyond his "Gates of Eden." Under Joan's attentive eyes, he put himself into a disciplined schedule. In the past, chaos and urgency were his stimuli to creativity. Now it was serenity. Down from Joan's cottage was a deserted cove, which they could reach in ten minutes in her sports car or in a half-hour's walk. There he loved to swim and ponder the Pacific. He could set up his typewriter in her house and work in the morning. Joan, fearful of intruding, left him to himself.

"I tried to get Bobby to look after his health," Joan told me later. When pressed in 1966 as to what Dylan really meant to her, she grew dark and thoughtful. Choosing words carefully, she said, with a touch of tartness: "He is a complicated, problematic, difficult person. I see Bobby with a slightly damaged diamond in his head. More fragile than the average person. When I was sitting and watching him play, how easily he could be blown apart by a comment or by something passing. But you never know that he feels these things, because he's very good at covering all that up. For some reason, in my opinion, he wants to relieve himself of all responsibility. Any responsibility, about anybody, it seems to me. To barely get by with what people have to offer. If you don't really care about yourself, then you don't have to care about anybody else. He is terribly, terribly bright, with a funny magnet inside him that makes you drawn to him. I mean, I love Bobby, and I would do anything for him, ever. Whatever went wrong between us, I really don't know. I don't know how Bobby feels about me. It obviously can't matter."

I looked down at Joan's Egyptian ring. "Is that a little gift from a pharaoh in Cairo?" Joan laughed: "Yes, it's the funniest thing. The fact of the matter is that … well, that's supposed to be a secret. Anyway, it's in the song. I have only the feeling that I wish that Bobby would be all right. I feel he is killing himself. I feel Bobby could have tremendous power for social good, but he could also have tremendous power to take a lot of people down in the hole that he's in, to coin a phrase. I've already asked him too many things. Even questions about his songs seemed to be imposing on something that he just didn't want to be bothered with. The split between us came on a professional level, but it made things clear in my head about what I wanted to do. At one point in our little scene," Joan continued, "when we were still doing concerts together … although I was enjoying those concerts, I froze up and said to him: 'Bobby, you'd be doing it as rock 'n' roll king, but I'd be doing it as peace queen.' And he was not even rock 'n' roll king then yet, but I just had the feeling he would be soon."

Dylan undoubtedly learned from Baez. He made some of his most candid comments in the long prose-poem on *Joan Baez in Concert, Part 2*, released in March 1964. In a fine piece of page writing, he mixed childhood memories with Joan's, showing how he learned a new concept of beauty from her. Previously, he had been able to say what Joan meant to him in songs only, a dozen classic songs.

In a stunning, two-disk album, *Any Day Now*, recorded in Nashville with musicians Dylan had used a year earlier on *John Wesley Harding*, Baez's

ABOVE

Dylan at the celebrated "We Shall Overcome" finale at Newport '63 with (from left) Peter Yarrow, Mary Travers, Paul Stookey, Joan Baez, Charles Neblett, Rutha Harris, and Pete Seeger.

"
The voice of the oppressed in America and the champion of the little man.
NEWPORT NEWS

"

interpretations of his work were deep and affecting. At that time, Joan hadn't spoken to Dylan for perhaps two years. The all-Dylan album was a letter to an old lover, telling him that she still loved him and his writing, even though that love worked better for her at a distance. From neither Dylan nor Baez, and certainly no observer or friend, can there be a *final* word on their relationship. Their most serious rupture came in England in spring 1965, and lasted years, even after *Any Day Now*. Yet they somehow managed to pick up the threads, well into the eighties. Joan told me at meetings in London in 1980 and 1982 of her contact with Dylan. She told the world about it in her finest song, "Diamonds and Rust." Whenever Joan talked to me about him, she would do the full-scale mimicry of his gestures. It was funny, and yet somehow sad, as if it were the only way she could get mastery over this impossible, elusive man.

At summer's end, Suze moved out of West 4th Street again. She needed to be alone. Meanwhile, Dylan had a major solo concert at Carnegie Hall, and suffered a trauma with the press. Billy James and John Kurland of Columbia publicity had approached *Newsweek* about a cover story. A *Newsweek* researcher, Andrea Svedberg, was impressed with the Baez-Dylan Forest Hills concert. Then Svedberg telephoned Billy in annoyance, saying she was having trouble reaching Dylan or Grossman. Billy: "She said they were very interested in determining certain things about Dylan's past. I tried to tell her that Bobby didn't like to talk about such things. I told her to let it lay."

The story, on November 4, 1963, turned into a hatchet job that led to a new era of tortuous relations between the musician and the media. Dylan turned from an accessible subject into a cagey game-player who toyed with interview questions, who developed the outrageous "anti-interview," saying shocking, even deleterious things he often didn't believe. He became dubious that even the emerging underground press could understand him.

The *Newsweek* story appeared, under the headline I AM MY WORDS. The adjectives were abrasive: "unscrubbed face … bewildered-hair … skinny frame … hip talk, punctuated with obscenities. His singing voice scratches and shouts so jarringly that

his success, at first, seems incredible … his knack for stirring audiences is unmistakable." Attributed to the words of his two hundred songs: "simple words that pounce upon the obvious." Admitting that "Dylan is practically a religion," the article challenged his believability.

The article was illustrated with a photo of Dylan recording, above the caption "Bob Dylan: What's in a name?" The "exposure" of his family was bad enough, but the imputation that he had stolen "Blowin' in the Wind" was the coup de grace. He lashed out at Billy James for having suggested the piece. He sniped at his parents for talking to Walter Eldot, not only for *Newsweek* but also for the equally irritating piece in the *Duluth News Tribune* a month earlier. Finally, Dylan blamed Grossman, who had unsuccessfully tried to bargain an interview in exchange for final approval.

I spoke to Dylan within an hour of his reading the article. Bob was nearly screaming: "Just wait till you read that piece in *Newsweek*. No, I won't read it to you. Read it for yourself and then you'll know why Joan told me not to even talk to *Time* and *Newsweek*. *Time* screwed up Joan's head for a year, and now it's my turn. I've got over five-thousand pages written of all sorts of things, poems and plays and a novel. I just want to be known for what I do." Dylan exploded with anger.

Dylan decided not to rebut *Newsweek* directly. After a concert in Boston, he went underground for three weeks, musing sullenly, and writing like a flood tide. He would face the press again, but his words often formed curious conundrums. Each reporter who got a "rare" interview hoped he or

OPPOSITE
Eric Von
Schmidt's poster
for the 1965
Joan Baez–Bob
Dylan tour was
commissioned by
Manny Greenhill,
its inspiration
drawn from a
photo taken
at Club 47 in
Cambridge.

> "His singing voice scratches and shouts so jarringly that his success, at first, seems incredible … his knack for stirring audiences is unmistakable.
> NEWSWEEK

she alone would persuade the sphinx to take the sand out of his mouth.

Amid all the offstage turmoil of 1963, Dylan gave solo concerts at Carnegie Hall, Philadelphia's Town Hall, and Boston's Jordan Hall. The Carnegie concert was singular in that "teenyboppers" surfaced. Previously, folk audiences dressed and acted differently than pop audiences. The first Beatles single, "Please, Please Me," was a hit in Britain in February 1963. Beatlemania erupted by October, just about the time the first wave of Dylanmania hit America. The Carnegie audience was younger, more exuberant and unruly than Kingston Trio fans had been. This wasn't a folk-campfire crowd. Dylan churned up his listeners. He used stage-center to lambast Fabian, soap commercials on TV, *Hootenanny*, censorship in general.

Leventhal gave a party later at his West 96th Street home for Dylan and friends, including a contingent of Suze's chums—then strong Castro supporters—and Ronnie Gilbert, a member of the Weavers since 1948. Ronnie told me: "Such passion! I've never heard such singing or such songs! It's more than just the topical movement, it's that Dylan is absolutely classic. He's in a class all by himself." The star was being toasted all around. Bob came over to me: "Well, man, you didn't think I could do it, did you?" I assured him I *had* thought he could do it, but he pushed right on: "Well, I did it, I did it!"

But with *Newsweek* his triumph soured. Somehow, amid all that intense work and limelight, Dylan began to lose his sense of whimsy, his youthfulness. Within a month, the assassination of President John F. Kennedy on November 22 plunged America into a troubled depression. Although some of Dylan's Castroite friends took the assassination with detachment, Dylan was stunned. To criticize a society where bullets could strike down even the mightiest and wealthiest reformers seemed pointless.

Clark Foreman's Emergency Civil Liberties Committee (ECLC) held an annual fundraising dinner marking Bill of Rights Day, and honored with its Tom Paine Award some public figure who, to them, epitomized the good fight for freedom and equality. In 1962, the ECLC gave the award to Lord Bertrand Russell. In 1968, the recipient was Dr. Benjamin Spock. The choice in 1963 was Dylan,

who felt it was more than he deserved because he had "only" written a few songs. He didn't want to be Joe Hill or Tom Paine. Nevertheless, he went to the dinner.

On December 13, 1963, Dylan began to drink too early. He saw the other dignitaries on the dais, among them author James Baldwin, dressed in suit and tie. The politics were different, but this could have been his father's B'nai B'rith Lodge. Bob looked at the faces and gray or balding heads of about 1,500 Old Left burghers in new middle-class security and mellowed radicalism. Presented with the Tom Paine award, Dylan started to speak. He hadn't prepared, and his almost disembodied voice began a Dylan truth attack:

> I haven't got any guitar, I can talk though. I want to thank you for the Tom Paine Award on behalf of everybody that went down to Cuba. First of all because they're all young and it's took me a long time to get young and now I consider myself young. And I'm proud of it. I'm proud that I'm young. And I only wish that all you people who are sitting out here today or tonight weren't here and I could see all kinds of faces with hair on their head and everything like that, everything leading to youngness, celebrating the anniversary when we overthrew the House Un-American Activities just yesterday— because you people should be at the beach. You should be … swimming and … just relaxing in the time you have to relax. [Laughter] It is not an old people's world. It has nothing to do with old people. …

Dylan talked about Cuba, saying that anybody should be able to go—Americans were prohibited from visiting. Then:

> I'll stand up and to get uncompromisable about it, which I have to be to be honest, I just got to be, as I got to admit that the man who shot President Kennedy, Lee Oswald, I don't know exactly where— what he thought he was doing, but I

got to admit honestly that I, too—I saw some of myself in him. I don't think it would have gone—I don't think it could go that far. But I got to stand up and say I saw things that he felt in me—not to go that far and shoot. [Boos and hisses] You can boo, but booing's got nothing to do with it. It's a—I just, ah—I've got to tell you, man, it's Bill of Rights is free speech and [Someone says to Dylan: "Time's about up."] I just want to admit that I accept this Tom Paine Award on behalf of James Forman of the Students Non-Violent Coordinating Committee and the people on behalf of who went to Cuba. [Boos mixed with applause]

The audience buzzed. Had this kid really been saying that Oswald deserved sympathy, three weeks after the assassination? Had he called them outdated, bald, old men ready for the junk pile of history? As the fundraising proceeded, Foreman realized the enormity of his gaff. Contributions were grudging and pale. Clark Foreman was crushed. He had been opposed within the organization for putting Dylan in such an honored position and now the words of the naysayers were coming back to haunt him. The outraged, bald old men weren't going to dig deep for an organization that would let that kid speak with such disrespect. Geno Foreman, Clark's son, who died three years later in an accident, told me that the collection was $30,000 short of expectations, although his father later told Dylan the sum was $6,000.

THE BROADSIDE

OF BOSTON

Vol. II, No. 17   Cambridge, Massachusetts   October 30, 1963

FOLK MUSIC AND COFFEE HOUSE NEWS ✹ TEN CENTS

ABOVE

The *Broadside* of Boston,
October 30, 1963. On
November 2, Dylan played
Boston's Jordan Hall.

As the repercussions broadened, Dylan realized the ECLC hadn't gotten his message at all. Like Kennedy going to consult Eisenhower, Bob went to talk with Harold Leventhal, Guthrie's agent and Seeger's manager. Harold, in his fifties, bald and Old Left, told Dylan those old-timers, who now looked so prosperous and well fed, had been fighting most of their lives. Harold recounted the McCarthy era, when many of these people had been blacklisted, had scuffled for a living, yet had remained socially conscious. Dylan listened, then went to his typewriter. He sent the Emergency Civil Liberties Committee an open letter, in which he described his moodiness and how futile it was for anyone to try to say what he meant, something he couldn't even do himself. He was only a songwriter, not a public speaker.

Late fall and winter of 1963 found Dylan at low ebb. Partly it was the letdown many stars experience right after they have made it, but he was also burdened by the general malaise that clouded America after the assassination. Dylan knew that nearly every day in the South, obscure black people were being shot, beaten, intimidated, harassed. His despair was deepened by increasing loneliness: Suze had moved out and became suicidal. All his "famiosity," as he called it, didn't spell happiness. He sat alone in his dingy West 4th Street hole, pouring out his songs and his back pages.

Around Christmas 1963, everyone tried to bury that dying year. On Christmas Eve, there was a dinner at Mrs. Rotolo's in New Jersey. Among the guests was Virginia Eggleston, one of the few at the Paine Award dinner who had actually approved of Dylan's unorthodox speech. On Christmas night, twenty people turned out for a party at the Avenue B apartment. Bob was very outgoing and friendly; Carla recalled that "he seemed to be at peace with himself Christmas Day, and I was his 'sister-in-law' again." The guests sang rock 'n' roll and had a cool Yule. Still, Dylan was planning an extended trip to California. The Rotolos were beginning to get a lot of telephone calls for Dylan from young girl fans, some very offensive. Anonymity for anyone close to Dylan was disappearing.

On New Year's Eve, a ritual that closed 1963 more than it opened 1964, Dylan was at a small party at the Van Ronks'. A year earlier Bob had been at a big, impersonal party at my place. Now, he wanted to be with very few people. Suze looked subdued, Bob haggard. I had been party-hopping, and the Van Ronks' was my final stop. Dylan and a half-dozen friends in their twenties sat as if at a wake. Bob had started 1963 filled with hope and ambition but now he seemed a lot less happy. Even Van Ronk's ribald jokes were not producing smiles. I went across the street to bed, and I thought of how very old and tired those kids seemed. If something didn't change, I felt Dylan would be dead before 1964 was out.

In autumn 1963, Bob had written a remarkable open letter to his friends at *Broadside*. It was the last time—for that period—that he was prepared to publish anything so personal. Dylan could speak honestly to Sis and Gordon Friesen, who always thought in human terms, not slogans. The Old Left, Gordon wrote to me in late 1970, "never did understand how to treat artists." Guthrie had been reprimanded for failing to show up at a certain corner to sell *Daily Worker*s as he had pledged to do. Shit! They couldn't comprehend that Woody's role was to write songs, not sell their paper. Gordon understood the plight of the artist in America: "Melville spent his last thirty years drudging away in a customs-house. Whitman worked away unrecognized, supported meagerly by the largesse of a friend or two. Nobody bought *Walden Pond* until Thoreau was long dead. Poe and Stephen Foster died in the gutter …" That was the compassion of Sis and Gordon, who published Dylan's letter in *Broadside* in January 1964. It was a remnant of the old Dylan, but hinted that the new Dylan was to be an even more solitary and tortured artist than he had been before the world took notice of him.

This was a soul-baring letter to friends. Through it one could see Dylan was the artist overwhelmed by fame, yet terribly lonely. He described his filthy flat and how he must move out of it amid falling plaster and rotting floorboards. But he could find a certain beauty in it, especially hearing Pete Seeger on his record player singing "Guantanamera." He called Pete a saint he loved more than he could show. And love lead to Suze, who had left, and he wished he could love everyone as he did her. He would be Christ-like if he were to love everyone as he loved Suze. He laughed at that idea and made his prayer for the acceptance of his many selves:

> *away away be gone all you demons*
> *an' just let me be me*
> *human me*
> *ruthless me*
> *wild me*
> *gentle me*
> *all kinds of me*

He bid a restless farewell to *Broadside*. But not without some old angers at *Newsweek* and the jealous gossipmongers. The nightmares he faced and his hates and angers suffused into his own hope for himself: "An I shall wake in the mornin an try t start lovin again." Much as he was denying it, in 1963 and '64, Dylan was flowering as a poet. By using the mass media in his special way, he was developing a new genre. The San Francisco beat poets had tried to wed spoken poetry with jazz—an experiment that scarcely got out of the basement. The French *chansonniers*, like Jacques Brel, had long known that song was an ideal vehicle for poetry, as had history's nameless bards, troubadours, minstrels, broadside balladeers, and buskers. Dylan saw "poets" all around him and was at the heart of the democratic folk tradition so well described by Guthrie: "I have a storm of words in me enough to write several hundred songs and that many books. I know that these words I hear are not my own private property. … You may have been taught to call me a poet, but I am no more of a poet than you are. … You are the poet and your everyday talk is our best poem by our best poet. All I am is just sort of a clerk and climate-taster, and my workshop is the sidewalk, your street and your field, your highway, and your buildings."

During 1963, I played editor to Dylan because I felt that he could handle any sort of writing job with speed, flair, and originality. My first assignment for him was a piece for the 1963 Newport Folk Festival program, which I edited under the pseudonym Stacey Williams. He chose to write an open letter to Dave (Tony) Glover, his old Minneapolis sidekick. Bob handed me the piece typed single-spaced on tired yellow sheets, written in a cross between Guthrie's folk-talk and his own invented punk-tuation. Roughly a hundred-and-fifty lines of free verse recollected the good old days and the friend "who knew me before I hit or got hit by New York City."

The Minneapolis group stood resolutely for the old music, mostly blues, and were alarmed by Dylan's drift into political slogans and protest and topical writing. Dylan recalled the old songs he and Glover used to sing, which came out of a time when, in Woody's view, there were only two roads to choose—"The American way or the Fascist way"—two sides to every question. Time changed that, he wrote. So Dylan couldn't then sing traditional songs any more, but rather "Masters of War," "Seven Curses," "Hollis Brown," and others. Yet, he emphasized he was not rejecting apolitical folk songs, for they "showed me the way … that songs can say somethin human."

In late summer 1963, I assumed the editorship of a folk-song magazine, *Hootenanny*, that slid into merciful oblivion after four issues, along with the craze that spawned it. I asked Dylan to do a bimonthly column, called "Blowin' in the Wind," for which he could choose any form, length, or subject. I offered him the princely sum of seventy-five dollars a column, which annoyed Grossman but seemed to amuse Dylan. "It's not the bread," Dylan told me, "it's the idea of it I like."

His first column appeared in early autumn 1963. Knowing that I was planning a magazine considerably broader than *Sing Out!*, Dylan appealed to folk fans to avoid hair-splitting debates about the music. "It just ain't healthy to let the music run yer life like that – /Yer life's gotta run the music. … Just get up in the mornin and go – /Just open yer eyes an walk." Then he hailed the natural beauties of the open country, from Monterey eastward. New York was stressful and ugly, yet possessed of a curious sense of beauty; Dylan was fascinated with its energy and variety. The neo-Guthrie tone of the piece was obvious, underlining the need to throw oneself into experience, life, and music, and to learn from them. Don't let the categorizers, analyzers, or rule-makers "boundary it all up."

By the end of 1963, Dylan told me he had so much work he couldn't continue the *Hootenanny* column. After one more issue, *Hootenanny* folded, because of bad management and lack of focus—it had attempted to reach everyone interested in folk music. The folk audience was already too fragmented to accept any single magazine. Although Dylan seemed to enjoy journalism, he was already working on *Tarantula*, and was feverishly writing songs and a few surprises for his next album. He knew that records had the greatest power to reach people.

When *The Times They Are a-Changin'* was released in February 1964, Columbia finally recognized that it had a star in Dylan. He had almost complete control over the album, which Tom Wilson produced. The jacket notes were a bold departure for a pop LP. Continued on a printed insert, "11 Outlined Epitaphs" constituted Dylan's first published poetry. The cover photograph, by Barry Feinstein, then Mary Travers's husband, showed an intense and tortured Dylan exuding sullen anger.

A strong sense of apocalypse dominates the album. Dylan's development of the topical song had far outstripped even his own previous efforts. "Hattie Carroll," "Only a Pawn," and "Hollis Brown" had been triggered by news items, but Dylan, brimming with confidence, was imbuing his more complex "stories" with larger vision and greater universality.

For all their artistry, *The Times They Are a-Changin'* and the Epitaphs showed critical reaction still divided. *Little Sandy Review*: "Forty-five minutes of gloom … by far his weakest album, musically." The "822 lines of free-association blank verse" were dismissed as "spiritual masochism." *High Fidelity* cautioned that "Dylan will not entertain you. That's not his line. But he will sear your soul." *HiFi/Stereo Review* had reservations about "this tortured hearer of

> **Dylan will not entertain you. That's not his line. But he will sear your soul.**
> *HIGH FIDELITY*

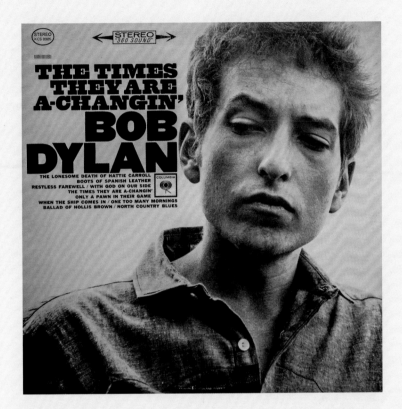

apocalyptic visions." This reviewer rated Dylan as equal to Guthrie, but feared he might "become only a mannered apologist for his own wounded self-esteem."

After an appearance in London in May 1964, Dylan made a lightning trip to Paris and then Greece. After returning in June, he recorded in only two nights a total of eleven songs, and wrote more poems for the sleeve. Columbia had originally scheduled a *Bob Dylan in Concert* album for release in early summer 1964 which would have been largely based on Dylan's October 26, 1963, Carnegie Hall concert, along with one song and his "Last Thoughts on Woody Guthrie" poem from his April 12, 1963, Town Hall concert. But this album was canceled, and in August 1964, *Another Side of Bob Dylan* was released.

Many critics were cool. The folk-Left saw him drifting into "too much subjectivity." Other critics carped for aesthetic reasons. *Another Side* was taped hastily, and the singing was not Dylan's subtlest. But the album does capture weariness, cynicism, and road *ennui.* It brings back Dylan's mocking wit,

notably absent on *Times Changin'.* Dylan reluctantly accepted Tom Wilson's album title.

The jacket notes for *Another Side* were titled "Some Other Kinds of Songs … Poems by Bob Dylan." As his songs extended page poetry, his page poetry extended his music. Columbia Records printed five of the poems in a cramped, telephone directory-sized typeface. *Writings and Drawings* offers a more readable text and the full cycle of eleven poems, the same number as the Epitaphs. "Some Other Kinds of Songs" further documents Dylan's experimentation with verbal music and his often elusive world view. The style is impressionistic and surreal.

For all their obscurities, these "other kinds of songs" show metaphoric daring, control of nuance, flowing rhythms. His seemingly random arrangements make his words into fortune-telling cards that reveal his emerging inner self. These poems were written in a period of personal loss and reorientation. Dylan has arrived at a major insight: the question can be the answer. Ahead lay the frenzied vision of his three great albums of 1965 and 1966, and the larger questions they posed.

06

SEVERAL SEASONS IN HELL

> ## I'm lucky. Not because I make a lot of bread, but because I can be around groovy people. I don't fear anything and nobody around me has to fear anything. That's where it's at: bread, freedom, and no fear.

In 1964, Bob Dylan decided to try rediscovering America. He was not yet twenty-three.

The journey that began in February 3, 1964, went from New York to California with a half-dozen detours to see embattled miners in Kentucky, a pilgrimage to visit a father-poet, New Orleans and Mardi Gras, and a linking of arms again with southern civil rights fighters. Only four concerts were scheduled. Dylan carried no compass, just "road-maps of the soul." After years of steering toward goals, Orpheus was descending for several seasons in hell. He rolled like thunder across America's landscape, right through Whitman's "Open Road," Guthrie's *Hard Travelin'*, and Kerouac's *On the Road*. Beyond the restlessness, curiosity and hunger for experience was Dylan's compulsion to keep in physical and spiritual motion.

He chose his companions carefully; the alchemy of four young men in a station wagon was not easy to balance. Later, Dylan told me: "I'm lucky. Not because I make a lot of bread, but because I can be around groovy people. I don't fear anything and nobody around me has to fear anything. That's where it's at: bread, freedom, and no fear." Doing most of the driving and keeping business affairs straight was Victor Maymudes. Tall, taciturn, with penetrating dark eyes, turbulent hair, and an uncanny ability to keep his mouth shut. Wanting to be an actor, or work in films, he often seethed in personal frustration but rarely criticized Dylan, even while his duties were often those of a flunky.

Pete Karman was a long-time friend of the Rotolos, seen by mother Mary as Mr. Responsible, with a job and a range of neckties. He came along for kicks. He had worked on the *Daily Mirror*, and later became a travel magazine editor. He never wrote about the Dylan trip, just talked of its madness and his disillusionment. The previous year, Karman had visited Cuba. "I used to call Dylan 'the punk.' I used to ask: 'How're you doing, punk?' I was twenty and he was only nineteen." By the time of the trip, Pete wasn't calling him the punk

anymore. Dylan later told me: "We had to kick Pete out and send him home on a plane."

Paul Clayton was an introspective singer and folklorist, with a Jesus beard and gentleness. A scholar and romantic, Clayton wanted to live his old ballads. With some twenty albums to his credit, he was once called "the most recorded young folk singer in America," yet he was scarcely known. Despite two degrees and encyclopedic knowledge of folklore, Clayton remained unpretentious, self-effacing; dedicated to his art and his friends, of whom none was greater than Dylan. Karman said that during this trip Clayton seemed to be traveling under some undefined personal burden. Paul had been going out with Carla, and at times he and Dylan, and the sisters had become so involved with each other that the problems of all the relationships were geometrically enlarged. According to Pete, Paul got stoned more often than anyone on the trip. (Succumbing to a dependency on drugs, Clayton was found dead in his bathtub, of electrocution, on April 6, 1967.)

The trip began unceremoniously. Victor loaded up with several thousand in traveler's checks. Pete showed up at Grossman's at 10 a.m., but with farewells to Suze and the Van Ronks and rounding up clothes for striking miners in Hazard, Kentucky, they didn't leave until dusk. The blue Ford was cluttered with suitcases, instruments, and old clothing. Once the clothes were delivered, Dylan often perched in the rear of that mobile writer's garret to scribble lyrics or a chord progression. Between talk and games, the foursome frequently fell into long silences. The solitude into which Dylan withdrew, a shell that created space around him, was palpable. He wrote at least two important songs on the trip: "Chimes of Freedom" and "Ballad in Plain D."

The first night's goal was Clayton's gracious old university town, Charlottesville, Virginia. Although Clayton had a rough country cabin outside town, the four stayed with Paul's friend, Steve Wilson. Buying two dozen copies of *Times Changin'* to hand out along the way, Dylan was recognized by students and sales people.

They left Charlottesville next morning for eastern Kentucky. Coal country. Near Abingdon, Virginia,

they picked up a young coal miner, Robert Swann, wearing a miner's lighted helmet, his face smudged with coal dust. Dylan gave the miner *Freewheelin'*. Swann was their introduction to Harlan County and the men of the other underground. They crossed Harlan County and looked for the strike leader, Hamish Sinclair, secretary of the National Committee for Miners. Sinclair, who had sung at benefits in New York, linked the pickets and their supporters. He greeted Dylan's group warmly; they unloaded the clothing. Hamish was up to his ears bailing people out of jail, seeing to strikers' welfare, organizing legal moves. Dylan wanted to contribute more than clothes—a benefit concert, perhaps. Sinclair was too preoccupied, and sent them to visit miners and picket leader Jason Combes.

They headed southeast. First night, a motel in Pineville, Kentucky; then, Asheville, North Carolina, birthplace of Thomas Wolfe, author of *You Can't Go Home Again*. Asheville was still segregated, although during store hours, the white shops welcomed black customers. The group went bowling in a black bowling alley, shot pool, and went to a nudie movie—Dylan recognized a girl who'd been a Gaslight waitress in the Village.

On to Hendersonville, near Flat Rock, North Carolina. They couldn't find the home of Carl Sandburg, the writer, but were directed to the home of a Sandburg who raised goats. Same man. Sandburg was a towering figure to his visitors. There was much that Dylan had in common with the eighty-six-year-old poet, biographer of Lincoln, collector and singer of folk songs. Much as the young Sandburg had revered Whitman, Dylan now revered Sandburg. In 1919, in a letter to French novelist and pacifist Romain Rolland, Sandburg had written words that might have come from Woody: "I am an IWW [Industrial Workers of the World], but I don't carry a red card. I am an anarchist, but not a member of the organization. … I belong to everything and nothing. … I would say I am with all rebels everywhere all the time as against all people who are satisfied."

When the travelers' station wagon pulled into Sandburg's 240-acre Connemara Farm, on the porch was a buxom grandmother figure out of Norman Rockwell, Lillian Sandburg. She didn't

seem startled by the hairy foursome. According
to Pete, Dylan announced: "I am a poet. My
name is Robert Dylan, and I would like to see Mr.
Sandburg." She disappeared into the house while
they looked over the serene, sloping pasture backed
by Sugarloaf Mountain. The Sandburgs and their
daughters lived there from 1945 until his death in
July 1967.

The waiting seemed interminable. Finally, the
poet appeared, a genial, slow-moving man. His
gray hair tumbled over his left ear, his face was
stubbled. Instinctively, his pale blue eyes locked
with Dylan's bright blue ones, saying: "You look
like you're ready for anything. I would like to
ask you about forty good questions. Your group
looks able to prepare for any emergency." Dylan
handed the old writer *Times Changin'* and Clayton
stepped forward with one of his albums. Sandburg
said he didn't know Dylan's work at all, but he
was interested in poetry and folk singing and
regarded them as kindred arts. The visitors praised
Sandburg for his pioneer song-collecting, indicating
familiarity with his *American Songbag*, 280 songs and
ballads first published in 1927.

For around twenty minutes, the five chatted on
the porch. Dylan had wanted the great writer to
"open up" and take them into his study. Sandburg
repeated that he'd listen to the two albums, and
Dylan reiterated that he too was a poet. Every
time the word "poet" was mentioned, Sandburg
seemed to prick up his ears. The old poet excused
himself, saying that he simply had to work on
some manuscripts and letters. Pete recalls: "We
had a definite feeling of disappointment, mainly
because Sandburg had never heard of Bobby. As
I recall, during the rest of the trip Sandburg was
never mentioned again. Dylan sank into one of his
quiet funks."

From Flat Rock into South Carolina, where
fireworks were sold legally. They filled the car with
rockets, whizbangs, and cherry bombs. Then,
Athens, Georgia—another university center.
Dylan, pinball wizard, headed for a pool hall, and
they played the tables and machines. Along the
streets, students recognized Dylan; some sidled
up for an autograph. Another record-shop flurry
of recognition soothed the disappointment of

> **I am a poet.
> My name is Robert
> Dylan, and I would like
> to see Mr. Sandburg.**

Sandburg's detachment. Next day, they looked around progressive Atlanta. That evening, Dylan's concert at nearby Emory University. The student audience knew nearly every song by its opening phrase. Afterward, a party, to which local *éminences grises* of folk music and southern radicalism were invited. Fresh from some picket line or sit-in were Freedom Singers Bernice Johnson and Cordell Reagon. Next day, Dylan visited them in Atlanta.

Westward through the Deep South black belt toward Mississippi: WHITE ONLY signs, garish billboards. They couldn't believe they were still in the United States. The South hadn't really changed all that much. Dylan scanned the roadside. He scribbled a few notes on small scraps of paper and heard "Chimes of Freedom" ringing in his inner ears. Crossing into Mississippi, a fork on their road. Should they join SNCC at Tougaloo College, as half-promised, or drift southward toward New Orleans and Mardi Gras? Excitement and curiosity pointed them toward New Orleans.

Many had made the pilgrimage to the fountainhead of jazz. New Orleans was the town of pioneers Buddy Bolden, Jelly Roll Morton, and Louis Armstrong. Here Mahalia Jackson learned to sing. New Orleans was the Jerusalem of all musical faiths, where the work-song mated with the spiritual to give birth to the blues, where the blues moved from country to city, where anything that could be banged, hit, struck, or blown through became an instrument. All that was vibrant and classic in American popular music was at home in this languorous, easy-talking "Crescent City." It was a carnival any time of the year, but especially at Mardi Gras.

Each year, just before the onset of Lent, New Orleans blows its collective cool in a multi-million-dollar festival that lures world visitors. Mardi Gras (literally, "Fat Tuesday") had passed from pagan to Christian to commercial. By tradition, Mardi Gras street revelry surrounds the parades, and everyone carries his own bottle. But another tradition of segregationist New Orleans soon became apparent.

The four had positioned themselves at a crowded corner where the view was good. Although the time was just after breakfast, each carried a bottle of wine, taking huge gulps. A costumed black dancer

passed, carrying candlelit flambeaux, aloft. The torchbearer stopped in front of Dylan's group, having danced for two miles he was exhausted and thirsty. He saw Dylan holding a wine bottle and pointed at it wordlessly; Bob handed him his bottle and the dancer took a generous gulp. The crowd around Dylan became uneasy. A kindly faced little old lady whined: "You mean that you would give a n***** a drink out of your very own bottle?" Dylan didn't reply. Several sailors moved forward menacingly. Pete said: "This is it, boys. We're all going to be murdered!" Dylan told his fellows: "Disappear into the crowd." When they reassembled, Dylan mused: "It's not the same country."

Although Mardi Gras madness made many lasting impressions on Dylan that appear in songs from "Desolation Row" to "Visions of Johanna," he only made passing specific references to it in his writings. In New Orleans too, 1964 was the year of the folk singer. Young white folknik pilgrims congregated on the street, strumming, singing, and trying to look like Dylan. On Bourbon Street, a kid was standing against a wall, playing his guitar and singing "Don't Think Twice." Dylan: "You sing that very well. Let's hear one more." The boy started to sing and Dylan and others joined in. The folk singer stammered: "You! I mean … it couldn't be. No, it's impossible!" Dylan repeated: "You sing that real well," and they moved on leaving one confused folk singer.

Back on the road again. Victor, at the wheel, knew there were only two days before the Denver concert. They had to put in an appearance in Tougaloo College, where the big Mississippi "Freedom Summer" was being planned. They zoomed in and out, time only to greet civil rights people, like Dorie Larner, Robert Moses, and Tom Hayden, who pulled together an audience. Dylan sang for an hour. After well-wishing, Victor made apologies for Dylan and hustled his group into the station wagon. They stopped to study road maps again. Jackson to Denver in two days! Dylan suggested they go by way of Dallas.

It was only three months after the Kennedy assassination, and the papers had been filled with reconstructions. As the freeway swung near Dallas, everyone was keyed up. They asked several people for the street on which Kennedy was shot, but no one seemed to know it by name. Even asking for the Texas School Book depository failed to bring a response. Finally, at Dealey Plaza, they appraised the theory that Oswald acted alone. Then, they took the station wagon along Kennedy's path, everyone but the driver looking back toward the depository from which the shots supposedly came. Pete recalled: "Everybody, including Bobby, started acting like a detective. We looked at that distant row of windows and we all pretty much decided that if someone had shot Kennedy from that window, he would have to have been a fantastic marksman."

On to Denver, via Forth Worth, through the Panhandle, toward Wichita Falls. Somewhere near the Texas-New Mexico border, they stopped at a little chili joint. A waitress, no more than nineteen, asked, "Where y'all from?" She'd never met anyone from New York. When somebody said Bob was a singer, she flipped. They gave her an album. She kept looking from the picture to Bob's face with total disbelief. A few hours later, another Texan roadside joint, near Claude. Sarcastically, they inquired: "What's been happening here,

lately?" "Ain't nothing happened here lately, but about a year ago we had a big fuss when Paul Newman and all them Hollywood people came in to shoot that movie *Hud*, right here." The swaggering, thumb-in-belt arrogance of *Hud* was one Dylan echoed in dozens of pictures taken by Barry Feinstein. They learned what they could about the filming.

In southern Colorado, Dylan spotted Ludlow on the map. Paul gave them some background about the site of a vicious 1914 anti-union massacre that inspired many ballads, notably Guthrie's. Dylan and friends stood before a memorial plaque put up by the United Mine Workers of America. The young man who had never paid much attention to history at school was getting his lessons on the road.

Denver: Dylan washed, shaved, and changed from dirty old clothes to clean old clothes for the performance at the Denver Civic Auditorium. Later, Bob's group made the rounds of the local coffee shops and folk hangouts, looking for Judy Collins. She was out of town, so Dylan took his

ABOVE

Backstage at Newport '64, with (far left) Bob Siggins of the Charles River Valley Boys, and John Hammond Jr., son of Dylan's Columbia producer.

companions up into the mountains to see Central City, his first return to the reconstructed boomtown since 1959. It was snow-clogged and ghostlier than ever. They went into the only open shop, a drugstore, to pick up some historical postcards.

Heading to San Francisco, they had to go over the Rockies in one of the winter's worst snowstorms. Loveland Pass: their tire chains broke under the effort. They spent a night in Grand Junction, Colorado, where the temperature was down to zero, yet they could run from the hotel and plunge into a naturally heated spring pool. Victor took the wheel from Pete. Before them was a long funeral procession of thirty cars twisting up a mountain road. Victor passed the funeral at more than seventy miles an hour. A police car led the procession. A chase began. "We panicked," said Pete. They hid all the smoking materials fast. Victor talked to the cop: "We're part of a singing group, have to be in Reno in a couple of hours or we miss out on a job." He showed the car's registration, and the cop, seeing the name of some unknown corporation, Ashes and Sand, decided to relent, and let them go.

The four roared with relief, but Dylan told Paul and Pete to share the driving. They arrived in Reno at 8 a.m. and tried the gambling tables. Pete quickly ran through his last thirty-two dollars and was then totally dependent on Dylan, who lost about a hundred dollars at blackjack. As they were leaving, Bob stopped in front of a slot machine and put in his remaining quarters. Suddenly the machine lit up like Times Square. Quarters came out in a flood. Pete reflected on winners and losers.

Somewhere near Reno, at a desert space—as in the film *Zabriskie Point*—they set up the fireworks from South Carolina. They giggled like kids at the magnificent bursting rockets and flares. When they got to the Sierras, they had one more boyish fling. Sitting in the swaying chairs of a ski lift, they climbed the side of a mountain—another freedom game. This was their farewell to spacious landscape. As they hurtled toward San Francisco, the roads were busier, and there were signs of farming and commerce. The trip was nearly at an end.

Dylan had a concert at Berkeley on February 24, 1964. Anyone with as free-floating a temperament as his would be at home on the West Coast. There was Berkeley's radical tradition, San Francisco's openness to new ideas, and the whole ambience of California, where people put no ties around their necks and few around their thinking. The leading West Coast critic had swung firmly into Dylan's corner. Ralph Gleason gave Dylan's concert at the Berkeley Community Theater a strong advance story and review, reporting that no concert in recent memory had stirred so much advance interest. He was beginning to see Dylan as a standard-bearer for the developing counterculture. Even to the Bay Area, where beats, bohemians, outsiders, and rebels were no strangers, Dylan's arrival meant something special. Wrote Gleason: "To the generations who were raised on solid Judeo-Christian principles, on the rock of moral values of our fathers, on the idea that cleanliness is next to godliness, the deliberate sloppiness, the disdain for what we have thought of as perfect by Dylan's generation is shocking. But we are wrong. Look where our generation has gotten us … a hard core of reality connects the music of Dylan, the best of

> **At Newport, perhaps no one felt let down more keenly than those who had earlier heaped praise on Dylan.**
> ROBERT SHELTON

RIGHT
With Bob Siggins riding pillion on
a borrowed bike at Newport '64.

jazz, of contemporary poetry, painting, all the arts, in fact, with the social revolution that has resulted in CORE and SNCC, Dick Gregory, James Baldwin and the rest."

Fariña was at the Berkeley concert, taking notes for a *Mademoiselle* story. His report augured his own motorcycle doom and Dylan's deliverance: "There was no sensation of his having performed somewhere the previous night or of a schedule that would take him away once the inevitable post-concert party was over. There was, instead, the familiar comparison with James Dean, at times explicit, at times unspoken, an impulsive awareness of his physical perishability. Catch him now, was the idea. Next week he might be mangled on a motorcycle."

After the Berkeley concert, the station wagon headed toward Joan's place in Carmel. Karman was, by this time, completely on the outs: "I'm not going on with this trip. If I do, I'll be going crazy," he said. The others were happy to see him replaced by Bob Neuwirth, the vagabond madcap artist/moviemaker/country singer who later succeeded Victor as Dylan's road manager. They arrived at Joan's with gifts of nuts and fruit. Joan's mother whipped up a beef stew. "The only overt reference to Dylan's music came," Fariña chronicled: "When Joan said she might want to record an entire album of his songs and he told her 'sure thing.'" The next day, Bob and Joan each headed toward southern California. Joan drove her Jaguar XKE while Dylan and the others continued on in the station wagon, staying at the Thunderbird Motel in Hollywood, drifting out to parties and local folk nightclubs between engagements.

Dylan was reluctant to return to New York. It meant more turmoil with Suze. The affair finally ended in March 1964. Despite depressions, he kept growing, professionally and artistically. The bust-up with Suze, the confusions with Joan, the anchorless feeling of being alone in front of thousands of people, all colored his life in dark shades. That year, he was often one very stoned rolling stone, apparently out of control, racing at his "own chosen speed." He was kept from spinning right off the road by the demands, urgency, and discipline of his writing.

May 1964: Off to England again. Dylan had had mixed feelings dating from his first trips there—December 1962 and January 1963, when he had been scheduled to star in a BBC play, *Madhouse on Castle Street*. Very much the bewildered young man from the provinces, he reported to London's Mayfair Hotel. Feeling uncomfortable, he checked out immediately and went looking for Philip Saville, producer of his play, and asked him if he would find some "groovy" people for him to stay with. Of his aloneness in London, Dylan said: "I knew then what it is like to be a Negro."

He drifted into a well-known London folk club, the Troubadour, and there met Anthea Joseph, who later became an official in artists' relations for EMI and CBS Records. "I was on the door, and these boots came marching down the stairs; large, brown leather boots. As those boots came down the stairs and were connected to legs and a body above them, I said to myself: *I know that young man!* Then I recognized the face at the other end of the boots. It came up to me and said: 'Are you Anthea? I'm Bob Dylan, can I come in?' 'Of course,' I said, 'providing that you sing for me; then you won't have to pay to get in.' I found him completely charming, great fun. Although he didn't talk a lot, he seemed to be enjoying himself enormously inside. He never stopped watching people, never stopped laughing. That was the day he had walked out of the Mayfair and he asked me if I knew where he could stay that night. I was amazed that no one had arranged a room for this waif. He went off with somebody he met at the Troubadour after singing there. Generally, people were terribly impressed by his singing; they thought he was marvelous."

Anthea took Dylan to the Singers' Club at the Prospect of Whitby pub, Gray's Inn Road. "Peggy Seeger *had* to ask him to sing because too many people knew who he was. She really didn't want to. They are funny people, Ewan MacColl and Peggy. After Bob sang 'Hollis Brown,' the audience almost fell apart, because they had never come up against anything so forceful in their lives. Hearing that terrifying chorus going through it every time, I, for one, felt the need for a good, strong drink. Peggy and Ewan just sat there in stony silence. Peggy went

OPPOSITE Town Hall, Carnegie Hall and now Philharmonic Hall: the poster for the now-legendary Halloween concert on which Joan Baez guested.

BOB DYLAN
AT PHILHARMONIC HALL
ONLY NEW YORK CONCERT APPEARANCE
ON SATURDAY OCTOBER 31ST AT 8:30PM
ALL SEATS RESERVED: $4.50, 4.00, 3.50, 2.75
ON SALE NOW AT PHILHARMONIC BOX OFFICE
Mail Orders To Philharmonic Hall, B'way at 65 St N.Y. 10023
ENCLOSE STAMPED SELF-ADDRESSED ENVELOPE
COLUMBIA RECORDS
240
MURRAY POSTER PRINTING Co. Inc., 221 W. 64 St NYC

up to him and said: 'Thank you, very much,' and that was all. I was shocked. Not one word of praise from her, and Ewan didn't even bother to say anything. We left straightaway. Bob didn't want to stay."

On that first trip, Bob instantly befriended Martin and Dorothy Carthy. Carthy's catholic approach toward modernized tradition put Bob at ease. Recalled Carthy: "I had read about him in *Sing Out!* Naturally, I asked him to sing. When the King and Queen audience heard his guest set, they fairly went mad. Strange, though, that after he left the club, that same audience started to put him down and said his appearance there 'was all a big mistake'."

The Carthys had written several times, but Bob only wrote them one long letter, in spring 1963, which showed how strongly he was thinking about the topical-song debate, the demands on his time, and his loving memories of them: "I remember Martin singing 'Lord Franklin' and I still got faith in singer and song to tell the truth and still be what they are. … I still remember Martin and Dorothy and getta feeling that no tongue can explain on the printed page, movie-house or record player. There ain't many folks like you."

Dylan went to Britain originally for the play, which had a role for "an anarchic young student who wrote songs." Having signed this unknown for what was then a large fee of £500, Saville discovered he'd also hired a would-be playwright. "We found he had trouble delivering the lines Evan Jones had written for him. Bob wanted to write his own lines," Saville told me in 1971. "At rehearsals, when he did show up, there was no problem with his saying his lines, but he was such an individualist that he wanted to write the play, or at least his part, over completely. Mutually, we realized that he just couldn't play it as written. We decided to make the central character into two people." David Warner, a rising Shakespearean actor, who later starred in the film *Morgan*, took the speaking role originally meant for Dylan. Bob and Warner got on famously. Staying at Saville's Hampstead home a few nights—one way Saville could guarantee Bob's appearance at rehearsals—Dylan began to run through his song repertoire. The producer, quite impressed, decided to have Dylan sing "Blowin' in the Wind" behind the opening and closing credits.

Several technical hitches developed in the play, and Saville told Grossman there would be a delay of several weeks. Albert said Bob had a commitment, and wrung another fee and round-trip airline ticket out of the BBC. "This became undoubtedly the most expensive money ever paid for a singer to do the opening and closing music for a play and to deliver only one spoken line," Saville told me. (The line: "Well, I don't know, I'll have to go home and think about it.") Nevertheless, Saville felt proud to introduce Dylan and "Blowin' in the Wind" to Britain. He was charmed with Dylan's "almost Buddhist inner concentration, and his little naïvetés about sophisticated London."

The extra time in London allowed Dylan to meet two old friends from Boston, Ric Von Schmidt and Richard Fariña, who were cutting an album on the Folklore label. They persuaded Dylan, as Blind Boy Grunt, to fill in with his traveling mouth harp on "You Can't Always Tell," "Xmas Island," "Cocaine," and "Glory, Glory." The sessions were at Dobell's Jazz Record Shop on Charing Cross Road on January 14 and 15, 1963. Dylan also played the Establishment Club, where his anti-establishment songs made him a triumph.

> **Strange, you can talk about a commercial artist, but you can't talk about a commercial poet. A poet has to be something holy as well as to have genius.**
> SIDNEY CARTER

Fifteen months later, Dylan returned to England. A booking at the Royal Festival Hall, May 17, 1964, perked him up. Anthea couldn't buy a ticket, so he insisted she come backstage. "You gotta come to this one, because the Rolling Stones are coming," he said. A line several thousand yards long stretched all the way to County Hall—the 2,700 seats had long since been sold out. Anthea: "He said: 'My God, I've never seen anything like it!' His admirers had hitchhiked from absolutely everywhere."

The concert was successful. Bob misplaced his capo and asked if his audience had one. There was a general surge forward. Dylan smilingly accepted one: "Don't forget that I have it, or you won't get it back." *The Times* said Dylan's drawing power put him in a class of "sheer personal magnetism," shared only by Callas, Segovia, and Count Basie. The *London Daily Sketch* headline: NO VOICE – BUT SOME SINGER. The singer heard cheers from an audience of intellectuals and beats who thronged around the stage door like pubescent fans. Dylan then taped a half-hour show for BBC TV's *Tonight*, and also recorded for BBC radio's *Saturday Club* and the TV *Hallelujah Club*. He left behind the makings of an articulate audience that, in 1965, would project him to superstardom.

The English singer-songwriter Sidney Carter told me: "Strange, you can talk about a commercial artist, but you can't talk about a commercial poet. A poet has to be something holy as well as to have genius. As difficult a role as this must be for Dylan, he definitely fits into that romantic concept of a poet, the listener to inner voices that are driving him. What the poets have been trying to do for a long time—to get through to a large public—the folk singers have done behind their backs." Rory McEwen, a veteran of the British folk scene, was as repelled by Bob as he was attracted: "I disliked his arrogance. … He can walk into a room and give the impression that he knows just a little bit more about the world than anyone in that room. He probably does, but it rankles a little that he should act as if he does." Elaine Dundy, writer, hostess and one-time wife of critic Kenneth Tynan, was smitten, calling him a genius. At another party, he met Robert Graves, who asked Dylan to sing and then talked throughout.

After Festival Hall, Dylan darted off for a few days in Paris, and then traveled with Victor to Greece for a short holiday. In the town of Vernilya, outside Athens, Dylan did a great deal of writing for *Another Side*. He was beginning to feel some calm. He wanted to stay on in Greece, but had too many commitments, so returned to New York and to Woodstock.

Newport '63 had been so Dylan-centered that, not surprisingly, Bob found the 1964 festival an anticlimax. He'd had time to consider the burdens of leadership and to decide that overtly political songs were only part of his work. No longer was he "writing songs for everybody else, but writing songs now for myself." As Dylan had grabbed the spotlight in 1963, he virtually shunned it in 1964. He was prepared, like Seeger before him, to step back from stage-center and feel wonder at the numbers who were working the same vein. Phil Ochs was coming on strongly as the chief political banner-waver, and wrote about the upsurge of topical song in the Newport program book.

In the year between the two festivals, topical songwriting had established itself. Ochs was becoming a campus darling; Tom Paxton, the careful craftsman, was not far behind. Len Chandler was a rising figure; and Buffy Sainte-Marie was emerging as the most adroit woman writer, while Malvina Reynolds was still the doyenne. Seeger remained the leader, although he was still away on a world tour. Other rising topical songwriters included Billy Edd Wheeler, Pat Sky, Fred Hellerman, Peter La Farge and Tim Hardin. Two newer talents had difficulties in establishing their own identities: Eric Andersen and David Cohen (also known as David Blue) began almost as replicas of Dylan. Although both were concerned about human folly and errant institutions, neither trod on Dylan's early political path. Their writing was more subjective and personal. Still in the background was thirteen-year-old Janis Ian, soon to cause a stir with "Society's Child."

Dylan performed publicly three times at Newport '64. On Friday afternoon at the topical-song workshop, he sang "It Ain't Me, Babe" and "Tambourine Man." No one seemed to mind that Dylan's two new songs were topical only to the singer. At that night's evening concert, Baez closed by bringing Dylan on for a duet of "It Ain't Me, Babe." The audience hankered for political inspiration and Joan obliged, leading "We Shall Overcome." Dylan's solo appearance was Sunday night, and he opened with "All I Really Want to Do." Many were glad to hear his wit surface again in a new "anti-love song." The rest of his set was not very well received; the longer he stayed on, the sloppier his performance became. "To Ramona" was so lackluster that I wrote a tentative question in my notebook: "Has the American Yevtushenko turned into the American Edgar Guest?" He sang "Tambourine Man," but so haltingly, between clenched teeth, that the floating imagery sagged. As he tuned between numbers, Dylan sometimes staggered onstage. Being stoned had rarely prevented his giving winning performances, but he was clearly out of control. He finished with "Chimes of Freedom," and then for an encore, called Joan on for a duet of "With God on Our Side."

The desultory performance surprised many, but not two friends backstage. Before he had gone on, Bob had been chatting with Tony Glover and Betsy Siggins of Cambridge. Tony had noticed that Bob was extremely uptight about facing the capacity audience of more than 15,000. Dylan said to Tony: "I don't care. I'll just do my music. I don't care." Dylan got his round of applause, but there was uneasiness. As I headed toward the press tent, I conveyed the general disappointment to Charlie Rothschild, who was trying to convince me I had just seen a great Dylan performance.

The evening emphasized something Bob already knew well: a performer must be always on his mettle. Critical ears won't accept mediocrity from masters. At Newport, perhaps no one felt let down more keenly than those who had earlier heaped praise on Dylan. Friends, old and new, began to give him pep talks in person or in print. In the November 1964 issue of *Sing Out!*, editor Irwin Silber wrote "An Open Letter to Bob Dylan," which summarized past veneration but expressed worry: "I saw at Newport how you had somehow lost contact with people. … The paraphernalia of fame were getting in your way. … I thought (and so did you) of Jimmy Dean … and I cried a little … for that awful potential of self-destruction. … In a sense we are all responsible for what's been happening to you. … The American Success Machinery chews up geniuses one a day and still hungers for more."

The letter cheered Dylan as much as a week's holiday in Hibbing would have. Everything he did seemed to displease someone. Minneapolis people hit him for carrying picket signs; then he was stoned for selling out. Now the preachy folksters were sermonizing. Many waited for the November release of *Another Side* to confirm that Dylan was "going apolitical." In December, a *Broadside* writer, Paul Wolfe, who Dylan had praised, treated Newport '64 as the point when Ochs emerged the political-song champion and Dylan "renounced" protest. Wolfe deemed "Tambourine Man" "a failure," and lambasted "Chimes of Freedom" for raising "bewilderment to the highest degree." The Dylan he sketched was

> **I saw at Newport how you had somehow lost contact with people. … In a sense [we] are all responsible for what's been happening to you. … The American Success Machinery chews up geniuses one a day and still hungers for more.**
>
> IRWIN SILBER

a Lonesome Rhodes—a trickster, hypocrite, and manipulator of his audience. Ochs leaped to Dylan's defense: "It is as if the entire folk community was a huge biology class and Bob was a rare, prize frog. Professor Silber and Student Wolfe appear to be quite annoyed that the frog keeps hopping in all different directions while they're trying to dissect him. … To cater to an audience's taste is not to respect them, and if the audience doesn't understand that, they don't deserve respect."

A key word in Silber's letter was "entourage," meaning that Dylan was now surrounded by payrolled sycophants. One member was Paul Clayton, whom folk moralists found difficult to criticize, who said: "He gave the appearance of expecting success, but he found himself before a public he wasn't ready to face. Once he had the public, he was frightened to death, mostly of all the questions people asked him. I remember a concert at Brown University. After the concert, Victor, Neuwirth, and I formed a cordon around him. Reporters ran after him with tape recorders, asking if he thought he was a folk singer! That's the sort of confrontation he feared." Clayton concluded: "There are about twenty people he feels safe with, and only about five or six of those whom he can spend much time with. Even with people around, he spends a lot of time with himself."

Around the Village, what *Eye* later titled "the Dylan Gang," were a half-dozen folk singers whom he felt to be kindred spirits—Jack Elliott, Eric Andersen, Dave Van Ronk, David Blue, Phil Ochs, Tim Hardin, and a very few others. These Villagers felt compelled to explain and defend Dylan when he did not do so himself. Ochs (describing him as "really Shakespearean in quality") remained the most articulate, even after the many times Dylan put him down. Summarizing Dylan's impact on his Village entourage, Michael Thomas wrote in *Eye*, August 1968: "Dylan made everybody aware of themselves, while he became aware of himself, and because he could hear the tambourine man, he was a prophet. He touched his contemporaries at the core of their ambitions. Some, like Ochs and Paxton and Tim Hardin, felt his energy and were energized; some, like Andersen and Blue, and others, like Richard Fariña, the destructive hero of his own life, and Paul Simon,

the last great sophomore, were stricken by Dylan, but he was not to blame."

After Newport '64, there was another round of controversy. If Dylan worked in blues, he was a white man stealing black music. If he developed Woody's talking blues, he was an imitator. If he adapted Anglo-Irish folk songs, he was a thief. If he wrote topical-protest songs, traditionalists thought he was a traitor, yet if he turned subjective, he was a self-involved existentialist.

Dylan's defenders came from all corners. In March 1964, Johnny Cash, the country singer then known only vaguely to the folk crowd, had leaped into *Broadside* with the demand: "SHUT UP! … AND LET HIM SING!" At Newport '64, Cash gave a stunning performance. The festival, in its finest hour, brought in an established Nashville star who also spoke folk. Cash was the real thing—off an Ozarks farm, tough as rawhide, tender as raw flesh. He was also a sophisticated man who would walk the line in several music worlds. Right after his performance on Friday night, Cash was hustled off to Baez's room at the Viking Motor Inn, where he and Dylan taped some songs for her. Cash, whose craggy, granite-hewn exterior made him look tough all the way through, was deeply touched to find that the two young stars of the folk world cared enough about him to spend the whole night taping him. To show his appreciation, he gave Dylan one of his own guitars.

The historic moments at Newport '64 tended to pass people by. Only when Dylan later appeared with rock backing, and, still later, went to Nashville, did all the pieces fit together. It was all brought back home at Newport '64, when Dylan went beyond topical songs, Cash sang of country troubles, and Muddy Waters brought on his band to show that music, if it's alive, is always in motion.

In summer and fall of 1964, Dylan had more time to spend in Woodstock. The barren pad on West 4th Street was too empty. He was anxious to move his few possessions. If he had to stay in New York, he could always stay at Albert's big apartment on Gramercy Park West or at the Chelsea Hotel. Woodstock was then an unpressured and uncrowded hamlet, and he had devoted friends there. He had a special room with a private entrance at Albert's large house in

Newport 1964: Robert Shelton (center) introduces Dylan to the fiddler Clayton McMichen.

> To cater to an audience's taste is not to respect them, and if the audience doesn't understand that, they don't deserve respect.

PHIL OCHS

nearby Bearsville, and a place to hang out, the Café Espresso at 59 Tinker Street, in Woodstock.

The Espresso was a bit of Greenwich Village in the country, owned by French-born Bernard Paturel, whose easy manner helped give the café and Dylan's Woodstock their informality. Bernard had moved to Woodstock in 1961; it reminded him of the French art colony in St Paul-de-Vence, in the hills above the Côte d'Azur. Hearing that the Café Espresso was up for sale, Bernard and his wife, Mary Lou, bought the place on credit. For live entertainment, folk music seemed right. There had long been a folk colony around Woodstock. Sam Eskin, an early ballad collector, was a veteran resident, and Billy Faier, banjoist-singer, had been a town mascot since the late fifties. Bernard called on Billy and a French folk singer, Sonia Malkine, to help him get singers. Among those who worked there were Paxton, who performed for three days for fifty dollars and food. The first Bernard heard of Dylan, he was causing a storm at Gerde's and making two hundred dollars a week, more than Espresso could afford. He first saw Dylan in his café one Sunday afternoon in summer '63. Bob was at a table with Joan and several others, tinkering with a wind-up phonograph. Establishing himself as a Mr. Fixit, Bernard repaired it for them and watched the old relic rotating at 78 rpm as Bob and Joan played an old spiritual.

Those were days when Woodstock was a refuge, not yet a zoo or a "nation." Dylan often practiced on the streets, sitting on a fence here, a bench there. Bernard soon saw Bob back in his club with Joan again. Bob had been drinking and his genial host politely escorted him upstairs to a large white room in the Paturels' apartment, where Bob slept off his binge. Dylan took an immediate liking to the room. It was quiet and secret, and yet so close to the club downstairs that it fought off loneliness. "He kind of moved in with us and held a symbolic key to the room," Bernard told me. "No rent involved, just a mutual understanding that he could stay there whenever he pleased."

After his hectic trips in winter and spring of 1964, Bob returned to Woodstock. He was getting ready to record *Another Side* and the refuge he found with Bernard and Mary Lou was duly acknowledged in "Some Other Kind of Songs." In Bearsville, Albert was always surrounding himself with people: his wife Sally, filmmakers Jones and Howard Alk, Peter Yarrow, John Court, visiting singers like Judy Collins, Odetta, and Ian and Sylvia. Among the amenities at Albert's was a swimming pool that Bob favored. He kept a motorcycle in the garage so that he could roar around the back roads. Sometimes Bob liked the "in-crowd" excitement around Grossman's, but he often needed to be alone. Although Albert's was only three miles from the Espresso, Bob frequently hid away in Bernard's room. He spent hours downstairs playing chess with Victor or Bernard, or drove with Bernard to Kingston, to a musty old poolroom over a Chinese restaurant.

In front of Albert's Bearsville house, a sign warned: IF YOU HAVE NOT TELEPHONED, YOU ARE TRESPASSING. Albert had three listed Woodstock phone numbers; Dylan had none. Dylan's own guest list was highly selective. Clayton used to come often in early 1964, but he was gradually ostracized. After Newport, Johnny Cash visited. Daniel Kramer went to Woodstock in 1964 and began several months' intermittent service as Dylan's court photographer. Later, Kramer was summarily dropped, and Jerry Schatzberg took over until *he* fell out of favor.

Dylan meets Beatles fans outside
the Delmonico Hotel, Park Avenue,
on August 28, 1964. The band was
about to play Forest Hills.

During Dylan's time in Woodstock in 1964–65, he turned out many songs. If we accept Wordsworth's commonplace about poetry, then Dylan recollected his emotions in Woodstock's tranquility. Concerts and recording sessions were always beckoning, so that he could only catch his breath in Woodstock. Had he remained in New York he might have lost his emotional equilibrium entirely. From Woodstock, he traveled to two major concerts in 1964.

On August 8, 1964, Joan sang at the Forest Hills Music Festival to an outdoor audience of 15,000. Her singing was typically smooth and orderly. In the second half, she slipped out of her shoes onstage then brought Dylan on. I have never heard him in such poor shape. Bob seemed to be struggling on one wing, never quite able to leave the ground. His voice was harsh, badly projected. Joan's cool only heightened his disorder. I had to write some stinging words about him. Later, Joan and her manager told me that after Dylan read the *Times* review he went on a rampage, swearing at me, vowing vengeance.

I had another chance to hear Dylan, on October 31, 1964, at New York's Philharmonic Hall, the so-called Halloween Concert. Dylan gave one of his greatest performances. For the first time in nearly six months, he was back at the tiller steering, not drifting I ended my review: "After half a year of detours, Dylan seems to have returned his enormous musical and literary gifts to a forward course. His developing control of those gifts and his ability to shape a meaningful program added up to a frequently spellbinding evening by the brilliant singing poet laureate of young America."

After the concert, Dylan gave a party at a banquet hall off Second Avenue. I arrived with friends. Joan and Bob, linked arm and arm, greeted me warmly; Dylan had apparently forgotten my harsh review in August. He knew he had just triumphed. He made sure that everyone had enough wine—Beaujolais of course. Among those present were poets Allen Ginsberg and Gregory Corso, and jazzman Ornette Coleman. It was not a celebrity party so much as a chance to see friends in post-concert relaxation.

Dylan preferred to battle his critics obliquely. Face to face, he was as polite as possible. Shortly after his weak performance at Forest Hills, I spent an evening with him in the Village. He made no reference to my negative review. Although slightly reserved, he had a bit of information and another bit of free advice. The information, stated in roundabout terms, was that he was about to gross his first million. He was clearly startled, even though he knew that he would be lucky to see twenty percent of the total, after paying his team and taxes. Turning the conversation to me, he asked what I was writing, and I told him about various projects, some for pleasure, some just for bread. Charlie Rothschild had told him that under the pseudonym of Adam Barnes I had written the liner notes on Linda Mason's mediocre album of Dylan songs. Bitingly, Bob said that if I ever got that hard up for money again I should ask him for some, which I never did. I told him of a book I was writing on country music and some other projects. He suggested I try my best to get beyond the bread-and-butter writing: "Find something that you feel strongly about and just write it," Dylan told me, as we sat in the Gaslight. I didn't realize it then, but he was obliquely leading me toward this book. He was strongly reminding me that my protégé no longer needed protection.

07

ORPHEUS PLUGS IN

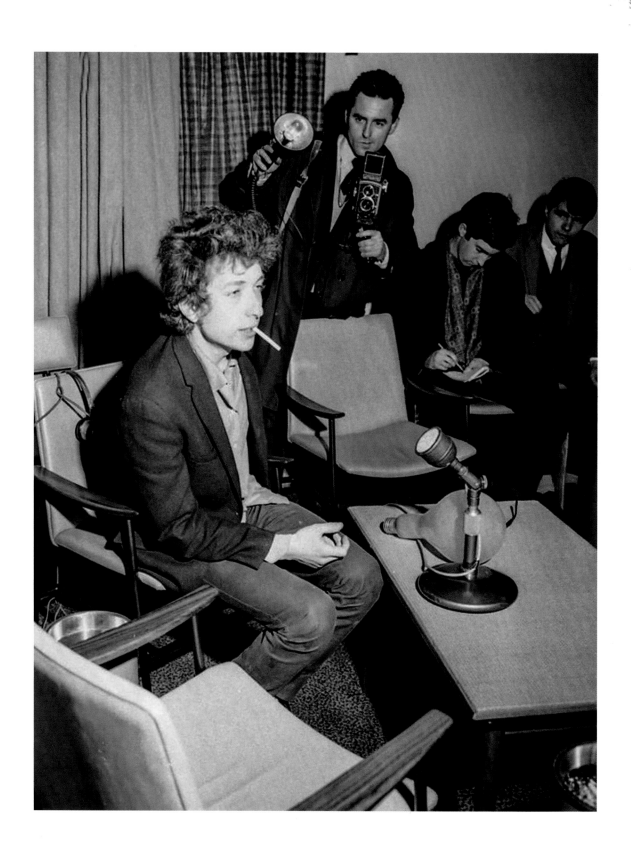

"Chaos is a close friend of mine. Truth is chaos. Maybe beauty is chaos."

As the "roads scholar" through time and space, Dylan had never really abandoned his highschool rock 'n' roll, his schoolboy radio music. In late 1964, the Beatles were only one of many new rock groups proliferating. By 1964, amid Woodstock's stillness, Dylan heard drum rolls, cymbals, thumping Fender basses, and metallic lines sliding from electric guitars. He didn't discard his old solo singing with acoustic guitar and mouth harp. He still knew the flow of his words, gentle or angry, was his greatest influence. He only wanted to put those words into a different context. But public and critical reactions to his 1965 albums, *Bringing It All Back Home* and *Highway 61 Revisited*, couldn't have been more extreme. He was traitor-opportunist to some, genius-messiah to others.

Dylan had not been surreptitiously manipulated. He alone decided to leap back into rock, taking with him folk song's storytelling and comment. The controversy over his adding a beat and subtracting topical sloganeering detracted from a significant development: Dylan was creating a new kind of expression, more sophisticated than that of his previous three years. His creation of "folk-rock" was a turning point in popular culture. Before Dylan's new work, most rock musicians, including the Beatles, had been using insipid, frivolous lyrics. While many folk slowpokes took time to assimilate Dylan's new approach, his new pop pastorate tuned in quickly.

Where was Dylan headed in 1965? I think his road maps pointed toward three aesthetic and philosophical concepts: exploration of the grotesque and the absurd in art; existentialism; dreams and hallucinations as mirrors of consciousness.

There are plenty of grotesques among Dylan's new dramatis personae. His rogues' gallery is distantly related to tortured figures in the paintings of Goya, Velazquez, Bosch, and Callot, as well as the French surrealists. Dylan had Coleridge's "shaping power of imagination"—the ability to create his own poetic otherworld, into whose dramas we enter half-fearfully. Rilke

OPPOSITE

Tea break
backstage at
Manchester's
Free Trade Hall,
May 1965.

saw his angels, Blake met his prophets Isaiah and Ezekiel; Dylan painted freaks and geeks. In finding artistic structures that could contain the absurd chaos he saw, Dylan somehow gained control over his world, his material, and attained a form of liberation.

Dylan now avoided political, social, or moral philosophizing. In 1964, earlier than most radicals, Dylan found picket-sign philosophy no longer serviceable. Following Sartre, Camus, and others, he traveled to a street existentialism that came less from ordered thinking than from emotional reaction. If we take existentialism out of the seminar and onto the highway, we can find compass points throughout Dylan's 1965–66 work.

For surrealist artists, dreams, imaginings, even hallucinations, natural or chemical, have helped broaden and deepen the scope of art. To these artists, life is sur-real, life is sur-earnest. This is the aesthetic of surrealism. The artist, as dreamer-in-chief, lends structure, shape, and color to the visions he will, at some point, share with his audience. The best art is a flame warming our own imaginations, a global campfire that irradiates some universal human experiences.

Innumerable Dylan followers have assured me it is impossible to understand much of Bob's 1965-66 work without dropping acid. The listener does not have to shop at the same drugstore as the artist. One does not need the same quantities of gin and fizz Fitzgerald required to savor *The Great Gatsby*. Dylan certainly asks of his listener intense concentration and at first, literal-minded folkniks were simply not prepared to let go and follow Dylan and his *Tambourine Man* into decadent, surrealist, existential sensation and vision.

Bringing It All Back Home, recorded in New York City on January 14 and 15, 1965, is not a series of intentionally "difficult" song-poems. The album title is a fine colloquial phrase which Dylan tattooed on to our language. It reminds Beatles and Stones fans, who vaguely thought sixties rock a British invention, that it all started in America. The phrase also means a homecoming for Dylan's own beloved rhythmic music. Trenchant protest returns, not for any sect, but for all of us. The dishonesties Dylan

sees leveled at American youth are cataloged to be fought and ridiculed. And the love songs are bringing Dylan back home to consider himself, his search for identity, his comprehension of what constitutes Eden. About this time, he said: "Chaos is a close friend of mine. Truth is chaos. Maybe beauty is chaos." Yet in portraying chaos, of the society or of the soul, he converts his "close friend" into artistic order.

Daniel Kramer's cover photograph is an essay in symbols. Dylan fondles his cat—named Rolling Stone. Behind him, albums by Ric Von Schmidt, Lotte Lenya, Robert Johnson, the Impressions. Far behind him stands his own last album. The attractive brunette is Sally Grossman, Albert's wife. Elsewhere, a fallout shelter sign, a copy of *Time*, a nineteenth-century portrait. Just left of center on the mantelpiece is Dylan's "The Clown," a glass collage he made for Bernard Paturel from fragments of colored glass Bernard was about to discard. On the back of the album, other photographs offer glimpses of the singer's life. Many regard *Back Home* as a high point of his recording career. Although several tracks have rock backing, an after-echo of the electric band resonates through the second, mainly acoustic, side.

Highway 61 Revisited was released in August 1965. There was no gap in Dylan's momentum, for "Like a Rolling Stone" had been released as a single in June, topping the charts for weeks. Despite that success, Dylan split with his second producer, Tom Wilson. For a time, he found an ideal match in Bob Johnston, a shy, soft-spoken Nashville cat. Johnston thought the record producer should extend help while allowing the maximum amount of freedom. "Dylan's king, and I'll not tell Dylan what I think of his material unless he asks me," Johnston once said.

Highway 61 generally has a cleaner ensemble sound than *Back Home*, giving more definition to individual instruments and the overriding voice. Another Kramer photograph adorns the album. Although Dylan poses indoors, his motorcycle T-shirt and colored silk shirt put him on the road again. On the back, three studio shots catch Dylan in the session.

In an elegiac March 1966 cover story for *Ramparts*, Ralph Gleason got Dylan to discuss his "complex" songs: "These songs aren't complicated to me at all. It's all very clear and simple to me. … There's nothing hard to figure out for me. I wouldn't write anything I can't really see. They're all about real people. I'm sure you've seen all the people in my songs at one time or another." Dylan still respected the complexity and subtlety of folk songs "based on myth and the Bible and plague and famine and all kinds of things like that which are just nuthin' but mystery and you can see it in all the songs—roses growin' right up out of people's hearts and naked cats in bed with, you know, spears growing right out of their back and seven years of this and eight years of that and it's all really something that nobody can really touch." Dylan tried to explain his changes and said that "'Rolling Stone' is the best song I wrote. I wrote 'Rolling Stone' after England. I boiled it down, but it's all there. I had to quit after England. I had to stop and when I was writing it I knew I had to sing it with a band. I always sing when I write, even prose, and I heard it like that."

Dylan's trip to England in spring 1965 was a turning point. Although he played to only 50,000 people in eight concerts, the April to June tour changed him from a folk star into an international pop superstar. At this time, most pop excitement emanated from England, and Dylan's shock waves flashed back to America. The first clue: In March, 7,000 tickets for his May 10 Albert Hall concert sold out within two hours.

ABOVE LEFT

Savoy shuffle: Dylan wanders in Embankment Gardens, London, in front of the Savoy Hotel, April 1965.

1965, headlined: BEATLES SAY — DYLAN SHOWS THE WAY. The story, with photos of Lennon, Harrison, and Dylan, was reproduced on the sleeve of the Columbia single of "Subterranean Homesick Blues," backed with "She Belongs to Me." It read, in part: "Two Beatles particularly go for Dylan in a big way. Harrison has all his LPs and plays them regularly and Lennon admires him too."

Coleman, later editor of *Disc* and *Music Echo*, and then of *Melody Maker*, wrote me: "1965 was the year Dylan conquered Britain, the year 'Wind' and 'Times a-Changin'' became favorites of the university students and the pop screamers. Dylan emerged from the relative obscurity of the folk world to the wider, more dangerous world of pop idol. For Dylan, it was fraught with trouble. I was among the hundreds who met Dylan at London Airport. He was bemused by it all. In seven major cities, Dylan faced an uncanny audience. Half was converted, half was the pop cult. Dylan made absolutely no concession to hit parade status. He commanded utter silence at his concerts. Even the noisy pop fans were stunned into silence by his words, the honesty of his performances. Bob consistently showed an endearing modesty. He wandered on stage with no sign of the 'big star' atmosphere we had come to expect from pop immortals. At Leicester's sensationally successful concert, a cross section of the audience agreed his performances were more electrifying, more important than his recordings. They clutched copies of *Back Home*. A student said: 'What made it for us was that he sang the words of his songs as if they had meaning. You see so many artists who perform like zombies, as if they're there for the money and that's all.'"

The build-up began long before his arrival on Monday, April 26. The March 19 *London Evening News* and next morning's *Daily Sketch* announced that his Albert Hall tickets were selling "like gold dust." The *Daily Mirror* did an advance story from the States. The pop weeklies ran background stories. Additional blessings from Manfred Mann and the Animals helped build anticipation. As Dylan's plane came into the London airport, two hundred fans waited in the rain, some wearing replicas of "the hat." They began to

If a single external factor triggered Dylan's British breakthrough, it was the Beatles' public endorsement, which wrought magic. If, as he once said, Dylan was "reborn in New York," then he was certainly reincarnated in England. Before then, in early 1965, he was doing concerts on both coasts. He was writing furiously and recording and, in February, made a brilliant appearance on the Les Crane WABC-TV show. When Dylan had played New Haven and Santa Monica in March 1965, there were local reviews, not the lionization he was to receive in the British national press. In a small country, excitement was like steam in a kettle. The pop and national press had a carnival. Reports were appalled, bemused, entranced. Dylan made good copy.

Dylanmania was probably triggered by Ray Coleman's article in *Melody Maker* on January 9, give him Beatles treatment, pulling at his hair and tugging at his clothes, virtually carrying him into the airport conference room. Police helped him through the mob; Dylan, looking somewhat shaken, said: "It's never been like this before! It was OK—they didn't hurt me. They just gave me a haircut. I'm ready to get drunk now." He carried an outsize light bulb, a prankish Diogenes lamp. Asked, "What is your message?" Dylan replied: "Keep a good head and always carry a light bulb." Brushing aside questions about Baez, the Beatles, and Donovan, he asked the whereabouts of Christine Keeler, who had been at the center of a political scandal.

Mike Hurst, who taped a ten-minute interview for the BBC, told me later: "He was a living myth before he got here. Many in the press were waiting to break the myth. At first, he was very vague. When I got down to his music, he really started to talk. He was almost interviewing me then." Dylan met the press at the Savoy Hotel, individually and in conference. "Mr. Dylan managed to exasperate practically everybody. … He wafted a red rose beneath his nose and could be heard … to say: 'Stiff, cold and mortistic,'" wrote Maureen Cleave of the *Evening Standard*. Cleave, who was friends with the Beatles, complained: "What do I do with him, how do you make him talk? He just says yes or no and rocks and sways as if he is masturbating himself."

A *Daily Mail* reporter was offered Dylan's heavy green glasses. Dylan: "See the world as Bob Dylan sees it. … I'm alone up here. I was over here three years back and on the streets. In two years, I'll be gone and you'll be talking to someone else." Why was he staying at the Savoy, a hotel where even minor clerks wear swallow-tailed jackets? Dylan snapped: "I can't live in a shack!" Grossman hustled the *Daily Mail* man into another room. Baez sat singing "Sally, Go Round the Roses." For the *Mirror*, Bob and Joan posed together on the balcony. One reporter wanted to know why Dylan sounded like a man of seventy-five who was always cross. Dylan: "I hate injustice, that's why I sing about racial discrimination and freedom, and I preach for people to be able to do the things they want. On some of my earlier records, I sounded cross because I was poor. Lived on less than two cents a day in those times. Now I'm cross because I'm rich. … I'm not spreading disillusionment by singing the truth. … I guess listening to me is like reading a newspaper. I wanna be entertaining as well as truthful."

Singer Martin Carthy told me: "All the times we went to visit him, only half a minute of the time could we actually contact him. The Savoy rooms were always filled with people. Bob became very, very detached; he had so many people to cope with. The more famous he became, the more he tended just to sit in his hotel." Dorothy Carthy added: "One very high window looked out over a stone balustrade. Pennebaker was in a corner with his camera. Everybody was eating and talking, when Bob suddenly came in through the window from the bathroom next door with an absolutely straight face. He walked along the tops of chairs, settees and whatever other furniture there was. He walked right out of the door and nobody else noticed."

The first concert, Sheffield, April 30, and the *Guardian* reported: "The audience … radiated a religious fervor … the second coming of Bob Dylan, their singing Messiah. … The times, they are a-changing … when a poet and not a pop singer fills a hall. For this ultimately is what Dylan is. … With his voice, the lyrics are astonishing; without it, in print, they are poetry."

The two Albert Hall gigs resembled the provinces. *Melody Maker*'s Max Jones: "Like a mysterious troubadour who'd lost his horse," Dylan had quietly taken over "with his weirdly compelling songs." Maurice Rosenbaum, in the *Daily Telegraph* and *Morning Post*: "There are better singers, better guitarists, better harmonica players and better poets. But there is no other twenty-three-year-old

OPPOSITE
Albert Grossman looks on as Dylan heads to the stage in London's Royal Albert Hall with a handful of harmonicas.

"Dylan emerged from the relative obscurity of the folk world to the wider, more dangerous world of pop idol.
RAY COLEMAN"

who does all these things with even a semblance of the power, the originality, or the fire … this haystack-headed young American has achieved in an age of more and more pictures, and less and less text, of emotional noises rather than meanings, an astounding popular victory for the word."

The tour gave Bob occasion to see old friends and to make new ones, including the Manfred Mann band, notably Paul Jones. During Dylan's tour, Manfred Mann's recording of "God on Our Side" was on the British charts. "Dylan's influence on the English pop scene was absolutely enormous," Jones told me later. "You can even look at the Beatles and see how much they were influenced."

Lennon visited Dylan late one night at the Savoy. He thought those who criticized Dylan for staying at such a plush hotel were fools: "What's wrong with staying at the Savoy? Does starving in a garret make his points any more valid? They say that to be ethnic as a folker you must also be poor and act the part. Absolute rubbish! Especially when you consider that the people he's sometimes having a go at—politicians especially—are probably twice as well off, anyway. If you've got a lot to say, like Dylan has, and if you want to make it heard, you've just got to elevate yourself and make yourself famous so people will listen. Earning a fortune's nothing to do with that side of it, but if he happens to do that as well, good luck to him." As soon as he discovered Dylan couldn't be served at the Savoy, Lennon invited him to his house in Weybridge, Surrey, for dinner one evening. Bob told me Lennon was "a full bold Beatle, a very untalkative cat, but very very clever." In the *Biograph* notes, Dylan said he and John tried writing a song together on a tape recorder.

On May 12, Bob went to Levy's Recording Studios on New Bond Street for a brief session that became a bootleg tape. Tom Wilson greeted James Craig of *Record Mirror*: "We're going to try a little experimental stuff tonight," he said, waving toward a piano and two organs. "Some new material Bobby wants to get on tape. Maybe we'll, get an album out of it, maybe not."

"I guess listening to me is like reading a newspaper. I wanna be entertaining as well as truthful."

ABOVE

Visions of Johanna:
Dylan and Baez in
Embankment Gardens,
London, April 1965.

In walked Albert and Sally, folk singers Nadia Catouse and Sidney Carter, Eric Clapton, Paul Jones, John McVie, Hughie Flint, bluesman John Mayall, and three female backup singers. Dylan cut "If You Gotta Go," for a promotional message to a CBS sales committee, and, reportedly, "Help!"

After a brief holiday in Portugal (referred to in "Sara"), Dylan returned to England in late May to tape a show for the BBC. It was delayed for a couple of weeks because Dylan had a viral infection and spent a few days in St. Mary's Hospital in Paddington. According to Richard Fariña, Joan came to visit but Sara (who Bob would marry in November) was in his room, and told her Dylan didn't want to see anyone. Baez had never appeared in Britain, and was keen to establish herself there. It was only natural that she would have expected reciprocity in getting some time on his concert tour. She didn't, and was visibly shaken, and her "farewell kiss" is her exit cue from *Dont Look Back*. Joan later said: "I thought he would do what I had done with him, would introduce me. I was very, very hurt. I was miserable." She should have left after the first concert she admitted, but felt an inner compulsion to stay.

Despite the breadth of his British triumph, the folk old guard was still ready to pounce. To the purists, led by Ewan MacColl and Peggy Seeger, success spelled compromise. In September 1965, in a *Melody Maker* interview, MacColl predicted: "We're going to get lots of copies of Dylan—one foot in folk and one foot in pop. … Dylan is to me the perfect symbol of the anti-artist in our society. He is against everything—the last resort of someone who doesn't really want to change the world. … I think his poetry is punk. It's derivative and terribly old hat. … Dylan songs accept the world as it is."

During the 1965 English tour, handheld cameras were focused on Dylan for about twenty hours, as he improvised dialogue and starred in his first feature-length film, directed by D.A. Pennebaker. Its title, *Dont Look Back*, suggests an arch twist on *Look Back in Anger*, the fifties play by John Osborne. The title also recalls the biblical story of Lot's wife. Released in 1967, the film earned as many raves as negative reviews.

Critical reaction centered on Dylan, not the film. Ralph Gleason saw it as "really about the problem of the artist in communicating with his audience and the problem of the Old World in communicating with the New Youth and vice versa. Dylan can be shown snarling, swearing, singing, smiling, shining, and sulking and still be the genius he is, and this honesty in portrayal makes the film very valuable." Richard Goldstein, in the *New York Times*, thought it showed Dylan "feeling around the edges of fame, like a chambermaid in a new mink coat." But Goldstein thought "Pennebaker's camera is almost too willing to play cinematic straight man. Without a program, you can hardly tell the vaudeville from the verité …"

After some years during which he was apparently embarrassed by the film, Dylan changed his mind. By 1971, Dylan told me: "In the last couple of years, I've come to like the film a lot more than I used to." Did he mean the man who said "don't look back" was ready to look back at a portion of his life? "No, I meant don't look back over your shoulder," Dylan joked.

At the Newport Festival in July 1965, Dylan starred in another kind of drama. All he did was play three songs with a rock backing yet he unleashed a storm. From the start, Newport '65 did not augur well. Baez sported her newest protégé, Donovan (whom she had met in London), on her arm. At an afternoon workshop, Alan Lomax, folk purist, and Albert Grossman clashed openly, over the way Lomax had introduced Grossman's soon-to-be clients, the Paul Butterfield Blues Band. After they had played to an ovation, Grossman belabored Lomax for his patronizing introduction. Invective began to fly, and shortly the giant of folklore and the titan of folk business were wrestling on the ground, before onlookers separated the two hulks.

Even before the Sunday night, Dylan seemed under some duress. Typically, he told few people about his plans, relishing the shock, the dramatic departure. But he couldn't envision a backfire; since January, his two electric singles and an album had done fabulously well. At Newport, the Butterfield Band and the Chambers Brothers

newport folk festival
july 22-25   1965

this year, and Muddy Waters the year before, had
shown that electric instrumentation and heavy
rhythm were not taboo. It was, to Dylan, "all
music, no more, no less."

To compound Dylan's difficulties, Seeger
announced that the Sunday night final program
was a message from today's folk musicians to
a newborn baby about the world we live in.
Unfortunately, this theme did not correspond
to Dylan's conception of his performance.
His Sunday segment was sandwiched between
Cousin Emmy and the Sea Island singers, two
very traditional acts. Cousin Emmy's high spot
was "Turkey in the Straw." Dylan had to fill his
appointed slot, without a sound check for his
pick-up band.

There's a lot of folklore about how the
band was picked up. Al Kooper's session work
had already impressed Dylan. At the festival,
Kooper was strolling about when Albert said
Bob was looking for him and gave him some
backstage passes (so giving Kooper a title for his
1977 memoir). Dylan told Kooper he wanted to
bring the "Rolling Stone" sound onstage. Three
members of the Butterfield Band were recruited:
guitarist Mike Bloomfield, drummer Sam Lay, and
bassist Jerome Arnold. At a Newport party, Dylan
completed his band with pianist Barry Goldberg,
and Dylan rehearsed this instant group until dawn
at a nearby mansion. They kept their plan secret
until they walked onstage, Dylan, in a matador-
outlaw orange shirt and black leather, carrying an
electric guitar. From the moment the group swung
into a rocking electric version of "Maggie's Farm,"
the Newport audience registered shock. What
happened next depended on where you were, but
I heard enormous vocal hostility all around me. As
the group finished "Farm," there was some reserved
applause and a flurry of boos. Someone shouted:
"Bring back Cousin Emmy!" The microphones and
speakers were all out of balance, the sound poor and
lopsided. For even the most ardent fan of the new
music, the performance was unpersuasive. As Dylan
led his band into "Rolling Stone," the audience
grew shriller: "Play folk music! Sell out! This is a
folk festival! Get rid of that band!" Dylan began "It
Takes a Train to Cry" and the applause diminished

as the heckling increased. Dylan and the group disappeared offstage, and there was a long, clumsy silence. Peter Yarrow urged Bob to return and gave him his acoustic guitar. As Bob returned to the stage alone, he discovered he didn't have the right harmonica. "What are you doing to me?" Dylan demanded of Yarrow. To shouts for "Tambourine Man," Dylan said: "OK, I'll do that one for you." The older song had a palliative effect and won strong applause. Then Dylan did "It's All Over Now, Baby Blue," the words taking on a new meaning, as if he were singing adieu to Newport, goodbye to the folk purists. He left the stage having vanquished the hostility of those who wouldn't accept his electric music.

As cast and audience left Newport '65 on July 25, a definite break in community brotherhood had occurred. Dylan had served another declaration of aesthetic independence. Later, in *Sing Out!*, Jim Rooney, a gentle Boston musician, wrote: "It

was disturbing to the Old Guard. … Bob is no longer a Neo-Woody Guthrie. … The highway he travels now is unfamiliar to those who bummed around … during the Depression. He travels by plane. … The mountains and valleys he knows are those of the mind—a mind extremely aware of the violence of the inner and outer world. 'The people' so loved by Pete Seeger are 'the mob' so hated by Dylan. … They seemed to understand that night for the first time what Dylan has been trying to say for over a year—that he is not theirs or anyone else's and they didn't like what they heard and booed. … Can there be no songs as violent as the age? Must a folk song be of mountains, valleys, and love between my brother and my sister all over this land? Do we allow for despair only in the blues? … The only one in the entire festival who questioned our position was Bob Dylan. Maybe he didn't put it in the best way. Maybe he was rude. But he shook us. And that is why we have poets and artists."

08

INSIDE THE COLISEUM

> # "I'm not really bothered by Newport, because I know in my own mind what I'm doing. If anyone has imagination, he'll know what I'm doing."

The booing didn't stop at Newport, but continued sporadically at Dylan's American concerts until October 1965, and resumed during his world tour until late spring 1966. The year beginning July 1965 was, for him, ridden with personal stress. Lionized now by the pop world, he was being rejected by many folkniks who had once deified him. Dylan was imitated, castigated, emulated, berated, upbraided, and celebrated. All he really wanted to do was write and sing. "Oh, the hours/I've spent inside the Coliseum,/Dodging lions and wastin' time" was surely heartfelt.

Dylan sustained himself with little sleep and food, and with what he once called "a lot of medicine." As public pressures devoured him, he was planning to marry. Debate about his going electric raged on internationally. Singer-actor Theodore Bikel said of the Newport debacle: "Dylan made a tactical mistake. He should have started with acoustic music, then gone into electric. He didn't bother to reach out. He didn't talk to the audience. A lesser person would have given up performing after such a reception."

Dylan remained silent about Newport until his August 28 concert at the Forest Hills Music Festival in Queens. Charlie Rothschild telephoned the *New York Times* to offer an interview. From my notes: "I'm not really bothered by Newport, because I know in my own mind what I'm doing. If anyone has imagination, he'll know what I'm doing. If they can't understand my songs, they're missing something. I'll have some electricity at Forest Hills. At Newport, whoever was in charge of the sound didn't know what was happening. This time I'll have a couple or three or four new songs. Time goes by very fast up there on stage. I have to think of what not to do, rather than what to do. I get very bored. I can't sing 'With God on Our Side' for fifteen years."

That summer, only Dylan, Sinatra, and Streisand had sold out the 15,000 seats at Forest Hills, grossing $75,000 for one evening. Dylan began an acoustic set with "She Belongs to Me." The reception was respectful, the applause generous. Dylan was in control. "Desolation Row" had a stunning debut, the audience hanging on every grotesque image. After intermission, Dylan returned with Robbie Robertson on electric guitar, Al Kooper on electric piano and organ, Harvey Brooks on electric bass, and Levon Helm on drums. The band and high-voltage singing raised a crackling intensity. At the end of each number, there were boos and shouts of "We want the old Dylan!" After "Maggie's Farm," someone shouted: "Traitor!" Others yelled: "Where's Ringo?" and "Play folk music!" In a confused jangle of music and audience discord, someone yelled: "Scum bag!" Dylan replied: "Ah, come on now." Some "listeners" threw fruit, and some young rockers were evicted. One prankster got onstage and knocked Al Kooper off his chair. Dylan told the band to keep playing the intro to "Thin Man." After five-minutes, the palliative worked. The muted backing for "It Ain't Me, Babe" elicited very few catcalls. By the time Dylan did "Rolling Stone," already a hit single, the audience mostly sang along. Critics of Newport '65 and the new music were proved wrong. At Forest Hills, the sound was right, the programming intelligent, the presentation persuasive. The problem lay with the audience.

The booing was virtually over in the East. When Dylan played Carnegie Hall on October 1, he heard cheers for the new music. Jack Newfield, writing in the *Village Voice*, observed "a new cultural tradition is evolving ... the opposite of High Culture. ... Seymour Krim once called it 'the culture of the streets.' Charlie Parker ... Allen Ginsberg and Lenny Bruce and William Burroughs contributed to it. And so, too, does Dylan, with his fusion of symbolic poetry and a new kind of folk music."

Folk-rock became a runaway music business trend and a clattering controversy. Another Dylan change that turned into a mass movement, it was a logical outgrowth of his art, and it revolutionized pop music. As a craze, folk-rock had run its course by the end of 1965, but dozens of styles that grew out of folk-rock are still flourishing. Its roots lay deep in the sociology, messages, protest, and social commentary of blues and country music.

Off campus, an even greater social malaise was developing, in American involvement in the Indo-Chinese war. Lyndon Johnson was leading America deeper into what Pete Seeger's song called "The Big Muddy." Without being consulted, American youth was about to be drained of its energy, its talent, its blood, its life. Peace campaigns affected more people than civil rights did. A rage for protest and comment made folk-rock considerably more than a simple merger of styles. In *The Making of a Counter Culture*, Theodore Roszak wrote that "one is apt to find out more about ... youth ... by paying attention to posters ... and dance—and especially to the pop music, which now knits together the whole thirteen to thirty age group." Earlier, Dylan had been regarded as the voice of his generation, although he spoke for only a radical fringe. Now, in front of folk-rock's greater audience, he represented his constituency.

The Byrds, who in 1965 cut "Mr. Tambourine Man," one of the decade's most successful singles, amplified Dylan's entry into rock, and later into country music. The chief Byrd, twelve-string guitarist Jim (later Roger) McGuinn, saw that in 1964 folk music "was getting very commercial."

ABOVE

March 1965, Dylan plays harmonica with the Byrds at Ciro's Nightclub, Los Angeles, as folk-rock dominates the airwaves. From left: David Crosby, Gene Clark, Michael Clarke (drums), and Roger McGuinn. The band's version of "Mr. Tambourine Man" took three months to reach the top of the American charts but it started a new trend.

In summer '64, McGuinn met Gene Clark at the Troubadour in Los Angeles, and they formed a group. David Crosby joined them, and they rehearsed as Jet Set. Chris Hillman and Mike Clarke rounded out the group. McGuinn: "I saw this gap, with Dylan and the Beatles leaning toward each other in concept. That's where we aimed." And that's where they hit. Their first attempt at "Mr Tambourine Man" can be heard on the 1969 demo collection *Preflyte*. The vocal harmonies are broadly in place, but martial-style drums distract from McGuinn's twelve-string Rickenbacker and the bass guitar counterpoint. In January 1965, signed to Columbia, the Byrds re-recorded the song with producer Terry Melcher, Doris Day's son. Dylan said: "Wow, man, you can dance to that!" McGuinn described Dylan as "astounded."

One of the ironies of the second recording of "Tambourine Man" was that, instrumentally, McGuinn was the only Byrd on the recording. The others couldn't make the session, so the famous bass introduction was by Larry Knechtel, with Hal Blaine on drums and Leon Russell on second guitar. Vocal harmonies were added later. The single was released in March 1965, while the Byrds were at Ciro's in Los Angeles. Everyone who was anyone, including Dylan, showed up. Columbia press releases had the song topping the charts "immediately," but it actually took three months in America and four in Britain, where the Byrds were the first American group to top the charts since the Beatles breakout.

The Byrds returned to Columbia's studios. They tried "Baby Blue" and "Times Changin'," and decided neither was right. Finally, they did Seeger's "Turn! Turn! Turn!," allowing its release after a reported eighty takes. In five weeks, it was number one.

Back in 1965, Dylan was soon appropriated by the music business as the trend of the year, "the biggest thing" since the Beatles. By September '65, eight Dylan songs, three of them his own recordings, made the Top Forty. Dozens of Dylan-inspired folk-rock hits had emerged that summer: Janis Ian, a fifteen-year-old *Broadside* alumna, wrote "Society's Child," a defense of interracial dating. Other folk-protest songs returned in folk-rock garb: Buffy Sainte-Marie's "Universal Soldier," and Ochs's "There But for Fortune." Only when Simon and Garfunkel overdubbed their acoustic "Sounds of Silence" with a rhythmic beat did they emerge from obscurity. Some established pop composers were striving to put substance into rock lyrics; Barry Mann and Cynthia Weil's "We Gotta Get Out of this Place," which protested black ghetto life, was recorded by Eric Burdon and the Animals. And the British charts featured Barry McGuire's "Eve of Destruction" and Donovan's cover of "Universal Soldier."

By 1966, *Look* called Dylan "Folk-Rock's Mr. Tambourine Man" and regarded him as "unchallenged as the teen-and-college crowd's Absolute Hipster, their own 'hung-up' idol, and singing annalist of a jingle-jangle reality that makes more sense to them than any secure, whitewashed American Dream." Dylan told *Look*: "I define nothing. Not beauty, not patriotism. I take each thing as it is, without prior rules about what it should be."

Although the folk-rock protest boom waned in early 1966, the music has persisted. Before 1965, many assumed that pop and rock were *supposed* to be about trivia, not only non-intellectual but *anti*-intellectual. This surface judgment belied a true understanding of popular music as social expression. Folk-rock, after its fad phase cooled, effected a major improvement of popular music. For that, one must credit Dylan.

What forced Dylan to battle prejudices among listeners who had once worshipped him? From mid–1965, he was treated by many as a heretic, an apostate. A heretic from what orthodoxy, an apostate from what creed? A brief look at folk orthodoxy shows how, in the name of purity, vast numbers held so rigidly to a dogma that they rose in outrage at Dylan's deviations from doctrine.

Although I had misgivings about performers like Barry McGuire and the Turtles, I took on the doctrinaires. In the Sunday *New York Times* on January 30, 1966, I swung a two-paragraph right hook at *Sing Out!* It unleashed such a personalized and vitriolic storm that some people asked the *Times* to remove me! I had accused *Sing Out!* of being "disturbingly narrow-minded," of not encouraging experimentation, of being opposed to the avant-garde. It reminded me "of Soviet cultural organs denouncing Yevtushenko for heresies, prodding him back to the pastures of orthodoxy."

After the folk-rock fad waned, and Dylan had surprised everyone with *John Wesley Harding*, the Old Guard ultimately relented. In Britain, in spite of initially rigorous objection to folk-rock, musical developments were even more imaginative. English, Scots and Irish groups like the Incredible String Band, Steeleye Span and Fairport Convention infused traditional materials with modern ideas. Eventually, on September 28, 1968, *Sing Out!*'s Irwin Silber rendered an eloquent mea culpa in American Leftist weekly, the *Guardian*:

> Many of us who did not fully understand the dynamics of the political changes … in America … felt deserted by a poet who—we had come to believe—cared. And Dylan did desert—not us, but an outmoded style of values which had become unequal to the task of reclaiming America. "This land is not your land," Dylan told us in 1965. But some of us raised on the songs of Guthrie and Seeger … inheritors of a superficial "Marxism" based on diluted Leninism and rationalized Stalinism were not ready to accept the revolutionary implications of Dylan's statements. Because if we accepted them … we would have to act on them!

Since Hibbing, Dylan had dreamed of having his own band. As early as the studio-combo sessions for his second album, Dylan was thinking about sidemen. From 1961 to 1964, he loved to jam. Forming the right band took time and work. One night in early 1965, Dylan, Neuwirth and I went to the Village Gate to hear the Paul Butterfield Blues Band. I'd heard them at the Gaslight and suggested Bob check them out, and he watched with fascination as Butterfield, who'd worked with all the great Chicago bluesmen, lead the band in some explosive R&B. Within a few weeks, Grossman had signed Butterfield. Dylan thought of working with Butterfield and his brilliant guitarist, Mike Bloomfield, but chemistry and career direction kept Dylan from hiring them.

Bob finally found his men in summer 1965, a Canadian-based group, the Hawks, later briefly known as the Crackers, and, ultimately, the Band. Dylan's involvement with the Band became what *Time* called "the most decisive moment in rock history." It developed into one of the most enduring relationships between a pop star and a supporting group. Their rapport began with musical ideas. Steeped in blues, country, R&B, the old rock 'n' roll, and the new rock, the Hawks provided Dylan with the camaraderie he'd enjoyed only fleetingly with other musicians. The group had been on the road—surviving, if not thriving—even longer than Bob. They had a maturity Dylan sorely needed in a trying year.

For Robbie Robertson, Levon Helm, Rick Danko, Richard Manuel, and Garth Hudson, the transition from years working out of Toronto with the raunchy Ronnie Hawkins to Dylan was a quantum leap. As the Hawks,

I define nothing. Not beauty, not patriotism. I take each thing as it is, without prior rules about what it should be.

they'd endured a grind only young musicians could romanticize. Dylan's world tour promised to be an enviable assignment, but folkniks still roared at Dylan's going electric, and his five wicked messengers were vilified for the electric shrieking and heavy thrust.

"Easy enough" to get together, Dylan once said, not mentioning the hours of jamming and rehearsing, discussions, exploring, and soul-searching to determine if the Hawks spoke Dylanese and if Dylan spoke Hawktalk. Robbie Robertson could only vaguely describe those important early meetings: "Let's just say that he didn't call us and we didn't call him. That's all I can remember. We'd had one of his albums and we all liked it, but it didn't snap us like that, you know. And we had no idea he was as strong as we later found out he was. We were a scrounge road group when we met him. He taught us about flying in airplanes, about meeting important people." Earlier, Robertson had said: "I think we were playing in Atlantic City. I didn't really know who he was or that he was that famous. I didn't think we could play with each other, at all. Then we jammed together and a lot of things happened. We've had a great effect on each other." Helm remembered a phone call to Somers Point, New Jersey, where the Hawks were playing. "You wanna play Hollywood Bowl?" Dylan asked. Helm said they had never heard of Dylan, and proceeded to inquire who else was going to be on the show. "Just us," Dylan said to the astonished Helm.

Onstage, the Band, a no-nonsense ensemble, kept theatrics to a minimum. Four could alternate lead singing, while Hudson often sang along on ensembles. Between them, they commanded seventeen instruments and used their technical skills to play music, not to whip up applause. On guitar, Robertson was a perfectionist technician, while Dylan remained primarily an expressionist who generally used instrumental technique as a vehicle, not an end. Vocally, Robbie soon joined the legions who felt the strong pull of Dylan's hydra-headed singing—the urgent, pained involvement, the hand-on-shoulder intimacy, the eccentric accentuation, the chilling directness and the raw bones of honesty.

After Robertson and Helm appeared with Dylan at Forest Hills in 1965, Bob signed the group for the world tour. When that ended, the Band followed Dylan's retreat to the country. They took a house called Big Pink, outside Saugerties, near Woodstock, to concentrate on their own new directions.

Dylan singled out Robertson to play on *Blonde on Blonde*. The first public indication of later recording collaboration was in 1967, on the bootlegged *Basement Tapes* of Dylan and the Band playing in Woodstock. The Band backed Dylan at the two-performance Tribute to Woody Guthrie on January 20, 1968, at Carnegie Hall. Dylan made a surprise appearance with them on July 14, 1969, at the Mississippi River Festival in Edwardsville, Illinois. Introduced as Elmer Johnson, Dylan sang three numbers, including the old hill tune, "In the Pines." He returned with the Band to do an encore of Buddy Holly's "Slippin' and Slidin'." A few weeks later, on August 31, 1969, Dylan and the Band appeared at the Isle of Wight, where they suffered from the Festival's vast, impersonal setting and general mismanagement. On New Year's Eve 1971, Dylan popped up, again unannounced, at an

December 1965: Dylan with (from left) Robbie Robertson, Michael McClure, and Allen Ginsberg
in San Francisco's North Beach neighborhood near the celebrated City Lights bookstore. Opened in
1953 by Lawrence Ferlinghetti, it was ground zero for the Beats, and City Lights' 1956 publication of
Ginsberg's *Howl and Other Poems* led to an obscenity trial which put it on the international map.

ambitious Band concert at Manhattan's Academy of Music. The most notable, sustained, and prominent evidence of the collaboration between Dylan and the Band was their tour in 1974 and the simultaneous release of *Planet Waves*, the collaborators' first commercially released album. Out of the tour came the double-LP set *Before the Flood*. Dylan appeared November 25, 1976, at the Last Waltz, the Band's farewell public concert at Winterland, San Francisco.

Among the many Dylan songs the Band recorded, the group gave four their official American debuts: "I Shall Be Released," "Tears of Rage," "This Wheel's on Fire," from *Big Pink*, and "When I Paint My Masterpiece," from *Cahoots* (1971). On *The Basement Tapes*, "Released" links *Blonde* and *John Wesley Harding*.

Given the close relationship between Dylan and the Band, it's strange that so much time passed between 1965 and the two albums of 1974. The collaborators may have agreed that detachment allowed air for more ideas to circulate with other musicians behind Dylan at sessions. There was some recording collaboration in 1965: the Band supplied backing on the single "Can You Please Crawl Out Your Window?."

The world tour of 1965–66 was Dylan's dance of life and death, choreographed for the eyes of thousands and orchestrated for the ears of countless more. Everything crowded in on him: three, sometimes four concerts a week; listeners hungering for a new album; acolytes awaiting new direction; businessmen demanding more product, more profit. No one stopped to think of the personal cost which, to Dylan, was high. From autumn through spring, as he careened around the States, Dylan continued to write new songs. During a concert break, he scribbled an idea in his dressing room. While the Band slept on the tour's chartered Lockheed Lodestar, in the back of a car, while others made small talk, Dylan saw visions beyond the passing landscape. In smoky motel rooms, he squeezed out a riff, a phrase from his guitar.

Although *Blonde on Blonde* was not released until May 1966, its material had been evolving for more than a year. Some ideas burst forth in the heat of a session, others had been simmering for months.

It was all pressure cooking, but Dylan seemed to thrive artistically under the deadline, giving first-rate performances and assembling the remarkable contents of his first double album. But every day the strain became increasingly obvious. He was chronically tired, boiling with anxiety under a surface he strove to keep cool. When I told John Court I was starting a book about Dylan, he replied sardonically: "You better hurry."

All of which heightens the achievement of *Blonde*, a hallmark collection that completes his first major rock cycle, which began with *Back Home*. No Dylan recording until then required as much studio time. Preliminary work began before Christmas 1965, continuing intermittently through the winter. Sessions began in Columbia's New York studios, where one eleven-hour taping yielded nothing. Not until the whole operation moved to Nashville in February 1966 did things jell. Nashville studios, "the Mayo Clinic of pop," have long proved therapeutic. Tennessee's capital is less abrasive, and quality sidemen can be corralled quickly. On the *Blonde* sessions were Wayne Moss, Charlie McCoy, Kenneth Buttrey, Hargus Robbins, Jerry Kennedy, Joe South, Al Kooper, Bill Aikins, Henry Strzelecki, and Robbie Robertson. Dylan went to Nashville for relief, but also because his producer, Bob Johnston, was based there.

Al Kooper said Johnston's faith in Nashville sidemen convinced Dylan to go south. At one point, Johnston wanted to do "Rainy Day Women" in Salvation Army style, but he needed a brass player instantly. At 4.30 a.m. McCoy made a phone call. Half an hour later, Kooper swears, a trombone player marched in, sat through three takes, and went home in an hour, the hit recorded. As usual, Dylan did a great deal of writing and rewriting in the studio, developing his songs from roughed-out versions he had brought with him. For "Johanna" and "Sad-Eyed Lady," Dylan hunched over a piano in his hotel room for up to five hours. Occasionally Kooper would come in, strum some chords to Dylan's work in progress, then teach the rest of the crew the changes.

There is a distinctive "sound" to the album, which Dylan later tried to recreate in *Street-Legal*. He described it as "that thin, that wild mercury

OPPOSITE

Less smoke rings, more smoke screen: at a press conference in Los Angeles in December 1965, Dylan jousted with a typically uninformed press corps.

sound." *Blonde* begins with a joke and ends with a hymn; in between, wit alternates with a dominant theme of entrapment by circumstance, love, society, illusions, and unrealized hopes. "We sit here stranded, though we're all doin' our best to deny it" describes the singer's position. "We see this empty cage now corrode" offers some hope. Dylan is "stuck" inside Mobile, inside roles in a highly personal album. He perhaps best summarizes his effort to remain strong and cool, despite his weariness, in "Pledging My Time":

I got a poison headache,
But I feel all right.
I'm pledging my time to you,
Hopin' you'll come through, too.

Lawrence Ferlinghetti's characterization of Dylan's work as "higher than surreal" certainly fits *Blonde*. Through the shadow and smoke we feel his doomsday imprisonment, as he pledges to go on living, loving, and singing. Still that battle against lifelessness.

There's a remarkable marriage here of a funky, bluesy, rock expressionism and Rimbaud-like visions of discontinuity, chaos, emptiness, loss, being "stuck." Words can be explicit, but also have a musical value beyond cognition. As Wallace Fowlie wrote of Rimbaud, we can think of Dylan here "bent upon subordinating words to their sounds and colors." If, as Fowlie maintains, one breed of modern poet "must be possessed by the night," then *Blonde* is Dylan at the break of midnight.

While determined to keep his new wife Sara from fans' fishbowl stares, Dylan revealed her through many songs. Dylan zealously guarded the privacy of his wife and their five children, yet Sara was often a prominent image in his work. While Lennon and McCartney made public rituals out of their respective marriages, Dylan kept his family life and artistic processes covert. Until he wrote "Sara" in 1975, he would talk only in metaphors about the "Madonna-like woman," whose sagacity, calmness, and warmth changed his life. Until "Sara," he never dedicated songs to her, never talked explicitly of her, relying on his songs only to proclaim his love or pain. There are specifics in "Sad-Eyed Lady" that reveal Sara.

Richard Goldstein wrote: "'Sad-Eyed Lady' is one of Dylan's least self-conscious songs … the most moving love song in rock. Even its foibles conspire to convey the paradoxical reality of its heroine; this sad-eyed lady who can be so nonchalantly strong, and so predictably weak; so innocent, yet so corrupted. … His sad-eyed lady is everyone's girl, and everyone's girl is what the love song is all about." The successive similes seem thoroughly successful at draping a subject in a richly brocaded tapestry of language. Dylan has brought high metaphoric development and literary allusion into rock. The sad-eyed lady, like Shakespeare's dark lady, is an elusive source of inspiration and wonder.

Blonde closed a period that, until 1974, has often been regarded as Dylan's most fluent, poetic, and experimental. He and others were turning rock into a new art form of vast horizons. Dylan's art stimulated a coterie of new commentators. One was Paul Williams, who launched *Crawdaddy*, a mimeographed, rough-and-ready bulletin. *Rolling Stone* and pop coverage in the *Village Voice* and other alternative periodicals reflected new acceptance of rock. Some fan magazines turned literary or sociological. Ellen Willis, who in 1968 became the *New Yorker*'s rock critic, wrote about Dylan with great insight. The *East Village Other* quoted the poet Frank O'Hara whom Dylan reminded of a young Auden, "in the sense of being a public poet. Even if the work was in the form of song, it was essentially presented as poem."

At the time of *Blonde*'s release, the older pop critics were reorienting their sights and the new rock critics were realizing that literature, art, and rock were all converging. Some performers, like Leonard Cohen and Richard Fariña, were flexing their muscles as singing *writers*. A few weeks before his death in April 1966, I interviewed Fariña: "The particular magic that Dylan has over, say, twenty million people, is the paradox and the inaccessibility of him. In his music, people are struck by something and yet they don't really seem to know what it is. That's always been the case with the most acute and exalted poetry. There are lines of Shakespeare like this, in which you don't have to know who plays what to be struck by the magic of words. Then the insight of the listener is followed by intense perplexity. We hear something that we finally realize is saying something we think ourselves and then we want to know more about the writer who can tell us something about ourselves. Joan [Baez], on the other hand, reinterprets what others have written in a way that makes us listen. Joan is a mother who gives birth to a new meaning in a song for us, and Bobby is the father, the one who does the fertilizing. While Hemingway has brought us the physical hero, whose presence and appearance are so exciting, Dylan has brought us the 'head hero,' whose brain attracts and compels our interest. But he is complicated! Everything he does and writes is complicated. How can you possibly be walking around upright on this earth and possibly be simple?"

Launching a tour after Newport and Forest Hills took nerve, but Dylan wanted to "show the audience what we're doing these days." Many in the heavily politicized audience wanted slogans, not the new beat. The times were indeed changing: On May 5, 1965, anti-draft demonstrations began at Berkeley, where forty students publicly burned their draft cards. More followed suit later in the month at a Berkeley teach-in, the protest highlighting America's immoral prosecution of the war. As such protests increased, Congress passed a law making it a crime to burn a draft card but the actions continued, a potent symbol of the growing opposition to Vietnam. At the University of Wisconsin, fifty students marched on Truax Air Force Base and tried unsuccessfully to arrest the commander as "an accessory to mass murder and genocide." At November 1965 anti-Vietnam War teach-ins, buttons and posters articulated youth outrage: MAKE LOVE, NOT WAR! POWER TO THE PEOPLE! YOU CAN'T TRUST ANYBODY OVER 30. Dylan had spent three years supplying marching songs for the campus protest against war, hypocrisy, and discrimination, but now he was changing the tempo, saying he wasn't "a schoolteacher, a shepherd, a soul-saver." He was looking for "salvation." So too many of his audience.

To heavily politicized youth, most rock ("the new numbness," Dave Van Ronk called it) represented escape to a palmier time before Vietnam. Dylan's *Blonde on Blonde* visions were very much in the new pop mood. Although most pop—shoddy Carnaby Street clothes, comic books—was disposable, Warhol's canvases became classics, and Dylan's art endured. But Dylan did not have an easy time setting out on his 1965–66 world tour in this jumbled environment of dope and Batman, teach-ins and screech-ins. Dylan later described it to me: "I was touring for a couple of years. That's a fast pace. We were doing a whole show, no other acts. It's pretty straining to do a show like that. A lot of really unhealthy situations rise up. I was just going out there performing these songs. Everyone else was having a good time. I did it enough to know that there must be something else to do. It wasn't my own choice. I was more or less being pushed into it—pushed in and carried out."

The first concert was at Hollywood Bowl, on Friday, September 3, 1965. Moving Dylan and the Hawks on the thirteen-seat, twin-engine Lockheed Lodestar took generalship. Bobby Neuwirth and Victor Maymudes alternated as road manager. When Neuwirth was aboard, Victor or Bill Avis

> **While Hemingway has brought us the physical hero, whose presence and appearance are so exciting, Dylan has brought us the 'head hero,' whose brain attracts and compels our interest.**
>
> RICHARD FARIÑA

served as Hawks' roadie. Two movers and truck drivers loaded eight crates of equipment and raced all night to the next stop, where they set up the $30,000 amplification system. Sporadically, *Variety* totted up the tour's receipts, calling Dylan "one of the hottest phenomena of show business today."

In early autumn, trouble began that continued for the remainder of the tour: most of the halls had inadequate sound balances. Sports arena acoustics were a far cry from those of theaters and concert halls. After each concert, Dylan asked: "How did it sound? I don't mean the songs, but how did it actually sound where you were?" From Newport to Albert Hall, concerts were plagued by distorted amplification. With better acoustics, the audience conversion to folk-rock might have been faster.

A high point of the year came on Sunday, December 12, when New York's two leading papers carried major features. The *Times* spread, by Thomas Meehan, was titled PUBLIC WRITER NO. 1? Finding Dylan the favorite American writer

of students at three Ivy League colleges, Meehan said: "Who needs Saul Bellow? There are those who say that *the* literary voice of our time—and a poet of high degree—is … Dylan." The *New York Herald Tribune* ran a major feature on the tour in which William Bender called Dylan "probably the greatest urban professional folk composer this country has ever known." Supplementing his piece was a six-page spread, billed as Daniel Kramer's "photographic portfolio." (Actually, Dylan's pal, Al Aronowitz, wrote the text and Dylan rewrote it.) This piece caught the non-sequential rock madness of the time.

This episode was not all fantasy. Shortly before Christmas 1965, I witnessed an evening almost as absurd. Paul and Betty Stookey gave a black-tie party at their lovely old brick house on Bedford Street in the Village. Scruffs were transformed into dudes. Grossman looked like a penguin headwaiter at an iceberg bar mitzvah. His lieutenant, Charlie Rothschild, fell asleep in the bathtub, while a chamber trio on the minstrel's gallery sawed away at the greatest hits of Boccherini, Corelli, and Vivaldi. As the party loped toward its finale, in marched a mob of uninvited street people. Heading the invading force was a very stoned Dylan in jeans and suede. Betty Stookey looked aghast as her careful planning evaporated. "Meet your hostess," I said, waving at Betty, and they glowered at each other. Dylan launched a heavy discussion with Albert, circling him so that the manager had to pan 360 degrees to listen to his client.

At almost 3 a.m. Dylan assembled Dave (Blue) Cohen, Phil Ochs, my date, Liz Newman, and me to depart for the next stop—an all-night club, the Clique, at 158 East 49th Street. The hangout fell silent as Dylan led us to a table.

Cohen was a comparatively new friend, who later took some acting honors in *Renaldo and Clara*. Just as Dylan was elevating Cohen, he was downgrading Phil Ochs, even though Ochs had revered Dylan for years. Two months earlier, Dylan had played his single "Crawl Out Your Window" for Cohen and Ochs. Dave loved it, but Phil said he didn't think it would be a hit. That night, Dylan stopped his limousine and

February 1966, Academy
of Music, Philadelphia,
Dylan looks sharp in tweeds
with his Fender Stratocaster.

Dylan with Al Kooper (left),
whose organ-playing on
"Like a Rolling Stone" is as
distinctive as Dylan's vocal;
and Doug Sahm, of the Sir
Douglas Quintet.

made Ochs crawl out the door, saying: "You're not a folk singer, you're just a journalist." Undaunted, Ochs was back, risking more abuse. Dave hung back, while Dylan attacked Phil's political-topical songwriting: "It's all wrong, you know. That isn't where it's at any more. It's way beyond that now." Ochs drank in the abuse, and while Dylan was away from the table, I asked him how he could take it all. Ochs said: "After all, man, if Dylan tells you something, you *gotta* listen." Dave split early, perhaps fearing he might be next on the carpet. Dylan returned to the table and continued the ax-chops. "Why don't you just become a stand-up comic?" he asked Phil. Dylan wasn't amusing; he looked ghostly pale, and was reluctant to go home to the Chelsea Hotel. As we hailed a taxi to the Village, Liz said: "My God, he looks like he's dying."

In the winter of 1965–66, Ralph Gleason agreed that Dylan looked close to death: "I was very worried about him. I figured he was in mortal pain. I wanted to ask him what was killing him. I was astounded he was still working, because I figured he would have had a breakdown. I thought he was having some severe abdominal pains, or a brain tumor."

The audience at Dylan's northern California series of concerts, beginning December 3 had no clue of Dylan's condition. Gleason ran the KQED-TV press conference and attended all the California events. At the first Berkeley concert, Gleason recalled, "in the front row were Larry Ferlinghetti, Ginsberg, Ken Kesey, and two Hell's Angels. The following week, there must have been a dozen Hell's Angels. Allen is very big with the Angels. In a way, he thinks he invented them."

What turned the Beat poets on to Dylan? "The San Francisco poets freaked out when they saw this Dylan thing happening. I thought Larry was a tragic figure that weekend, a shaken and embittered man. You know. What is that stringy kid doing up there with his electric guitar?' I mean, 'I am a major poet, and this kid has thirty-five hundred kids in this hall.' And Larry has been mumbling to himself ever since. The rest of them just flocked around. This is the first time the poets ever showed up. Allen made Dylan and the Beatles respectable. Dylan and Allen had long talks about 'Desolation Row.' There's Dylan sitting in the corner, and on the floor, like some ancient tribe of hill people about to go on an assaulting raid, is this mob of bearded Hell's Angels with all that leather and medals dripping off them. Obviously, Dylan couldn't talk to them. He just kept repeating: 'Good seats? Got good seats?' When Dylan's cigarette and leg start going, they're a thermometer of his tensions."

By the time of the Berkeley concerts, the single of "Positively Fourth Street" had charted at number seven. Gleason could report in the *San Francisco Chronicle*: "Dylan's band went over like the discovery of gold. … Dozens of university professors were scattered in the audience, some looking rather shattered by the experience … the audience lingered. … They simply didn't want to go home. Something most certainly *is* happening here." Four paintings by Neuwirth hung above the Berkeley stage, an early attempt to heighten rock visually. Gleason thought each painting was "an abstraction of Dylan's own image, or so it seemed to me after two glasses of milk and a Hershey bar."

During visits to Los Angeles in autumn 1965, Dylan befriended producer and songwriter Phil Spector. Gleason again: "In a certain sense, Dylan

appealed directly to Spector for help. There are so many parallels in their careers. The type of help that Bob was looking for was 'tell me how to live.'" Indeed, Bob told me: "When I first got really, really famous, I looked around for who else was like me. And of the people I saw, Phil Spector was one. He's young and made all his bread on his own."

Getting to see Spector was no easy matter. He was in the throes of producing "River Deep, Mountain High" at the Gold Star Studio. We drove to a modest Hollywood restaurant. The chauffeur sat, not eating, waiting for his master's voice and, midway through supper was dismissed. Afterwards, Spector drove me to his home tucked away behind a Hollywood Hills driveway and heavy iron gate. Intermittently, for the next six hours, he talked on about Dylan and the pop life. "Songwriting is poetry, but the only poet around is Bob Dylan. The Beatles should play Dylan's records five hours a day and learn what he's doing. Dylan doesn't compete, he doesn't care. It's very easy to talk a poem, but very difficult to sing a poem. Dylan is a reporter, a philosopher. A unique talent, the most piercing and the most aware insight at work today. His genius lies in his insight into the truth and the phony. If he were only in the hands of someone who really knew how to record him." Would he like to produce Dylan? Spector's eyes gleamed assent.

"Dylan doesn't owe anyone anything. What he was writing three years ago, he was living. They poisoned Socrates. What happened to Jesus the last time he went out in public? Two or three years ago, they said Dylan was a social-protest singer. Now, he becomes a possession. Dylan's going through things I went through a couple of years ago. He is nervous and he is suffering. The most amazing thing, I think, was when Dylan and Baez were doing 'With God on Our Side.' The hardcore American is one of those Midwestern coal miners, the flag-wavers. With that song, he challenged everything they believed in. I am surprised there aren't more outraged pickets outside every one of his concerts. He sang an atheistic song in a country that has 'In God We Trust' on every penny."

One evening, in December 1965, Dylan,

Neuwirth, and Suze Rotolo sat at the back of the Kettle of Fish with filmmaker Barbara Rubin. Suze and Bob were having a pleasant reunion as old friends. Dylan was ranting on about the "literary establishment": "Those cats at the Poetry Center want me to go up on their stage now. Where were they all a few years ago? Now, they are just getting on the bandwagon, but I couldn't care less." Lurking at the bar was a gentle man in a black leather jacket, Andy Warhol. He shyly waved at Dylan, who waved back but made no effort to draw Warhol to his table.

A black-leather motorcycle type—a Hell's Angel in spirit if not membership—approached Bob with photographs. I assumed he was showing pictures of his girlfriend or baby. Dylan remarked approvingly of each picture, and when I asked to see, Bob handed over a pile of snapshots of the guy's motorcycle.

Dylan's conversation was hardly sequential. He raved about Michael McClure and sang the praises of Ginsberg. "Read 'Kaddish,' man, if you want to read something really great." He had seen the anthology of Woody Guthrie writing, *Born to Win*, which I had edited. "I like it, all right," Dylan said, "but that was for a particular time and place." I told Bob I was heading to Britain in January and wanted to get started on the British aspects of his biography, so he scribbled a note to Martin Carthy and his wife, telling them they could speak openly with me: "This man is an old friend here—he is happening right now to be a reporter." Then he said goodbye to Suze and we left for a party at some East Village pad. We found a taxi and, as we got out, no one made a move to pay, so I fished out the fare. "I never carry money," Dylan said. "Never."

Soon he was back on the road again. I joined Bob on tour in St Louis in March 11, 1966. I checked in to his hotel, the Holiday Inn Downtown, and headed for the Kiel Municipal Auditorium, a fine hall with good acoustics that made for a thrilling concert and a standing

Dylan doesn't owe anyone anything.
PHIL SPECTOR

ovation. He was impressed by "some of the mail that comes in. It's amazing! I couldn't ever hope to read it all, let alone to answer it all. From people all over, talking about my songs and records. And talking about their problems and their heads and how they're stuck somewhere and want to get out." Back at the Holiday Inn, I asked Bob if I gave him the feeling of being followed. "Glad you could make it, man. How did you get here? I'm not too happy with our plane. I fly it only when I have to. I'm thinking of buying a DC-3 instead." He said he'd see me on it the next night—tonight they were fully loaded.

Lincoln, Nebraska, March 12, 1966. Plumb dead center in the Great Plains, Dylan was on Middle America's home ground. Population 120,000, 98 percent white. Flour mills, creameries, meat packing, insurance companies, grain and cattle markets, brick and tile works. Cultural center: Nebraska State University. The big news, aside from basketball: President Johnson said spending

on Vietnam was running below estimates. In Laredo, Timothy Leary got a thirty-year sentence for transporting marijuana. No Dylan news, but the manager of the Pershing Memorial Auditorium was still delighted: "It's really amazing, how much press that boy gets. None here in Lincoln, mind you, but a lot nationally."

By now, Dylan had enforced rules: I had to park my Marantz in the hall manager's office. The audience filed in for the electric set. Dylan plugged in his black-and-white Fender, chatted with Robbie, turned his back to the audience. The listeners stared motionless. Dylan turned his toes in like a pigeon. His longish hair fell down to his collar. His trousers bore an impeccable crease. As he led the band behind him into the song, he spread his legs so far apart you feared he'd do the splits. Another standing ovation.

Back at the hotel, I found a note from Victor to call Dylan in his room. Two dozen kids were in the corridor outside. Dylan: "Bob, you're older, maybe they'll listen to you. Tell those kids I can't see them. Tell them I'm really tired." I tell the kids and half leave; the others hang about. Dylan explains the tape recorder ban: "You wouldn't believe what's happening. Tapes are going out of my songs in concerts before I even record them! And people copy the tapes and copy the songs!" Bob talks about my book: "I'll go along, if it's a respectful book. I resent it when they try to treat me like a kid. I resent being placed in some little pigeonhole as some sort of 'rock-star millionaire freak.'" Victor comes to tell Bob there's room on the plane. I race to pack my bag.

Two cars heading for the Lincoln airport waited in front of the hotel. Half of us went down the stairs while Dylan and the rest took the elevator. In the lobby, fifty fans clustered. We rushed for the cars, so quickly the fans said: "There he is. There he goes!" We took off like bank robbers. Victor smiled as wheels screeched from the curb. "That wasn't too bad," Dylan said. "Sometimes you can't even get to the car."

09

ONE FOOT ON THE HIGHWAY

> # There was never any change. No instrument will change love, death, in any soul. My music is my music.

It was just past the break of midnight, a Saturday, mid-March, 1966. Dylan, five members of the Hawks, two roadies and one guest were in two cars speeding toward Lincoln Airport. As we arrived, runway lights flashed on and mechanics busied themselves around Dylan's plane. Denver was next, then back to New York for some studio work, then up to the Pacific Northwest, Hawaii, Australia, Scandinavia, Ireland, England, and France, and back to the States. This was the beginning of the end of one of Dylan's many careers.

Dylan walked into the dark canteen. He took a cup of muddy coffee from a machine, then stood at the window beside a mechanic in white overalls. "It must get lonely out here," Dylan said to the mechanic. Both looked at the field, not at each other. "It does," the mechanic replied, "but it's a job. I just take the hours they give me." "I know how that feels, I really do," Dylan said, as they both stared across prairie land. Soon he walked on to the field. He'd just evaded fifty fans at his hotel lobby, but a half-dozen were clustered around the plane.

He scribbled his autograph a few times. A shy youth, about seventeen, approached him. He wore glasses, a neat white shirt, and tie. "Mr. Dylan," he said, nervously, "I'm interested in poetry, too." "Yeah, is that so?" Dylan replied. "Yes, sir," the boy answered. "I was wondering if you could spare a few minutes, sometime, to read some poems I've written." "Sure," Bob responded. The young man handed Dylan a large envelope stuffed so full it bulged like a football. "Are all these poems?" Dylan asked. Proudly, the boy said: "Yes. I've been writing more since I began to study your songs." "Well," Dylan said, "thank you. I'll try to read some tonight. Is your address on the envelope? I'll let you know what I think of them." The boy glowed: "That's wonderful. I hope you like them."

Inside the plane, the band were dozing off. Bob probably needed sleep more than anyone, though he had revived now and seemed eager to use the minutes until the plane was ready to depart. Literature: "Rimbaud? I can't read him now. Rather read what I want these days. "Kaddish" is the best thing yet. Everything else is a shuck. I never dug Pound or Eliot. Shakespeare was commissioned to write. He wasn't a mystic, just one of the arch-queens of all. I dig Shakespeare. A raving queen and a cosmic amphetamine brain." On his new music: "There was never any change. No instrument will change love, death, in any soul. My music is my music. Folk music was such a shuck. I never recorded a folk song. My idea of a folk song is Jeannie Robertson or Dock Boggs. Call it historical-traditional music. I want to write songs now. Until *Bringing It All Back Home* songwriting was a sideline. I was still a performer. Then I knew I had to write songs. I don't have to look to anyone to tell I'm good. I know, I'm honest. Get some of those literary people, some of those poetry people to sit down with my records, that would be good." On civil rights: "Look at the South. Blacks are taking over the town. But how groovy is it? Power, that's all it is. Rich blacks will take over. The kids are just a start. If I was black, I don't know if I'd want to go to school with whites." The words poured out of him. "It's bullshit. All is death, I'm afraid. I don't want to see myself die. I'd just as soon drive a car off a cliff than do something I don't believe in. Got to beat the pressure. … I saw Chuck Berry at St. Louis Airport. You can listen to Buddy Holly when you're all alone, but Chuck Berry? You have to be out on the highway."

Dylan and I sat face to face. On one knee, he held the proofs of *Tarantula*, sent him by his publisher for approval. On the other was the fan's envelope. I knew he probably wouldn't open either that night. I held the mic a foot away from him. His eyes were slits. He was exhausted, but he told me he wouldn't have slept, even if I hadn't been there. He just had too much to do.

"It takes a lot of medicine to keep up this pace," Dylan said. "It's very hard, man. A concert tour like this has almost killed me. It's been like this since October. It really drove me out of my mind. I never had it like this before. It's been a very weird time, and it really had me down. I'm really going to cut down. Next year, the concert tour is only going to last a month … or two. I'm only doing it like this, this year, because I want everyone to know what we're doing." Dylan sipped his tea, sent a cloud of cigarette smoke over his head, tugged his shirt-collar, and continued: "It's just absurd

for people to sit around being offended by their own meaninglessness, so that they have to force everything else to come into the hole with them, and die trying. That's the hang-up here. But I'm not involved with that any more. I've told you that many times. I don't know if you think I'm kidding, or if you think it's a front. I really just don't care— honestly just don't care—what people say about me. I don't care what people think about me. I don't care what people know about me. It matters nothing to me.

"Playing on the stage is a kick for me now. It wasn't before, because I knew what I was doing then was just too empty. It was just dead ambassadors who would come and see me and clap and say: 'Oh, groovy, I would like to meet him and have a cocktail. Perhaps I'll bring my son, Joseph, with me. Joseph clapped a lot. You liked the program, didn't you, Joseph?' And Joseph, of course, said: 'Oh, yes, father, father. Yes I did—oh, whoopee!' And then they ask: 'Can I bring Isabella?' And the first thing you know you've got about five or six little boys and girls hanging around with Coke bottles and ginger ale bottles and you're confronted by some ambassador who's got his hand in your pocket trying to shake your spine and give you compliments. I won't let anybody backstage any more. Even to give me a compliment. Give me no compliments. I just don't care."

The speech rhythms and the vitality of his thoughts began to rouse Dylan. His eyes cleared as he continued: "You can't ask me about how I sleep. You can't ask me about how I make it, and you cannot ask me what I think I am doing here. Other than that, we'll just get along fine. You just ask me anything and I will shoot right back. Now, we have one thing straight about the book. I'm going to tell Albert we have come to an understanding about the book. I'll give you as much time as I can. I'll come very quickly to the point in all the things that I want done, but you can easily go back on me. You can easily do it any way that you want. But I won't forgive you for doing that, man. It's not going to be a biography, because I'm not dead yet. It's going to be a timeless thing, right?

"Nobody knows about me. What do people really know? That my father's name is Zimmerman and my mother's family is middle class? I'm not about to go around telling people that this is false. I'm not covering up anything I did before. I'm not going back on anything, any statement or anything I've ever done. I'm not copping out on anything I've ever done since I was born. I've given up trying to tell anybody that they are wrong in their thinking about anything, about the world or me, or whatever it is. I don't care. You can write anything you want to write. There is nothing that anybody can expose about me. Everybody thinks that there is such an exposé, on millions of little tiny things, like name-change or anything. It doesn't really matter to me."

Twisting restlessly, Dylan was getting animated now, angry at the phantoms that haunted him, angry at the hungers of his audience. He seemed to want to explain himself. He tried a new beginning: "I think of all that I do as my writing. It cheapens it to call it anything else but writing. But there is not a person on the earth who takes it less seriously than I do. I know that it's not going to help me into heaven one little bit. It's not going to keep me out of the fiery furnace. It's not going to extend my life any and it's not going to make me happy."

"What do you think will make you happy?" I asked. "I'm happy, you know, I'm happy to just be able to come across things. I don't need to be happy. Happiness is a kind of cheap word. There's some kind of happiness that is very, very snobbish. Let's face it, I'm not the kind of cat that's going to cut off an ear if I can't do something. I would commit suicide. I would shoot myself in the brain if things got bad. I would jump from a window. I sure as hell wouldn't cut off my ear, man, I would shoot myself. You know, I can think about death openly. It's nothing to fear. It's nothing sacred. Death is nothing sacred. I've seen so many people die." I asked: "Is life sacred?" "Life's not sacred either," Dylan replied. "Look at all the spirits that actually control the atmosphere, which are not living and yet which attract you, as ideas, or like games with the solar system. Or look at the farce of politics, economy and war.

"It's become so easy for me to do everything, you have no idea, man, everything at my command. I can make money now doing absolutely anything. But I don't want that kind of money. I'm not a millionaire now, in terms of everything I have. But it is really close. This next year, I'm going to be a millionaire, but that means nothing. To be a millionaire means that next year you can lose it all. You must realize that I have not copped out on one thing. It is very hard for somebody who does what he does not to have to cop out on some things. I mean, I love what I do. I also make money off it. Hey, I sing honest stuff, man, and it's consistent. It's all I do. I don't give a damn what anybody says. Nobody can praise me and have any effect on me and nobody can criticize what I do that's going to have any effect on me. Nobody. I'm not going to read anything for me or against me that can possibly have any effect on me. So, therefore, I never really read what people say about me. I'm just not interested.

"When I first really knew that I had money that I couldn't see, I looked around to see what a few of my agents were doing with it. First of all, I like chauffeurs. When I came back from England last time, I didn't buy a chauffeur, but I sure rented one. I make no bones about it. I need the money to employ people. It all works hand in hand. If I had no money, I could walk invisible. But money now is necessary. It costs me money now to be able to walk invisible. That's the only

> **I've given up trying to tell anybody that they are wrong in their thinking about anything, about the world or me, or whatever it is. I don't care.**

reason I need the money. I don't need the money to buy clothes or nothing." Again his anger mounted. "I'm sick of giving creeps money off my soul.

"Oh, if it's not the promoter cheating you, it's the box office cheating you. Somebody is always giving you a hard time. Even the record company figures won't be right. They are never right. For one reason or another, they are never right. Nobody's going to be straight with you because nobody wants the information out. Do you know that up to a certain point I made more money on a song I wrote if it were on an album by Carolyn Hester or anybody than if I did it myself? That's the contract they gave me. Horrible! Horrible!"

He worried he was going to get to the point where "nobody else is going to be able to sing my songs but me. Like, I'm going to drive myself right out of business. I'll have to put out 10,000 records a year, for God's sake, because nobody will record the songs I write." Did he influence young people because he broke the rules? "It's not a question of breaking the rules, don't you understand? I don't break the rules, because I don't see any rules to break. As far as I'm concerned, there aren't any rules.

"You just have to make it. When I say 'make it,' I don't mean being a popular folk-rock star. 'Making it' means finding your line. Everybody's line is there, someplace. People think they just have to go through living hell on earth, but I don't really believe that attitude. The only people who believe you have to go through living hell on earth, or that life is a tragedy, are the people who are simple, close-minded people who have to make excuses for themselves. Everybody's line is there. Despite everybody who has been born and has died, the world has just gone on without them, I mean, look at Napoleon—but we went right on. Look at Harpo Marx—the world went around, it didn't stop for a second. It's sad but true. John Kennedy. Right?"

Isn't the difference, I asked, in what people did when they were here on earth? "Don't you see they did nothing? Has anybody done anything, really? Look at anybody who you think has done anything. Name anybody you think has done something." Shaw, I said. "George Bernard Shaw," Dylan slowly repeated one name at a time. "Who has he helped?" "He helped a lot of people to use their heads,"

I replied, adding, "You've helped a lot of people to use their heads and their ears." "Well," Dylan rejoined, "I don't think I have, that's all. It's funny that people think I have. I'm certainly not the one to go around saying that that is what I do. At one time I did read a lot of the stuff that was written about me, maybe three or four years ago. Now, I don't even read anything any more. So I have no idea what people say about me. I really don't. I do know that a lot of people really like me. I know that."

Eight miles high, flying over the Great Plains, Dylan jiggled his knees, like the trays of a scale, proofs of *Tarantula* on one knee, the Nebraska boy's poems on the other. An unconscious seesaw of literary weighing-in. Did he think *Tarantula* was going to be accepted by the establishment literary people, by the serious poets? "First of all," he said, animatedly, "you have to realize that if you are going to write for poets and literary people—" He stopped short. "I think a poet is anybody who wouldn't call himself a poet. Anybody who could possibly call himself a poet just cannot be a poet. They have just settled for the romance of their ancestors and their historical knowledge of facts that never were. And they would like to think that they are a little above it all. When people start calling me a poet, I say: 'Oh, groovy, how groovy to be called a poet.' But it didn't do me any good, I'll tell you that. It didn't make me any happier.

"Hey, I would love to say that I am a poet. I would really like to think of myself as a poet, but I just can't because of all the slobs who are called poets." Who was a poet, then? Allen Ginsberg? "He's a poet," Dylan fired back. "To be a poet does not necessarily mean that you have to write words on paper. Do you know what I mean? One of those truck-drivers that walk down the stairway of a motel is a poet. He talks like a poet. I mean, what else does a poet have to do? Poets," his voice trailed off in inchoate formulations, ideas running too fast for his tongue. "Poets, old people, death, decay, people like Robert Frost, poetry about trees and branches, but that isn't what I mean. Allen Ginsberg is the only writer I know. The rest of the writers I don't have that much respect for. If they really want to do it, they're going to have to sing it. I wouldn't call myself a poet for any more reason than I would call myself

OPPOSITE
May 1966: Dylan contemplates Kronborg Castle, Elsinore in *Hamlet*. In his Nobel speech, Dylan later said of Shakespeare: "When he was writing *Hamlet*, I'm sure he was thinking about a lot of different things."

> I don't break
> the rules, because
> I don't see any
> rules to break.
> As far as I'm
> concerned, there
> aren't any rules.

a 'protest-singer.' All that would do would put me in a category with a whole lot of people who would just bother me. I don't want to be in their category. I don't want to fool anybody. To tell anybody I'm a poet would just be fooling people. That would put me in a class, man, with people like Carl Sandburg, T. S. Eliot, Stephen Spender, and Rupert Brooke. Hey, name them—Edna St. Vincent Millay and Robert Louis Stevenson and Edgar Allan Poe and Robert Lowell.

"I know two saintly people," Dylan continued. "I know just two holy people, Allen Ginsberg is one. The other, for lack of a better term, I just want to call 'this person named Sara.' What I mean by 'holy' is crossing all the boundaries of time and usefulness. Hey, I dig a lot of people, I love a lot of people, but I certainly don't consider them poets." Two other writers he admired suddenly occurred to him: "William Burroughs is a poet. I like all his old books, and Jean Genet's old books, but I'm talking about writers of this country. Genet's scholastical lectures are just a waste of time, they are just boring. But if we are talking now in terms of writers I think can be called poets, then Allen must be the best. I mean Allen's "Kaddish" not "Howl."

"Allen doesn't have to sing "Kaddish," man. You understand what I mean? He just has to lay it down. He's the only poet that I know of. I can't really tell you all my feelings of him because they are just too total. He's the only person I respect who writes, that just totally writes. He don't have to do nothing, man. Allen Ginsberg, he's just holy, one of the two people that I know are holy." How is Sara holy? "I don't want to put her in this book. I want to keep her out of this, I don't want to call her 'a girl.' I would rather refer to her, if I refer to her at all, I can't really refer to her by any other name than—I don't mean to come on, I know it's very corny, but the only thing I can think of is, more or less, 'Madonna-like.'"

I was beginning to think that he had forgotten my tape recorder, when he asked me: "Are you getting it all? How much tape do you have left? Is it still running?" I told him we had hours of fresh tape and he plunged on: "Love and sex are things that really hang everybody up. When things aren't going right and you're really nobody, if you don't get laid in one way or another, you get mean, you know. You get cruel. Now, why in the world sex should force this is beyond me. I truthfully can tell you that male and female are not here to have sex, you know, that's not the purpose. I don't believe that that's God's will, that females have been created so that they can be a counterpart of man's urge. I just can't really believe that. I can't believe that it is that way. There are too many other things that people just won't let themselves be involved in. Sex and love have nothing to do with female and male. It is just whatever two souls happen to be. It could be male and female, and it might not be male and female. It might be female and female or it might be male and male. You can't turn your back on it, man. You can try to pretend that it doesn't happen, and you can make fun of it and be snide, but that's not really the rightful thing. I know, I know."

Inevitably, music displaced all other topics, even though he had remarked to me before we got on the plane "music is only 20 percent of what I am."

"I want you to have explanations of my songs in your book," Dylan said. "Things nobody else will ever have." "Such as," I broke in, "who Mr. Jones is to you?" "Well," Bob parried, "I'm not going to tell you that way. I'm going to tell you about the stuff that I want to tell you about. I could tell you who Mr. Jones is in my life, but, like, everybody has got their Mr. Jones, so I can't really say that he is the same for everyone. I can't give Mr. Jones a name, you understand. I know he's there—" and he plunged into the subject of "Ballad of a Thin Man" and "Like a Rolling Stone." Nothing struck me so strongly as this passage from the surge of Dylan's two-in-the-morning flood: "Mr. Jones's loneliness can easily be covered up to the point where he can't recognize that he is alone, suddenly locked in a room. It's not so incredibly absurd, and it's not so imaginative, to have Mr. Jones in a room with three walls with a midget and a geek and a naked man. Plus a voice, a voice coming in his dream. I'm just a voice speaking. Anytime I'm singing about people, and if the songs are dreamed, it's like my voice is coming out of their dream.

"Why, I don't even want to talk about college. I have no respect for college. It's just an extension of time. I hung around college, but it's a cop-out, you know, from life, a cop-out from experience. A lot of people started out to be lawyers, but I venture to say that a hundred percent of the really groovy lawyers haven't gotten through school the way they ought to. They've always been freaks in their school, and have always had a hard time making it; so many lawyers just take people for what they're worth. They all make deals and all are very criminal, but doctors, lawyers, all these kind of people—they're just in it for money, and for resentment. They put in their time and they're going to get it back. I agree with them that way. But I'm sure it could be done in other ways, and it's not—I've known people who've been really loaded down with burdens and who have been in the right to collect, and who have been so innocent, that when they got lawyers to get them what they deserve. … Do you follow me? The party's lawyers they are suing make deals with their lawyers. Like, it happens all the time, man. How anybody could have respect for lawyers baffles me! I have lawyers working for me I never see. I don't see my lawyers. Anytime they see the chance, they jump on it."

Did he want to talk about Joan Baez? Or would he bite my head off? "Me and Joan?" Bob asked. "I'll tell you. I hope you do explain it, if you can do this book straight. She brought me up. I rode on her, but I don't think I owe her anything. I feel sorry for her. I want to explain this. I want you to print that, because I am not joking. I feel sorry for her, knowing that I don't have to feel sorry for her because she would definitely not want me to feel sorry for her, or anybody to feel sorry for her. I feel bad for her because she has nobody to ask, nobody to turn to that's going to be straight with her. She hasn't got that much in common with the street vagabonds who play insane instruments. She's not that kind of person. Her family is a very gentle kind of family. She's very fragile and very sick and I lived with her and I loved the place. Can you write all this in your book? If you can't man, it's a waste of time. I mean, is your book going to be a mature book, or is this all just a waste of time?" I reassured him.

He talked of an earlier time, when we had knocked around the Village together. "After Suze moved out of the house, I got very, very strung

> I have not arrived at where I am at now, I have just returned to where I am at now, knowing that it's the only way. What I am doing now is what I must do before I move on.

out for a while. I mean, really, very strung out." But, he told me, he'd survived those emotionally straining periods.

"I can do anything, knowing in front that it's not going to catch me and pull me, 'cause I've been through it once already. I've been through people. A lot of time you get strung out with people. They are just like junk. The same thing, no more, no less. They kill you the same way. They rot you the same way." I didn't press him as to who could rot him and kill him, but I suggested that it reminded me of the line in Sartre's *No Exit*, "Hell is other people." Dylan joked: "Whatever it is, man. I don't know Sartre. He's cross-eyed, that's all I know about him. Anybody cross-eyed can't be all bad." He hit the bottom, saying: "I have a death thing, I know. I have a suicidal thing, I know."

Later, I asked him if he wanted to leave all this despair on the record. He said: "I haven't explained those things I said against myself. I'll explain them, and you better well use them, you can put in what I talked about it, if it's in context. Nobody knows about where I was at. A lot of people think that I shoot heroin. But that's baby talk; I do a lot of things. Hey, I'm not going to sit here and lie to you, and make you wonder about all the things I do. I do a lot of things, man, which help me. And I'm smart enough to know that I don't depend on them for my existence, you know, and that's all. Man, that's where it lays, like that."

I'd been thinking then of how, one night at the Gaslight, Dylan had once advised me "to just write about something that is really important to you." At that time, I couldn't envision that it would be a book about the man who'd given me the advice. Dylan continued: "I can't be hurt, man, if the book is honest. No kidding, I can't be hurt. I want you to write an honest book, Bob, I don't want you to write a bullshit book. Hey, I'm trusting you. The only reason that I am here with you now is that I know that you are the man who, if there is anybody I want to do it with, is you."

Our conversation drifted to the folk-song "movement." We were bitter then because the folk world was so hostile toward his merging of folk and rock. "Nobody told me to go electric," he said emphatically. "No, I didn't even ask anybody, I asked not a soul, believe me. Hey, I went electric on my second record. Why don't you bring that out in the book?" The *Freewheelin'* album, released in May 1963, Dylan reminded me, had "four electric songs. The only reason they cut out the electric ones was because I didn't write them. Columbia still has them; they are trying to retouch them." Before the Beatles were known in America and before the "folk-rock" craze of 1965, Dylan had tried to show he was not a performer to nest in any pigeonhole. "I hate all the labels people have put on me, because they are labels. It's just that they are ugly, and I know, in my heart, that it's not me. I have not arrived at where I am at now, I have just returned to where I am at now, knowing that it's the only way. What I am doing now is what I must do before I move on."

Dylan began digging his heels in about the music world and his early attraction toward folk music. I scarcely needed to ask questions; he was monologuing now. "I hate to say this, because I don't want it to be taken the wrong way, but I latched on, when I got to New York City, because I saw a huge audience was there. People I knew I was not taking advantage of. I knew I wasn't going to stay there. I know it wasn't my thing. Many times I spoiled it.

Many times I went against it. Any time they tried to think I was like them, I knew I wasn't like them. I just told them whatever happened to be in my mind at the time. I didn't have any respect for any of the organizations. In New York City, they are all organizations. I had respect for the people. Woody turned me on romantically—Woody used his own time, in a way nobody else did. He was just a little bit better, just a little smarter, because he was from the country. I met Woody and I talked with him. I dug him, I would dig him, I imagine, if he were around today."

He cited some reservations about Guthrie's style, and I asked if Woody's work then seemed too simple for him. Dylan shot back: "No, not simple at all. The fundamental objection is that I can see why he wrote what he wrote. I can see him sitting down and writing what he wrote, in a very calm kind of a way. I am not putting him down. You can print all this, man. I'm not copping out on my attraction to him, and his influence on me. His influence on me was never in inflection or in voice. What drew me to him was hearing his voice. I could tell he was very lonesome, very alone and very lost out in his time. That's why I dug him."

Dylan stressed that at the height of his involvement in the folk world, he still loved rock 'n' roll. "Suze Rotolo could tell you, because Suze knows more than anybody else that I played, back in 1961 and 1962, when nobody was around, all those Elvis Presley records. She'll tell you how many nights I stayed up and wrote songs and showed them to her and asked her 'is this right?' Because I knew her father and mother were associated with unions and she was into this equality-freedom thing long before I was. I checked the songs out with her. She would like all the songs. Suze is a very talented girl, man, but she is very frightened."

We talked about *Sing Out!*, the folk-song magazine that had lionized Dylan, then turned against him. In defense of Dylan's changes, I had wrangled with them. He cautioned me against my wasting time with polemics. "Don't you understand? If you're smart, you just gotta keep going, you're just not going to stand still. Everyone else is going to die. I don't mean die. I mean, they are going to decay and go crazy. If I could help them, I would love to see them straightened out. But I know in my heart that it is impossible to straighten all these people out, because they are all so nine-to-five, and so involved with that life that it is impossible. I don't want nothing to do with it. *Sing Out!* has a big organization; they know they control a lot. They have a very big hand in a lot of money. They have an establishment. Believe me, Bob, they make a lot of money. The only person in that organization I respect is Moe Asch, who is old and hip. He's the only one who knows that he's not serious, that he is not a clown, that the whole world is not a circus. He knows. The rest of the people there don't know it. They have power—fake, phoney power. They're dumb, man. They're clods. I never signed their petitions. Hey, dig it, man. They're gonna decay. If you're out of it, groovy! But I'm telling you, man, get out of it. It's not that you have to put them down to leave it."

He eyed the packet of poems from the Nebraska fan, knowing he wouldn't read them that night. I told him how touching it was when he told that airport mechanic how lonely it got out there. "Well, I loved him, man," Dylan replied.

> "Don't you understand? If you're smart, you just gotta keep going, you're just not going to stand still. Everyone else is going to die. I don't mean die. I mean, they are going to decay and go crazy.

"He's a poor cat. What's he doing out there in Nebraska? I just wanted to know. I was just curious. Hey, it's lonesome everyplace. The people that can't live with it, that can't accept it—they are just going to blow up the world, and make things bad for everybody, only because they feel so out of place. Everybody has that in common—they are all going to die."

He told me he'd withdrawn, for a while, from Woodstock: "I moved out a long time ago. Before the summer [of 1965] ended, I moved into New York City. I couldn't make it up there any more because it wasn't private any more. It will never, ever happen again. I'm never going to tell anybody where I live again. People want to tear me apart, man. Hey, I don't take people up to the country now, because the country is a very alone place. And if you don't dig being alone, if you haven't got something to do, you're just going to take the bus back. You're going to get bored and go back. I can be alone as long as I have to be alone. I don't give a shit about being with people. I don't have anything to say to anybody. But it's hard for other people like that."

Dylan's search for the place to be "alone" has kept a lot of real estate agents and moving men busy. He asked me: "Do you know what I did when I got back from England, man? I bought me a thirty-one-room house. Can you imagine that? It turned into a nightmare, because, first of all, I wrote *Highway 61 Revisited* there and I don't believe in writing some total other thing in the same place twice. It's just a hang-up, a voodoo kind of thing. I just can't do it. When I need someplace to make something new, I can't go back there because—have you ever smelled birth? Well, I just can't stand the smell of birth. It just lingers, so I just lived there and tried to go on, but couldn't. And so the house is up for sale now, and I've moved back into Albert's."

On this tour, I'd seen a lot of cracks developing in Dylan's relationship with his manager. "There are some things that Albert tries to push on me. There are some things Albert and I naturally agree on, and some things that I have to tell him to agree on. He's only come across once on his side. The rest of the time, I don't want him telling me shit." I suggested that people should realize a manager is a

star's employee, not his employer, but Dylan flared at that. Like the man who grumbles about his wife but wouldn't let anyone else criticize her, Dylan leapt to Grossman's defense: "It's not that Albert works for me. People who put Albert down ought to be—I mean, critic people. First of all, did you know—Sara told me this, and it's true—that in hell there is a special place for critics? Did you ever know that? That was before Dante's time. Before the 'Inferno' and before the Black Plague. And when you think about it, it is very weird. Obviously, now, you see the ragman walking around a couple of thousand years BC did not like to be confronted with a bunch of mouths. That's still where it's at."

Dylan's wide swings in mood were something I'd grown accustomed to long before. Only after the fact could I figure out what was elating him or depressing him. After one encounter on this trip, in which he expressed what I could only view as his deep and pervasive pessimism, I tried to counter his depression. A few days later, he scorned me for misunderstanding his moods. "I am not pessimistic," he told me. "I am just trying to get that across in the shortest, most concise way possible. If I am pessimistic, I am not even going to talk. I'm just going to go in the corner. One thing I have never done and will never do is force my moods on other people. Why should I sit around and talk to somebody for hours and then have them think that I am pessimistic? That's an insult!

"I'll tell you what the drag is, what hangs everybody up is that I'm not stopping. They call me dead. It is very silly for them to call me dead, and they know it. There was a time, last year, when it just went overboard. Everybody recorded my songs and it would have been very easy for me, at that time, to have written up another huge batch. Everyone would have done them. They would have just lapped them up," he said of the great folk-rock surge of 1965.

Dylan's ambivalence has confounded and confused everyone who's ever been close to him. It sometimes confuses him. As late as 1976, he was saying that his Gemini personality "forces me to extremes. I'm never really balanced in the middle. I go from one side to the other without staying in either place very long. I'm happy, sad, up, down, in, out, up in the sky and down in the depths of the earth." At least that was consistent for, ten years earlier, as we rode on this plane, he was swinging widely. When I said I'd like to interview Phil Spector, Dylan said, "Sure, sure, go see him." Then he told me how Spector had annoyed him but "tell him that when I think about him, I really love him." Another area of ambivalence is the press, critics, tastemakers and opinion-molders. Dylan dislikes them and repeatedly taunts them, even as he is ineluctably drawn to them.

Sic transit the Fourth Estate, in the estimation of one who has used the press with much artfulness. I sought to move to an area of his enthusiasm, black musicians. "Ask Aretha Franklin about me, man," Dylan said, "or talk to the Staple Singers. Why don't you talk to Mavis Staples? I'd be interested in what she says. And to Purvis and Roebuck Staples, too. Remember that night when Mahalia Jackson came out from the dugout in three limousines? Remember, from the dugout [at a 1962 gospel festival at Randall's Island in New York] with her goddamn maids, who lifted up her dresses and opened up her doors? She sure has class.

"A lot of people think that the modern black musicians are getting a raw deal. A lot of them are, because there are real genius people playing in dives. A lot of them are. But an awful lot of the records you hear are all copies. They, too, are imitating who they think they should think they should imitate. That don't mean you have to give them a million dollars and a house in the suburbs and a golf course. That's what we're talking about here. We're not talking about equality, or enough food to eat."

Why had he become so hopeless about the civil rights movement, when it had once so engaged his energies and songwriting? "I'm not pessimistic about it. No, no, I don't want to be misunderstood about it! I don't think that anybody who is taught to get his kicks off a superiority feels—man, that's a drag! But the word 'Negro' sounds foolish coming from my mouth. What's a Negro? I don't know what a Negro is. What's a Negro? A black person? How black? What's a Negro? A person living in a two-room shack with twelve kids? A lot of white people live in a two-room shack with twelve kids. Does this make them Negro? What's a Negro? Someone with African blood? A lot of white people have African blood. What's a Negro? An Ethiopian kind of thing? That's not a Negro, that's an ancient religious pajama-riding freak! I've got nothing against black rights. I never did."

Dylan immediately reminisced about a string of his black friends from his early days in New York: about Mel and Lillian Bailey, who had treated him like a son and brother; about Jim Foreman, the former leader of the Student Non-Violent Coordinating Committee. He spoke nostalgically about some other young blacks from Albany, Georgia, whom he had worked and played with, like Bernice Johnson and Cordell Reagon. "Put their names in the book. I love Cordell. He's a madman. He's the only faithful madman, the only madman— let me put it this way—that really looks bad, that can wipe you out with pure strength, who I could trust to go anywhere with. I never get to see so many people. That's why I would like you to say things about a lot of people that I loved. Say that I said good things about them. Hey, I've turned down everybody, Bob. I'm giving you all this. I'm trusting you to go along with me. Hey, I've never

been wrong. I'll tell you something about this book. If I tell you something, I'm not trying to horn in. I don't want any of your bread."

Knowing how mercurial Dylan was, I tentatively began to explore with him how he changes his mind about people, about his own music, his own past work. I said: "You have always been wildly enthusiastic about the recording you have just finished, and then you turn around a few months later and say it was nothing. At least, you always did that in the past." "No, no," Dylan flashed. "I like the last record. Hey, I made *Bringing It All Back Home*, and I love that record. I made *Highway 61 Revisited* and I love that record, I love the *Blonde on Blonde* album. What I was trying to do on my fourth album, on *Another Side of Bob Dylan*—well, I was just too out of it, man, to come across with what I was trying to do. It was all done too fast. All done in one session. I liked the idea of it. No, I don't like the first album. You know, though, I've done some stuff on that first record that still stands up. Like my harmonica playing. Like in 'Man of Constant Sorrow,' the arrangement of that I like. 'In My Time of Dying' still stands up. But as a whole, it doesn't make any kind of sense, you understand? It's not consistent."

Wasn't he really his own worst critic? "Of course I am my own worst critic! Those aren't my words, those are your words. A lot of the stuff I've done, man, as far as I'm concerned, the last three things I've done on records, is beyond criticism. I'm not saying that because I think I'm any kind of god. I'm just saying that because I know, I just know. I've been at it too long. I wanted to call that album *Highway 61 Revisited*. Nobody understood it. I had to go up the fucking ladder until finally the word came down and said: 'Let him call it what he wants to call it.' I have to fight for songs on the album. I put them on there because I know it is right. And sure enough, it turns out to be right."

One thing that repeatedly disturbed Dylan on this tour were the problems of sound amplification, despite the brilliant setup that engineer Richard Alderson had assembled. Acoustics had still been giving them trouble, especially in sports halls. Dylan continued: "This year, I'm doing the tour because I want everybody to know what we're doing. It turns out that we have wasted a lot of time, because

it took me so long to realize that no matter how groovy and good it is, if it can't be heard, then it doesn't do anybody any good. Then, the only people behind you are your loyal fans. Those are the people you just have to react to. But now, and you have heard it yourself, there is nothing in the world like this sound system we are using." He asked me in detail my reactions to the sound at the various concerts I'd heard. He said he wanted, at the end of this tour, to bring the show into Carnegie Hall. I jokingly suggested he try, for really great acoustics, the Metropolitan Opera House. Dylan laughed, then asked: "How many people does it hold?"

Our talk drifted back to some things he'd written about himself, like the 1962 prose-poem memoir "My Life in a Stolen Moment." Dylan wove a web of ambivalence: "I don't disavow it. Please don't get me wrong. I don't disavow it. It is just not me. Somebody else wrote that. But I am not that person of five years ago. It's almost as if I were him," he said, pointing at one of the sleeping band members. "I remember all of it. I remember the drafts. I remember the words I used to write then, thinking they might someday be novels. I remember why I did them. I remember all the reasons. I remember all the shucks and all the cons. All the cute, funny things. Like, man, I am so lucky now. I wouldn't be lucky if I couldn't produce. That's what I thought the last six months. Oh, I was really down. I mean, in ten recording sessions, man, we didn't get one song," he said, referring to *Blonde on Blonde*. What slowed things down? "It was the band. But you see, I didn't know that. I didn't want to think that. I'm not saying it was a mistake, because I know I'm going to do it all again. If I go back to Nashville, man, and everybody down there can't make it, I'm going to take a plane until something else happens. That's just the way it is. You can't blame

> **I know how that boy feels. I know what it's like being a boy in a small town, somewhere, trying to become a writer.**

anybody else. I don't have the right to blame anybody else. It's not that I blame myself, man, it is just that I was down, I was down."

I chanced a Hollywood star–interview question—just what does he do with his money? I held my breath for his outraged response. "Tell them," Dylan said, making his first and last full financial disclosure, "tell them to check their pockets." We laughed. I asked him what he saw in his future. "I can't talk of the future," Dylan said slowly. "I can only talk a little more about it than I used to be able to talk about it, but, still, I can't talk about it all that much. I know there's a movie. I'm going to make a movie, and it's going to be groovy, you know. Then, there's this book for Macmillan," Dylan said, tapping one of the envelopes still resting on his lap. "It's already been fucking publicized and written about, and everybody's expected it and that kind of stuff," he went on, eyeing the *Tarantula* envelope warily. "Every time I look in the paper, there is something about this book. And I gave away the title, which I shouldn't have done. So, I'm thinking of changing it now. You know, I just don't like the obvious. Obvious things are a step backwards. Nobody should step backwards because nobody knows what's behind them. The only direction you can see is in front of you, not in back of you."

The plane's vibrations had been diminishing, even though it hadn't been descending sharply. We'd forgotten that Denver is so high, the ground comes up to meet a plane from the East. The Hawks stirred themselves, wiping sleep from their eyes. They looked at Dylan, surprised he was still wide awake, still talking. Bob gave directions to Victor and Bill about deplaning. He asked Robbie Robertson if he was up to a few hours' work when they got to the motel, and Robbie nodded. As the plane touched down, Dylan kept talking. He looked at the package of poems from his fan in Nebraska, and said he'd have to read them some other time. His eyes went back and forth between the two envelopes of writing on his lap. "I know how that boy feels. I know what it's like being a boy in a small town, somewhere, trying to become a writer."

The landing at Stapleton Airfield was almost imperceptible. At the airport, Dylan called Sara in New York. Luggage assembled, cars rented, the convoy sped off to the Motel de Ville on West Colfax Avenue. The rooms were reserved for Ashes & Sand. Dylan took room 102, Robbie 104, and I was up the corridor at 108. Although there had been a time change, it was nearly 3 a.m. now, and I thought Dylan was finished for the night. "Give us about ten minutes, Bob," Dylan said, "and then come down to the room."

Robbie and Dylan were again sprawled out on twin beds, each holding acoustic guitars, starting an hour's jamming. I drank some coffee and tried to bring myself to life to tape them at work. It was all new material; I couldn't put a title on anything. When Dylan came to "Sad-Eyed Lady," he said: "This is the best song I've ever written. Wait till you hear the whole thing." Robbie's face was gray with fatigue. I had to get to bed and assumed that tomorrow would be a long sleep-in. Dylan said: "Let's go out to Central City tomorrow morning. You'll like it. Meet me here at about eleven."

Next morning Bob was on the phone to Grossman in New York. "I've got five new songs to tape," Dylan told the telephone. "Uh-huh, uh-huh. I don't think they're giving us a fair count. Yeah, yeah. Sinatra wants it? What about Otis Redding? I'd rather he do it." The trip to Central City seemed to relax Dylan but he was quiet on the drive and I thought he was depressed. "I want to save my voice," he explained. "It's hoarse this morning."

Bob sat in the front of the car, looking like the *Blonde on Blonde* cover, his frizzy electric halo, which Hendrix and others soon affected, surrounding a lean face drawn with fatigue. "I don't know how it will look to me today," Bob said to me, "but when I first went up there, Central City looked like paradise. It seemed so far away from anything I'd seen or done before, it was sort of magic to me. Imagine a kid just out of high school coming up here in the mountains! Feeling like he was discovering the world." We passed a jerry-built shack of corrugated iron, tar-paper, and wood scraps. "Look for the TV aerial, just look for it!"

ONE FOOT ON THE HIGHWAY 215

Bob commanded. First we saw a bearded recluse puttering with his goats and pigs—and then the aerial. Bob fingered the dial until a DJ's voice poked through the mountain passes. "Here's the latest hot single from Simon and Garfunkel, 'Homeward Bound.'" Dylan listened silently.

Within a few turns, we were back in 1859: worn stone buildings, gingerbread wood houses on hillsides. In May 1859, nine Georgia prospectors, led by one John Gregory, struck gold here.

We parked near the old courthouse, ambled down Eureka Street into Main. "Nothing's changed. It's almost exactly the way it was," Bob said. We passed the opera house, like a film crew sizing up a location. Some tourists ogled Dylan. A teenager yelped, "What's he doing here?" Up Main Street, a small nameless bar was dark. It had a large, circular window front, like an aquarium. "This was the place," Dylan said. This was where the Gilded Garter had been, where Dylan had "scuffled" for a few dollars that summer.

We edged away from the saloon. "Oh, it only lasted a few weeks," Dylan said, "but I suppose I'll never forget it. They paid me very little, but they threw in sandwiches and drinks, and all the strippers I could watch. All the noisy drunks were thrown in free too." We went in to a little curio shop where Dylan spent fifteen minutes rummaging for mementoes. He bought some postcards with a dollar he'd borrowed from me and, with the change, a tiny cowboy hat. There was an original snapshot of John Dillinger, the public enemy shot down in his prime. The shopkeeper told him it was twenty dollars, "a very rare item." Dylan studied the picture, like a still from *Bonnie and Clyde*: "I'll think about it and let you know." After a quick lunch of eggs and hamburgers, we headed back to Denver. "The time has gone so fast," Dylan mused. "It almost seems like it happened to someone else."

We returned to the motel. I assumed Bob wanted a nap before the concert but he said I should come down in half an hour. When I did, he was puttering around in a faded old shirt and jeans—we were suddenly back four years to simple times in the Village. I turned on the tape recorder and threw questions at him for another two hours. He was less frenetic than he'd been in the airplane, but no less

The time has gone so fast, it almost seems like it happened to someone else.

articulate, no less candid. We talked about Hibbing, New York, Dinkytown, Woodstock, Memphis and London. Dylan flicked on the television and, without ever losing the continuity of his thread, became engrossed in a horror film. Some miscreant was brewing an evil potion. "Hey, look at that!" he exclaimed boyishly, "He's going to get his back full of cyanide!"

He shuffled around the room, hanging up some of his clothes, one eye on the TV. We talked about his hat, his first gigs, and the folk scene then.

"How the hell can you get any work done on a tour like this? How can you write?" I asked. "It's very hard, man. It's killed me, ever since September, and it really drove me out of my mind. I never really had it like that before. It was a very weird time. It really had me down." He would cut down next year, he said. "It embarrasses me to talk about the career thing, because it's very hard to talk about. It's been so dumb. Because in my own mind, I know how lucky I am, and I don't know how long it could go on."

We talked about people who had been important to him along the way. "Suze, I will be kind to her the rest of my life. Suze, any time she wants anything, she could always come to me." But he had no patience with some others: "Just con people—they shouldn't be associated with me, because they are just going to get hung up by idiots that know they have known me." We ranged wide and free, in time and in geography.

Time passed quickly and I was afraid I was wearing him out. "Don't worry about it, I'm OK." He played around with the little cowboy hat he'd bought for his daughter, then dramatically pulled out his "rabbit suit," brushing it off for another

April 1966: Dylan and the
Hawks arrive at Arlanda
Airport twenty-four hours
ahead of a concert in
Stockholm. They had flown
from Australia, where they
played seven shows.

night's performance and saying how unusual it
was to be dressing up for a concert. He laughed at
himself. I turned off my tape recorder. "I wish you
could come down to El Paso next week," Dylan
said. I told him I had to see a dozen people on the
West Coast first. He said two concerts in Oklahoma
had to be cancelled because of further work on
Blonde. "You couldn't make it to Europe in May,
could you?" Dylan asked. I said I doubted it—I had
to work. "Well, I've got to go to work. Drop back
after the show."

Dylan's reserve of energy to tackle another
concert for 3,000 people amazed me. After the
Denver concert, I returned to Dylan's crowded
motel room. Some fans began calling up, and
friends dropped in. Bob was expansive, but couldn't
conceal his fatigue. I decided it was time to quit and
he saw me to the door.

Grossman should have guessed that Australia,
even more middlebrow and muddled than Middle
America, would spell trouble for Dylan. But the
Kingston Trio and Peter, Paul and Mary had sold
there—why not Dylan? After concerts in Seattle,
Tacoma, Vancouver, and Honolulu, Dylan and the
Hawks arrived in Sydney on April 12 for a fifteen-
day tour. The *Melbourne News Weekly* greeted them:
"Manly boys and sweet girls are OUT, now. Young
men who look like girls soon begin to think like
girls; young girls who look like men eventually try
to play the role of men … whenever this happens,
civilization falls apart, and a more primitive virile
race takes over."

There was not much advance notice that
Australian civilization was about to fall apart.
Pre-tour publicity was minimal, and disc jockeys
were not spinning Dylan. Newspaper stories
seemed more like counterattacks than reports. At
the arrival of Flight 305 in Sydney, some fifty fans
joined the press. Dylan signed a few autographs
as "The Phantom," then his ringleted hair and
shades provoked this: Why have you started playing
rock 'n' roll? "Is that what they call it?" Are you a
professional beatnik? "Well, I was in the Brigade
once—we used to get paid, but it didn't pay enough,
so I became a singer." Why don't you see your
family? "I wouldn't know where to find them." Why
do you wear those outlandish clothes? "I look very

normal where I live." Does it take a lot of trouble to get your hair like that? "No, you just have to sleep on it for about twenty years." Throughout Dylan's tour, the Australian press indicated he didn't deserve publicity, but they grudgingly gave it to him.

The most balanced and sympathetic reporting was in the *Sydney Morning Herald* by Craig McGregor, whose report to me was later reworked into the Introduction to *Bob Dylan: A Retrospective*. Dylan spent most of his time writing, reading and playing new material, but he made tentative efforts to meet compatible people, holding court in hotel rooms. A road manager invited McGregor to the first Sydney concert and backstage, on April 13, in the 10,000-seat Sydney Stadium, where Dylan was somewhat unnerved by a revolving stage which swept a full ninety degrees after each song. McGregor found him during the intermission, squatting on the floor, chain-smoking, and tried to explain to him that he was "a writer," not a member of "the press," which Dylan was rampaging against.

Dylan's main Australian support came from Sydney artists and writers, including the founders of the underground magazine *Oz*, Richard Neville and Martin Sharp. Among folk fans, controversy ran high, but the *Australian*'s folk critic, Edgar Waters, wrote sympathetically: "Dylan remains the most effective voice for the feelings of the most intelligent and sensitive people of his generation. The ugly sound and the hysterical tone are essential for what he has to say."

For his final Sydney stadium concert, which was sold out, the sound system was better and the audience more appreciative. Dylan was beginning to feel somewhat more at home. The following morning, Sunday, as the *Sun-Herald* headlined: DYLAN NOT HERE TO WIN HEARTS, the troupe flew to Melbourne for two concerts where audiences were puzzled rather than annoyed by the rock segments.

Dylan headed to Adelaide. During the show's electric segment a few people walked out. The next day, he flew two thousand miles westward to Perth. On arrival, a barefoot Dylan said: "I had a choppy flight across your desert." Around a hundred people met him. Another press conference found him in good, bitter form.

After a concert at Perth's Capitol Theatre on April 23, Bob went to a party briefly, then returned to his hotel to find a young actress, Rosemary Gerrette. Her mother was the *Canberra Times*'s features editor and, although Rosemary knew virtually nothing about Dylan, she wanted an interview. She heard a lot of literature talk and observed Baudelaire, Durrell, Australian poetry, and a Norman Mailer work strewn around the room. Dylan and crew left Perth on a twenty-seven-hour flight to Stockholm. Ripples in the Australian press continued for some weeks. "Rainy Day Women" was duly released, and duly banned.

Heavy with fatigue and jet lag, Dylan and the Hawks arrived in Stockholm for a one-nighter on April 29. Scandinavian audiences were surprised by the presence of "the Group," which some saw as a sellout.

Dylan's May 5 concert in Dublin's Adelphi Theatre was a critical disaster. By now the show was truncated to ninety-five minutes, the last forty-five minutes electric. The Anglo-Irish form of derision, the slow handclap, resounded. Even the music press was taken aback. *Melody Maker*: "It was unbelievable to see a hip-swinging Dylan trying to look and sound like Mick Jagger … for most, it was the night of the big letdown." The *Irish Times*: "a minor [poet] were he to publish in slim volumes without … a guitar, harmonica and publicity machine, it is something to sell poetry to a mass-audience at all."

By the time Dylan arrived in London, his camera crew had taken over. They shot a one-hour, 16-mm color film that was originally scheduled for the ABC-TV series *Stage 67*. The film, *Eat the Document*, has rarely been shown publicly. After Dylan's and Howard Alk's editing the film ran fifty-four minutes, Jonas Mekas wrote in the *Village Voice*: "About the richest … the best, of all films on rock … we can feel his attitude … a combination of expectation, exuberance, and great joy of living."

During the shooting, Donn Pennebaker was again nominally in charge, but he later told me that *Eat the Document* had "become Dylan's film. He took over. He was quite dragged by the performances, but I thought the songs were extraordinary. The original title was *Dylan by Pennebaker*, but Dylan changed it to *Eat the Document*, from a line by Al Aronowitz.

This time, Dylan got much more involved in the actual filmmaking. Some of it was shot at the Olympia in Paris. I think some of the very best footage was at Bob's birthday party. In Scotland, I stayed right on stage shooting—an incredible thing to do. The best was probably in Glasgow. The halation effect from the fast film was incredible. It really caught the psychedelic aura of drugs and rock on stage."

The first English concert was on May 10 in Bristol's Colston Hall. Walkouts among the capacity audience, no encores, and uniformly bad reviews. The Welsh audience at Cardiff's Capitol Theatre showed more respect. While ironing out amplification problems, one of the British roadies evicted all press and even theater staff: "One would not expect to be allowed to see Marlene Dietrich before she was completely ready."

In Birmingham the show started forty-five minutes late. There were huffy walkouts, cries of "Folk phony," "Traitor," "Give us the real Dylan," "Yank, go home," and "We want folk." Then to Liverpool, the Beatles' turf. No advance publicity and precious little notice he had been there. When one heckler shouted: "Where's the poet in you?" and "What's happened to your conscience?" Dylan retorted: "There's a guy up there looking for a saint." After a successful first half in Leicester, jeers of "get them off" greeted the Hawks, along with whistling and walkouts. In the *Illustrated Leicester Chronicle*, David Sandison, later press chief for Island, EMI, and CBS Records: "Dylan has a great band to support him … probably one of the greatest young poets alive … doing what … Ginsberg and Corso have been doing in free verse. … Dylan is producing poetry. … Perhaps those who spoiled … the concert will also mature … and realise … their prejudice is almost as great as the prejudices Dylan used to campaign against."

The Manchester Free Trade Hall was another station of the cross. Dylan apologized that the sound was too loud, but this didn't quell the hostility. Although there were hecklers and walkouts at the Glasgow Odeon, those who liked the new music shouted down those who didn't. Someone yelled: "We want Dylan." Bob replied: "Dylan got sick backstage. I'm here to take his place."

Nowhere did the press gallivant as in France. The day Dylan arrived, some 10,000 young people were attending a festival at Oullins organized by the French labor unions. Hugh Aufray, whose Barclay recording of Dylan songs had made him the leading Gallic interpreter, announced the arrival, "at this moment," at Le Bourget airport, of "my friend" Dylan. Remarked the Lyons paper *Le Progrès*: "The applause doubled in intensity. The star, one sensed, was Dylan, not Aufray." Other references compared Dylan to Rimbaud, Proust, James Dean, François Villon, and Homer. The French "hipoisie" had an especial affinity for Dylan because of their chansonniers, poet-singers like Jacques Brel, Gilbert Becaud, and Georges Brassens. Even Johnny Hallyday, then the twenty-three-year-old Gallic rock star, felt Dylan was *un ami*. He spent one night taking him around Paris, and gave him a Turkish water pipe for his birthday. Paris has more astrologers than psychotherapists, and the French press relished the coincidence that Johnny, Antoine, and Dylan were all Geminis.

The French also liked Dylan for his allegiance to peace, for his fondness for Beaujolais and Bardot, and for his poetics. Philippe Labro in *Elle*,

May 6: "He … sings of the America of backstreets, dirty little bars, back-room pool-players … air filled with smoke, heavy and sweaty … snatches of speech … nothing actually happens, but it is from this that the greatest books (Steinbeck, Caldwell, Faulkner) and the greatest films (Rossen, especially) have come. … Dylan is an authentic poet, a writer. He is, in this milieu, the only true writer."

In Paris, an old friend surfaced—Mike Porco of Gerde's Folk City. Returning from his native Calabria, Mike went to considerable lengths to see "Bobby." Heading toward the George V, Mike ran into Grossman, who said, "Dylan isn't seeing anyone. He is tired. I don't think it can be arranged." Mike persisted and got into Bob's suite, where he received a gracious welcome. "Bobby couldn't do enough for me, just the opposite of what Grossman had made me feel. He introduced me to everyone, and said I was like his father, like his uncle, like his pal. It really made me feel good. It was funny, remembering what he'd looked like here, to see him in that hotel in Paris."

Dylan's Paris Olympia concert was on May 24, his twenty-fifth birthday. Two-thousand seats costing up to sixty francs sold out a month in advance. Some tickets went to French performers Johnny Hallyday, Charles Trenet, Françoise Hardy, Hugues Aufray, and Antoine. The concert was anticlimactic. The audience tended to be unruly, but Dylan wasn't passive to heckling. Someone had draped the stage with a large American flag. Many shouted: "Happy Birthday!" When he took time to tune his guitar (some said fourteen minutes), jeers were silenced by Dylan saying: "I'm doing this for you. I couldn't care less. I wouldn't behave like that if I came to see you."

The Olympia crowd seemed to like the electric set but most reviews were vitriolic. *Le Figaro*, under the headline THE FALL OF AN IDOL, suggested that the audience had heard Dylan's double, an ill-looking puppet "unable to overcome his narcotism." *Paris Jour* took umbrage at Dylan's remarks during tuning breaks. Rouen's *Liberté Dimanche* acclaimed Dylan because he had "re-established poetry for the masses. He is in some way, the Homer of the twentieth century."

At London's Royal Albert Hall, with its notorious acoustics, its antediluvian pomp and impersonality, Dylan's first world tour ended with two contentious concerts, May 26 and 27, that followed the provincial pattern: rapt attention for his solo acoustic work and anger during his electric set. Ray Coleman reported that "Hundreds walked out during his final show" which was "a shambles of noise. We just couldn't hear his words. It was tragic."

Coleman wrote me that Dylan exploded to his listeners: "Aw, it's the same stuff as always—can't you hear?" Evidently completely fed up at the heckling and the growing storm over "Rainy Day Women," Dylan stormed back. The "Rainy Day" single was being blacklisted by American radio. Home Secretary Roy Jenkins had received an appeal to ban it in Britain, along with the Byrds' "Eight Miles High." According to *Melody Maker*, Dylan lashed back during the acoustic set: "I'm not going to play any more concerts in England. So I'd just like to say this next song is what your English musical papers would call a 'drug song.' I never have and never will write a 'drug song.' I don't know how to." Finishing with "Rolling Stone," he fairly yelled the line about having to get used to it. Summarized Coleman: "The crowd who stayed, the loyal ones, cheered. He had conquered again, all right, despite the outbursts."

Dylan and the Hawks limped back to America in June, dispirited, exhausted, and angry, only to find that Grossman had scheduled sixty-four concerts in the States for the immediate future.

Late Friday night, July 29, I received a telephone call from Hibbing. Dylan's father sounded distraught: "They just called me from the radio station here. They said they had a news bulletin that Bob's been badly hurt in a motorcycle accident. Do you know anything about it?" I said this was the first I had heard of it. "The Grossman office won't help me one bit on this," said Abe. "And I can't get through to Sara. Would you please see if you can find out something—anything— and call us back, collect? Bob's mother is very worried—and so am I." Four months earlier, a similar phone call had informed me of Fariña's death in a motorcycle accident. I rang the *New York Times* for more information.

10

LISTENING TO THE SILENCE

BOB DYLAN

DONT LOOK BACK

A Film By D. A. Pennebaker
with Joan Baez • Alan Price
Produced and Released By
Leacock Pennebaker *Inc.*
Albert Grossman • John Court

Woodstock was a daily excursion to nothingness.

Details about Dylan's motorcycle accident on July 29, 1966, were not easy to ascertain. It was widely reported that Dylan nearly lost his life. To me, it seems more likely that the mishap *saved* his life. The locking of the back wheel of Dylan's Triumph 500 started a chain of redemptive events that allowed him to slow down.

Journalists speculated endlessly. A Tokyo journalist even published a hospital-bedside "interview," which Dylan emphatically told me never happened. What most confused things was that Grossman was sending out one set of signals, Dylan another.

Dylan emphasized the serious after effects. Albert said that although Bob had broken his neck, he would need only a couple of months before resuming work. Even this got garbled. His brother told me: "Bob never said he broke his neck. Albert broke his neck." So, I speculated in print that the accident's effects had been exaggerated. Immediately, David came down from Woodstock insisting: "There *was* an accident. There definitely *was* an accident." Hubert Saal, music editor of *Newsweek*, interviewed Dylan in early 1968 and concluded: "Dylan's current reluctance to give concerts has nothing to do with the accident, from which he appears fully recovered. 'I have more responsibilities now,' he says."

Dylan told me only: "It happened one morning after I'd been up for three days. I hit an oil slick. The damp weather still affects the wound." To others, he said he was riding along Striebel Road, not far from his Woodstock home, taking the bike into the garage for repairs, when the back wheel locked and he hurtled over the handlebars. He was rushed in a friend's car to Middletown Hospital with reported broken vertebrae of the neck, a possible concussion, and head and facial bruises. A major concert at the Yale Bowl, scheduled for eight days later, was canceled. Only Dylan knows just how severely he was hurt, and at what point in his convalescence he discovered that he wanted to reorganize his life, spend time with his family, and listen to the silence. Even if it was as bad as reported, the accident became a metaphor, the start of seven-and-a-half years of withdrawal to a more tranquil existence.

The music business machine doesn't like "undisciplined" performers who fall off motorbikes. Grossman is reported to have said after the accident: "How could he do this to me?" His aide, Charlie Rothschild, asked me: "Do you know how much work was involved in setting up sixty concerts?" When I told Bob about Grossman's remark, he laughed: "That shows you where he was at, worrying about those concerts!"

Allen Ginsberg visited in late September, bringing some Emily Dickinson and Bertolt Brecht books, and said he didn't think Dylan was seriously hurt. Donn Pennebaker, the filmmaker, told *Melody Maker:* "I know he wasn't as sick as he made out. This provided the basis of an excuse for delaying delivery of that TV show, which is what he wanted to do. But I know he was at a doctor's. I went to see him a number of times and he was in a brace. … I knew he'd been hurt in other ways, so in either event, what he was doing was recovering."

The first reporter who did get through was Michael Iachetta of the New York *Daily News.* Dylan told Iachetta, in May 1967, that he'd been "seein' only a few close friends, readin' little 'bout the outside world, porin' over books by people you never heard of, thinkin' about where I'm goin' and why am I runnin' and am I mixed up too much, and what am I knowin' and what am I givin' and what am I takin'. And mainly what I've been doin' is workin' on gettin' better and makin' better music, which is what my life is all about." The *News* story described him as "emotionally and physically scarred."

During Dylan's retreat in Woodstock and New York City until the end of 1973, his creative work flourished. He immersed himself in the family life so often denied the pop star. Apparently in retreat behind a cloud of mystery, he was continually sending out messages to friends in random interviews and in songs. A handful reveal Dylan's changing world view. "Too Much of Nothing," with its Lear-like stress on nothingness, and its "waters of oblivion" line, indicted the vacuous rock scene from which he was detaching himself.

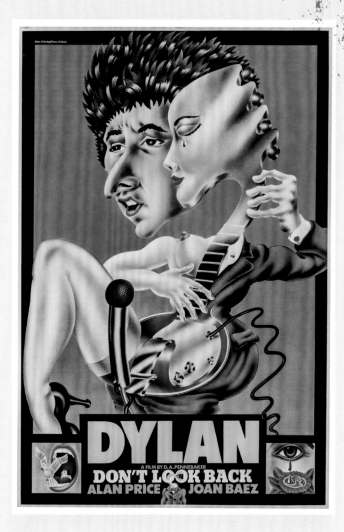

ABOVE

Alan Aldridge's poster for *Dont Look Back*. Aldridge was art director at Penguin Books, creating many iconic covers, and in 1968 set up Ink Studios with Harry Willocks. They worked with the Beatles, the Who and many other rock artists.

"I Shall Be Released" was clearly a search for personal salvation. "The Drifter's Escape" was a transparent parable about a person, trapped by a role, who awaits a sentence of doom before a hostile crowd, when he is almost magically delivered from the courtroom. The song's "bolt of lightning" could be Dylan's accident. In "Watching the River Flow," a man changes from participant to observer. The audience couldn't understand his need for privacy, and felt rejected. Dylan was repeatedly compelled to justify his withdrawal.

As late as spring 1975, Dylan was explaining to Mary Travers on her radio series that "we needed to dry out." Dylan was saying that there must be another way of life for the pop star, in which *he* is in control, not *they*. He had to find ways of working to his own advantage, with the recording industry, his book publisher, the TV network. He had to come to terms with his one-time friend, long-time manager, part-time neighbor, and sometime landlord, Albert Grossman.

> ## The royalties were twice anything we'd ever paid before, but it was worth it to keep Dylan.
> CLIVE DAVIS

Dylan's Columbia recording contract had run out. Grossman had asked the new Columbia chief, Clive Davis, for an enormous guaranty for a long-term contract. When Davis asked why the figure was so high, Grossman reportedly said: "Because it is there." In 1966, Davis was a master at pressuring his employees and artists. He wanted to keep Dylan under contract, but did not want to get involved in the high-money sweepstakes Grossman was playing with MGM and Capitol, among others. Davis felt he held the trump card because he knew that Dylan's influence then ran considerably ahead of his actual sales.

By Christmas 1966, MGM was announcing that Dylan had been signed. According to contract provisions, Dylan owed Columbia another fourteen tracks, or one album. In the *New York Post*, Nora Ephron revealed that a flaw in Dylan's contract would allow Columbia to dump an enormous amount of past royalties on him in one year, delivering about ninety percent of his profits for that year to the taxman. In April 1967, Columbia halted all Dylan's sales. This suspension was settled almost immediately, with Dylan committing himself to supplying the songs.

Meanwhile, Grossman and Dylan were having second thoughts about MGM. Grossman went back to Davis offering Dylan for double his former royalty. Davis wrote in his 1974 autobiography, *Clive: Inside the Record Business:* "I thought it was a perfect solution, and I grabbed it. The royalties were twice anything we'd ever paid before, but it was worth it to keep Dylan." On August 21, 1967, Columbia proudly announced it had re-signed Dylan to an exclusive, long-term contract. Soon Bob was back in the studio, recording *John Wesley Harding*.

The post-accident period also saw problems between Dylan and ABC-TV over the two-hour special for its *Stage 67* series, the film that later surfaced as *Eat the Document* and which was shot in Britain during Dylan's 1966 world tour. In April 1967, an ABC spokesman said the show had been canceled because of a disagreement over format. For a $100,000 advance, ABC had received

footage in November 1966 that the network described as "totally unsatisfactory." ABC was contemplating legal action.

The accident also delayed publication of *Tarantula*. Dylan had been appalled by Macmillan's pre-publication publicity and still had reservations about the book. He told *Sing Out!:* "I learned not to do a book like that … where the contract comes in before the book is written, so you have to fulfill the contract. … There was no difficulty in writing it at all, it just wasn't a book, it was just a nuisance."

Dylan's relationship with his manager was in delicate shape. In November 1965, they had organized a music publishing company, Bob Dylan Words and Music, to follow his three-year contract with Witmark/Music Publishers Holding Corporation. Artie Mogull managed this enterprise,

for a time. Grossman and Dylan were otherwise tightly linked but, by early 1968, Dylan wanted to be free. During the Guthrie memorial concerts in January 1968, Albert and Bob scarcely spoke.

In late 1970, Woodstock buzzed with reports of the falling-out of its two glamorous residents. Taxi drivers and motel owners talked of an unverified "huge settlement" that ran to more than a million dollars. Bernard Paturel, owner of Woodstock's Café Espresso and friend to both, asked me later: "The poet and the stern businessman—how long could it last?" In spring 1971, Charlie Rothschild told me that Naomi Saltzman, an executive secretary at Grossman's, had played "an important role in Dylan's split with Albert." She denied this to me. Dylan subsequently hired Saltzman as his music publisher. In May 1971, Dylan was

ABOVE

Watching the river flow: Dylan outside his Byrdcliffe home, near Woodstock.

ABOVE

Carnegie Hall,
January 20, 1968:
the two Woody
Guthrie tribute
concerts were
Dylan's idea.
The 6,000
seats sold out
within hours.

expressing relief that his contract with Grossman was finally settled, and that he'd be free by June. Bob told me: "I finally had to sue him. Because Albert wanted it quiet, he settled out of court. He had me signed up for ten years … can you believe that? For part of my records, for part of my everything. He only had me for twenty percent. There were others who had to give him fifty percent." Although the three years in Woodstock after the accident may have looked idyllic, Bob told me afterward: "Woodstock was a daily excursion to nothingness."

Woodstock, some 130 miles up the Hudson from Manhattan, in New York's Ulster County, at the eastern fringe of the Catskills, was originally an arts-and-crafts colony and a rural theatrical center inhabited by descendants of Dutch settlers, successive waves of artists, craftspeople, dancers, musicians, urban dropouts and rebels looking for a green alternative to Greenwich Village. In the early sixties, Pete Yarrow seduced several people up the Woodstock Valley, and soon the place had a new pop-music mystique pasted atop its old art frame.

Dylan's efforts at finding refuge, rest and restoration in Woodstock spread over six years, from 1963 onward. But his sanctuary turned into a zoo. For a recluse who really likes and needs people, the secret of where he lived was difficult to keep. Although famous artists had been migrating to Woodstock since the early twentieth-century, none drew as many pilgrims. Bernard Paturel, who "changed fuses, drove the Cadillac or the baby-blue Mustang" and tried to keep Bob's privacy, reflected: "There's a magic here, an emanation.

Lots of musicians, artisans, and writers. A gifted person would feel these vibrations, and get support from people like that living there. There is something in the air. You can visit someone who might have the same spirit, the same attitude. But all this could be lost with over-saturation. Many people are coming up here who having nothing to *give*, they're only here to *get*. Some are trying to just bring the city up to the country."

Public and private Woodstock are different entities. The "scene" in Woodstock is behind shrubbed driveways and closed doors. The pilgrims rarely got that far. At the time of the Woodstock Festival, living in and around Woodstock were Dylan, the Band, Van Morrison, Frank Zappa and the Mothers of Invention, Tim Hardin, and a fluid roster of Grossman's musicians, aides, and roadies.

Friends drifted up or lived nearby: Ginsberg, in bare feet and white robes, wafted about, and Gregory Corso, Happy Traum, and filmmakers Howard and Jones Alk.

"Until Sara, I thought it was just a question of time until he died," Paturel continued. "I was afraid for his life and for his mind. But later, I had never met such a dedicated family man. There's so many sides to Bob Dylan, he's round." In the hospitable Woodstock atmosphere, the family man pursued his painting. His proud father told me in 1967 that Bob was turning out canvas after canvas: "There's a guitar in every one."

The Woodstock period was a time of sickness in America but a time of healing for Dylan. I think his motivation for holing up in Woodstock was philosophical as well as personal. When he left

ABOVE

Poster advertising *Sing Out!* and the October/ November 1968 issue's interview with Bob Dylan, its cover featuring a painting by him.

> ## "The greatest album in the history of American popular music. JOHN ROCKWELL, *NEW YORK TIMES*"

and moved into a house on Macdougal Street, he found for a time in the Village both a certain connectedness and a privacy that Woodstock could no longer give him. The "scene" in Woodstock for Dylan was not physical so much as spiritual. It could take place on a hillside, in wooded acres, in farmland. In quiet visits with the guys in the Band, with stray artist, writer, musician friends. The "scene" and "soul" of Dylan's Woodstock couldn't be photographed or filmed. It could, however, be taped in a basement.

Anyone concerned about Dylan's personal or artistic health in 1967 could have looked at the bed chart provided by *The Basement Tapes* and seen a patient who had *not* cracked up, vegetated, abdicated, or run out of inspiration. For nearly eight years, all but one of his *Basement* songs

circulated illegally, as publishing demo tapes or in bootleg collections. In July 1975, the Dylan tapes, in modified versions, plus six previously unknown songs by the Band, emerged from below ground and were officially released as a two-LP set: *The Basement Tapes*. Comment ran to superlatives at the songs' variety, vitality, richness, and evergreen pertinence. John Rockwell in the *New York Times*: "The greatest album in the history of American popular music." The material was taped on a home recorder in the basement of the Band's house, Big Pink, in West Saugerties, near Woodstock. Their roughness, which pleased many, contrasted starkly with the Beatles' studio extravaganza, *Sgt. Pepper*, another 1967 landmark. Charlie McCollum of the *Washington Post* likened them to "the first draft of a Doctorow novel or the rough cut of an Altman film."

Dylan's sixteen tracks surfaced initially like snapshots from home, a peek into his Woodstock wilderness. Originally intended as demos to interest other artists in recording some new Dylan songs, the cellar compositions take a pivotal position between *Blonde* and *John Wesley Harding*. Without the transitional evidence of *The Basement Tapes*, the leap made between the two other albums could be exaggerated. The LP carries an overwhelming impression of the joy of jamming, with flawed ensembles, rough-hewn singing, unkempt instrumentalism, distortions, the lot. This isn't Sunday parlor neatness, just basement scuffling. Sheer bravura, intimacy, and excitement is caught, much as in jazz sessions. The bizarre cover echoes *Tarantula*—a dwarf, a sword-swallower, a weight lifter, an Eskimo, a gypsy, a clown, a fat lady, a nun, a belly dancer, and a ballet dancer. Song characters Tiny Montgomery, Mrs. Henry, and other eccentrics provide another link. Dylan has moved away from the death-heavy atmosphere, the trapped chaos of *Blonde*, into a communal feeling, somewhere between a bar-room rumpus and a gospel choir. The wonderment of these sessions can only increase when we realize that, soon after, the Band recorded *Big Pink* and Dylan twelve other songs for *Harding*. Links forward and backward make this an important album historically.

Dylan's *Basement* songs fall into two principal categories. The first is songs tinctured with the search for salvation, including, "I Shall Be Released." The second is songs of joy, signaling some form of deliverance and including most of the remaining titles: "Million Dollar Bash," the single from the album, certainly embodies this feeling. "You Ain't Goin' Nowhere" would easily fit in with the last two gentle love songs on *Harding*.

Divide the Dylan songs on *The Basement Tapes* as you will, light or heavy, soul-in-bliss or wheel-of-fire, this album could have been titled "Roots." What a massive catalog of chanteys, old blues, early rock, and truck-driver, hoedown, gospel, and folk songs! The Band rarely sounded brighter, and more spontaneous and involved, than on *The Basement Tapes*. Here, the Band and Dylan were relaxed and joyous, breaking the country silence.

In January 1968, the release of *John Wesley Harding*, which he later called "the first biblical rock album," created several new myths about Dylan and desecrated several music business myths. In the wake of the frenzied trilogy of 1965–66, the album brings to mind one of Blake's *Proverbs of Hell*: "The road of excess leads to the palace of wisdom." We've seen Dylan's excess of piled-up images, of wild living, of spontaneous action. Now, in his post-accident period, he was contemplative, compassionate, exuding a sense of musical, physical and spiritual calm. The elliptical tale on the album cover is a contemporary Christ parable in ironic reverse: the Three Kings come to get, not to give. This album ushered in a period in which Dylan's life and work would reject past excesses and embrace moderation in all things. Dylan, who once said he accepted chaos, was now saying: "I believe there should be an order to everything."

The surface order belies the songs' underlying complexities. In his Woodstock study, Dylan kept a huge Bible open on a wooden lectern, and the songs of Hank Williams near at hand. He had assembled the cast of Colin Wilson's *The Outsider*—the outlaw, outcast, loser, victim, the oppressed, lonely, and alienated. From these elements he sketched a series of studies in allegory, psalm, parable, symbol, metaphor, and morality. Biblical allusion, style, and syntax mixed with commonplace language and folklore run throughout the album.

The album's sparse music startled everyone. In a period of wild musical explorations, Dylan had turned to folk-country simplicity of melodic line and laconic backing. His dramatic change of music styles flew in the face of the Beatles' *Sgt. Pepper*, a daring foray into studio techniques. Dylan's spare, effective background was supplied by only three Nashville session men—Pete Drake, pedal-steel guitarist; Charlie McCoy, bassist, and Kenny Buttrey, drummer. Here was Dylan whispering in a climate of shout and scream. He had pulled the plug on electric music.

Finally, Woody Guthrie's wasting, decay, trembling, and pain ended. On October 3, 1967, he died, after fifteen years of illness. His long-time agent, Harold Leventhal, briefed the press on Woody's turbulent career. The fragmented folk movement seemed to close ranks at the death of its elder statesman. Leventhal told me: "A lot of people got in touch to say how sorry they were, but only one singer actually suggested that we *do* something—Bob Dylan." A benefit concert seemed the appropriate tribute to a ballad-maker. The proceeds could help fight Huntington's chorea, or start a library in Woody's hometown of Okemah.

With Dylan pledging his time, the concert was easily arranged. Millard Lampell, screenwriter and former Almanac Singer, wrote and directed the production. Will Geer and Robert Ryan, two Hollywood actors who had known Woody, were narrators. In December, an unobtrusive notice in New York papers announced twin concerts at Carnegie Hall on January 20, 1968. Listed were Dylan, Judy Collins, Jack Elliott, Arlo Guthrie, Richie Havens, Odetta, Tom Paxton, and Pete Seeger. Some 6,000 seats sold out within hours.

Dylan's return threatened to upstage the concerts' purpose. Audience and press were keyed up not to mourn the death of Guthrie so much as to celebrate the return to life of Dylan. At the first concert, in the afternoon, Dylan sidled on from stage left, and was not immediately recognized.

Wearing a Jesus beard and moustache, he was dressed in a conservative gray suit and light-blue dress shirt, open at the neck. He looked very serene. As the audience started to recognize him, it erupted in a series of whoops and shouts.

The heroic celebration of the Guthrie legend began. Lofty ideas in simple words, angry feelings in cutting phrases. Always the rub of the language, the American language that perhaps no other writer since Mark Twain had caught with such gritty idiom. One by one, or in varying combinations, the singers interpreted Guthrie's songs, taking over where Lampell's narration or Woody's words left off. The transition from singing prose to singing lyrics was easy, for there was melody to both. Some of Marjorie Guthrie's dance students performed to one song, and slides of the Pacific Northwest accompanied the federal bard's scratchy old voice singing "Talking Dust Bowl." In a period of harsh politics, acid music, pop art, and assassinations, Woody's words sounded like scripture.

The lights went out for ten seconds after Ryan finished, and there was some shuffling at stage right. The lights rose and a country jamboree ensued. Dylan and the Band jolted out "Grand Coulee Dam." Real hillbilly, strong, shouting, crackling with tumult, Dylan picking his acoustic guitar one minute, then raising it up high to the mic, or raising his right arm to "conduct" the Band with decisive ax chops. Seeger sat, chin on fist, like "The Thinker." Odetta smiled broadly, like another spotlight onstage. Dylan and the Band sailed into "Mrs. Roosevelt."

After the applause subsided, Dylan steered his drifters into "I Ain't Got No Home." It was startling to hear Woody's songs done as rockabilly! Vocal harmonies with the Band brought it all back home down in contemporary country. At intermission, everyone was chattering about Dylan. Only thirteen minutes onstage, and he'd upstaged everyone but Woody.

In one of the dressing rooms, Dylan was sitting near Robbie and Jack Elliott. Everyone looked nervous except Ramblin' Jack, who was cracking wise. I greeted Bob, and he stood up to shake my hand, a rare concession to manners. We were

OPPOSITE

Cowboy booted and suited, Dylan on *The Johnny Cash Show*, June 1969.

talking about the weather and the outlook for
spring crops when Grossman hove into view and
handed Bob a piece of paper, which Dylan read,
then laughed at. My first impression on seeing Bob
that day was like his brother's in Hibbing later that
year—"like a fifty-year-old man, so calm."

At both performances, the singalongs exuded the
spirit of a revival meeting. The faithful tried to find
some hope in Guthrie's words that we were, against
all the evidence, "born to win." Everyone sailed
into "Bound for Glory." Dylan took his verse,
momentarily forgot the lyric, smiled, recaught the
line, and everyone joyfully sang on. Finally, the folk
national anthem, "This Land is Your Land." We
all tried hard to believe what it said. A few cried;
most clapped, stamped, jumped to their feet, or
shouted themselves hoarse. Gone for the moment
was fractionalized, suspicious, partisan, self-seeking
individualism. We were all together around the
campfire of brotherhood and sisterhood, turning
on to the fantasy of hope for a real democracy.

Between concerts, Dylan and the Band relaxed
at the nearby Sheraton-Plaza Hotel. Robbie had
told me "just wait for tonight," and he was right,
for the excitement of their segment was even
greater. After the second show, a party for about
a hundred members of the cast and friends was
held at Robert Ryan's apartment in the Dakota
on Central Park West. Leventhal was subdued,
the reality of Woody's death having finally hit.
About midnight, Bob came in with Sara, Happy
Traum, and a few friends. He was wearing his Ben
Franklin glasses, looking relaxed but drawn inward.
Conversation almost stopped when he entered.
He began to make the rounds of old friends and
acquaintances, including Alan Lomax. Allen
Ginsberg spent a considerable time slumped in a
chair in meditation. I chatted with Dylan about
the concert. He called almost everything "great,
just great." I noticed that he wasn't shunning small
talk, and had almost become quite good at it.

Eventually, another version of the Carnegie
Hall tribute was mounted at the Hollywood Bowl,
on September 12, 1970. The cast added Baez,
Country Joe McDonald, and Earl Robinson.
Sharing the narration with Will Geer was actor
Peter Fonda. Two recordings of the twin shows,

only pale reflections of the events, were released in April 1972, *Volume One* by Columbia and *Volume Two* by Warner Bros. Proceeds went to the Huntington's chorea fund and toward a Guthrie library.

Where would the late sixties take rock? By 1969, everybody had to get stoned and make it to Woodstock, cut a psychedelic album, prove they were disturbed by Vietnam by freaking out. Then, a quiet young countryman made his way down to Nashville's Music Row, picked up a few sidemen, went into a studio and, in a few days, cut an album of gently crooned country love songs in a voice he'd never used before. While most of his fans were still stalking Desolation Row, Dylan turned the corner into Redemption Street.

Nashville Skyline proclaimed, in April 1969, a man reformed, subdued, and very much in love. One more sudden experiment unsettled and disoriented. Many reviews stressed what was *not* on the album: no protest, no bitterness, no druggy symbolism, no hipness. How could he *do* this to us? Many thought he'd lost his cutting edge because he'd turned soft and plump. Artists create better work when they are suffering, and they should, indeed, suffer for their audiences and their art.

Dylan told *Newsweek*: "These are the type of songs that I always felt like writing. The songs reflect more of the inner me than the songs of the past. They're more to my base than, say, *John Wesley Harding*. There I felt everyone expected me to be a poet so that's what I tried to be. But the smallest line in this new album means more to me than some of the songs on any of the previous albums I've made."

I had always found Dylan more aware of the country currents than most other city folk singers. In December 1961, when I returned from my first visit to Nashville to begin work on my book, *The Country Music Story*, Bob asked who I'd seen and heard. He often alluded to Hank Snow, Hank Thompson, Bill Anderson, Dolly Parton. In September 1968, he stole in from Woodstock to catch Johnny Cash at Carnegie Hall. He repeatedly told associates that he regarded country music as the coming thing, long before he cut *Skyline* on his fourth set of working visits to Nashville.

Dylan's first Nashville session after *John Wesley Harding* was in Columbia's Studio A on September 24, 1968. *Skyline* was taped from February 13 through 17, 1969. Session men included Charlie Daniels, dobro steel-guitar player, Johnny Cash, and a passel of Nashville sidemen. Six weeks after its release, the album reached number one.

He could have had no more influential a "sponsor" in country music than Johnny Cash. On the last evening of the sessions, Big John ambled into the studio and the two jammed. They put down twelve to fifteen tracks together, including "I Walk the Line," "One Too Many Mornings," and "Understand Your Man." The only public results were the duet on *Skyline*, a brief segment of Dylan in a theatrical-TV film on Cash, and Dylan's appearance on the premiere of Cash's TV series. Dylan told a reporter "it's a great privilege to sing with Johnny Cash." The Dylan-Cash relationship reached its apogee in 1969 with their opening track of *Skyline* and Dylan's appearance on *The Johnny Cash Show* reaching millions.

Bland and serene, optimistic as the "howdy neighbor" picture on the cover, *Skyline* is certainly without pretense. It begins a trend that continued until 1974—a retreat from "significance." Except the significance of an old truism: "Love is all there is/It makes the world go round." It is a reactive album, saying again that for him, the "moderate man," his happiness in retreat has been the rediscovery of some basics about life and love.

The influence of *Nashville Skyline* was unimaginable. At the end of the sixties, pop and rock were looking for new directions, and strong

> These are the type of songs that I always felt like writing. The songs reflect more of the inner me than the songs of the past. ... The smallest line in this new album means more to me than some of the songs on any of the previous albums I've made.

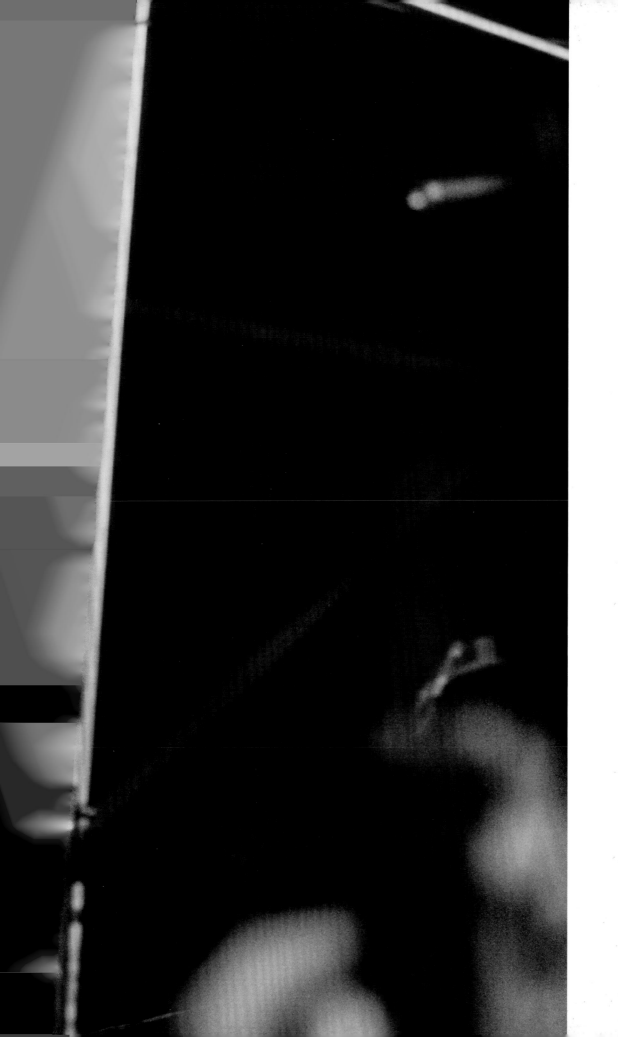

LEFT
Dylan and
Robbie Robertson
of the Band,
onstage at the Isle
of Wight Festival,
August 31, 1969.
He played for
only an hour
when fans had
been hoping for
a super-jam.

elements of country had always existed in Anglo-American pop. A good part of the pop and rock of the seventies explored country music. Soon Nashville studios were crowded with performers who had earlier disdained country as corn. Baez started to record there with *Any Day Now.* Ringo Starr followed, choosing for his mentor producer Pete Drake, who had worked on two Dylan Nashville albums.

Within months of *Skyline,* a new flock of Byrds was taping *Sweetheart of the Rodeo.* In the next few years came hip country artists and rock musicians gone country—Poco, the Flying Burrito Brothers, the Nitty Gritty Dirt Band, Tracy Nelson, Captain Hook and the Medicine Show, Kris Kristofferson, Chip Taylor, Kinky Friedman, Commander Cody. The country influence was firmly rooted by a major seventies group, Crosby, Stills, Nash and Young. Dylan himself remained interested in both the recording environment of Nashville and such country performers as Ronee Blakley, featured on Dylan's 1975 tour, and Emmylou Harris, who came dramatically on. The brilliance and the bias of Robert Altman's film *Nashville* reflected the old and new country music that met in Dylan's *Skyline* sessions.

The influence of *Nashville Skyline* dwarfed the album itself. Dylan had helped trigger a major shift in taste and style, and was privately amazed at the effect the album had on other musicians. As for the audience, by the time they got to Woodstock, its most celebrated resident had become almost an honorary citizen of Nashville.

Ending a remarkable decade in pop music, 1969 was the year when several giants of rock resurfaced and the international audience showed what an elephantine monster it had become. During the summer of 1969, Elvis Presley, unseen on stage since the fifties, sang for a live audience in Las Vegas, John Lennon resumed concerts, and the Rolling Stones gave the first free concert in London's Hyde Park. The sage of Woodstock, who had been pondering a stage return for some time, got an offer he chose not to refuse—one gig in late August in the Isle of Wight. In the aftermath of the Woodstock Festival, held partly in Dylan's honor on his

own doorstep, he was appearing three thousand miles east at Europe's own Woodstock. Even in absentia, he cast a long shadow.

If Dylan wouldn't work on Max Yasgur's farm in Bethel, New York, some 450,000 others would. The spontaneous combustion of Woodstock was, in the words of *Time,* "the moment when the special culture of US youth … displayed its strength. … It may well rank as one of the significant political and sociological events of the age." Woodstock inspired more hyperbole: Ginsberg called it "a major planetary event." Yippie Abbie Hoffman saw it as "the birth of the Woodstock Nation and the death of the American dinosaur."

Two weeks later, like a muted European echo, came the antiphonal response from the second Isle of Wight Music Festival. From all over Europe, perhaps as many as 200,000 young flocked. Among them were most of the Beatles and Stones, Jane Fonda and Roger Vadim, the Paris cast of *Hair,* and a huge press corps. There were hints that a mellowed Dylan was going to be quite chatty.

Two brothers both in their early twenties, Ray and Ron Foulk, had lured Dylan to the Isle of Wight. "We realized we couldn't attract him with money, so we decided to sell him the island," Ray said. A third brother, Bill, twenty-two, made a color film of its beauty spots, the festival site, and the house they'd rent for Dylan.

The Dylan family boarded the *Queen Elizabeth 2* in New York on August 13. During a small farewell party, Jesse, then four, suddenly lost consciousness. The ship's doctor reportedly wouldn't accept responsibility for Jesse's ability to make the voyage, and Bob lifted his son on to his shoulders and rushed him to a New York hospital for observation. The boy soon revived, his condition "not serious." A few days later, the Dylans flew into Heathrow, and were soon ensconced in a sixteenth-century farmhouse, Forelands Farm, near Bembridge. It had a swimming pool, and a barn for rehearsals. Gates and guards kept the public at bay. Chris White of London's *Daily Sketch* got past them long enough to ask Dylan what attracted him to the Isle of Wight. Tennyson had lived there, Bob replied, and he'd always wanted to visit. "Basically, we are just having a holiday."

Bob gave a twenty-minute press conference. Some reporters seemed to want to provoke an old cat-and-mouse session, so they asked him about drugs and his marriage, whether he was becoming square, why he was there. He stuck to Tennyson. His longest comment: "My job is to play music. I'm just going to take it easy. You've got to take it easy if you're going to do your job well."

The festival began Friday, with Nice and the Bonzo Dog Band. Saturday was dominated by the Who and Joe Cocker, and also included the Edgar Broughton Band, Marsha Hunt, Family, and Bloodwyn Pig. Sunday opened with the Liverpool Scene who mixed pop and poetry, the Third Ear Band, and Indo-Jazz Fusions. Christopher Logue, Anthony Haden-Guest, and Jeff Nuttall read contemporary poetry, not Tennyson, between

the acts. One surprise was the impact of Tom Paxton—his folk-topical songs had an audience reaction that *Melody Maker* called "amazing." More folk styles followed with Pentangle, Julie Felix, and Richie Havens.

I was backstage chatting with Gloria Emerson and Clive Barnes, both of the *New York Times*. Dylan's convoy arrived and there, smiling, trying to looked relaxed and very mortal, was Dylan. I noted the time: 7:23 p.m. Dylan had been ready to go on at 7:30, which was noteworthy, since later there was widespread anger at his late entrance and brief appearance. The press seats had to accommodate perhaps five hundred reporters, VIPs, friends of the high and mighty, when probably fewer than half that number was available. I avoided that mob scene and went

to the back of the crowd. To get a good spot, I had to climb over hillocks of empty beer cans, around piles of rubbish, over prone, stoned bodies. One tent encampment of fans was signposted DESOLATION ROW. From my location, the figures onstage looked like ants. About 9:30, compère Rikki Farr announced that Grossman's party could come forward to their seats. The Band did not come on until 10:00 and suffered the same problems that vexed Dylan's appearance—bad sound, impersonality, too distant. From my post, the Band was very slow to kindle. A bit of their punch came through on "Brazos" and "Don't Ya Tell Henry." By 10:35, while they were playing "I Shall Be Released," many in the audience were shouting for Dylan. By 10:50 and "The Weight," they'd adjusted to their surroundings, but then their set ended.

After interminable mic testing, Dylan walked on with the Band. Standing ovation, flashbulbs and flashlights, Roman candles. Dylan was in white, tieless, with a pastel-colored shirt. He slid into "She Belongs to Me" in a soft jazz-crooner voice that sounded unfamiliar, even after *Nashville Skyline.* Dylan's longest comment to a roaring crowd was: "It's, ah, great to be here. It sure is." During "I Threw It All Away" with acoustic guitar, he didn't appear nervous so much as formal. He played "Maggie's Farm" in a bluesy vein, with strong Band harmonies. Especially for British listeners, he played "Will You Go, Lassie, Go" (or "Wild Mountain Thyme"), taking some florid vocal lines unaccompanied. "It Ain't Me, Babe" and "To Ramona" were rather introverted, but the audience seemed to catch his mood and reached toward him. By "Tambourine Man," they were in his hands. He then sang "St Augustine," "Lay, Lady, Lay," and "Highway 61." The audience, more appreciative than ecstatic, seemed to be waiting for fireworks. Then came "One Too Many Mornings," "Immigrant," the predictable excitement with "Rolling Stone," a country lullaby on "Baby Tonight," and a bit more extroversion on "Quinn" (with a nod to the Manfred Mann recording), and "Rainy Day Women." Evidently, he remembered the 1966 "Rainy Day" ruckus. He split just before midnight, returning for encores, and repeating "Rainy Day" for the final encore. The crowd thought it was only the beginning. Dylan briskly said, "Thank you," and departed. Rikki Farr bleated: "I'm sorry! Dylan has gone! He came and he did what he had to do!"

Dylan left Britain in a very disappointed mood. By the time he touched down at Kennedy Airport, he said he had no wish to return. "They make too much of singers over there." He called the Isle of Wight a warm-up for future American tours. During Dylan's first major appearance in eighteen months, he found himself in a situation he could not fully control. In retrospect, I think the festival had a great deal to do with his holding off further live appearances until early 1974, though he turned out for George Harrison's Concert for Bangladesh in August 1971. When he did return, he wasn't doing low-key introverted work, but reaching out boldly for an audience that demanded much greater excitement.

> "I'm sorry! Dylan has gone! He came and he did what he had to do!
>
> RIKKI FARR"

11

RUNNING FREE

> ## Bob Dylan is still the most consistent artist there is … every single thing he does represents something that's him.
>
> RAY COLEMAN, *MELODY MAKER*

"It's the price of fame, I guess," Dylan told me sadly at the height of the Scavenger's campaign against him. "We loaded up our garbage with as much dog shit as we could—mousetraps, everything—but he still keeps going through my garbage!" The Scavenger was, in the words of Jerry Rubin, John Lennon, Yoko Ono, and John Peel, "leading a public campaign of lies and malicious slander against Dylan."

The Scavenger was a would-be anarchist star, a wheeler-dealer of the freaked-out New Left, a self-promoting, speedy-talking hustler named Alan Jules Weberman. From 1968 through 1971 Weberman led delegations to Dylan's home in the Village, telephoned him at weird hours, taped conversations with him then distributed these tapes and transcripts around the world. He formed the Dylan Liberation Front and then the Rock Liberation Front. He researched Dylan's finances, finding royalty check vouchers from Columbia, unearthing Dylan's alleged real estate investments. Estimating that Dylan had earned more than twelve million dollars, he called him "the singing real estate broker."

By 1971, the Scavenger seemed to feel that Dylan had somewhat redeemed himself with the "George Jackson" single and his appearance at the concert for Bangladesh; thereafter the attacks diminished. Others, less extreme than Weberman, repeatedly felt betrayed by Dylan after 1966, for his rock star indulgences. When Dylan dropped out, he relinquished millions of dollars from concerts and their stimulus to record sales. He turned down TV and film offers that would have swelled his income. In retreat, Dylan refused more money than many pop stars made in a career.

One of the Scavenger's charges disturbed the most: "Dylan supports the racist and counterrevolutionary organization, the Jewish Defense League, a militant organization whose aim is to attack anyone they believe to be anti-Jewish." Even Weberman admitted that the JDL stated that Dylan had never given this group any money. Still, the allegation stuck. After the 1967

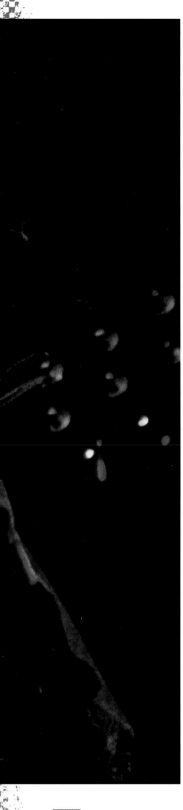

war, leftists of all backgrounds challenged Israel as an imperialist-maintained military government. Many Jews were alarmed by Israeli denial of Palestinian rights. I saw Bob just before his trip to Israel in May 1971, which he went to great pains to keep private. He only hinted at an interest in the JDL. He also talked of Jewish writers he was reading, of attending a Hasidic wedding. He certainly didn't appear to be endorsing Zionism.

According to Stephen Pickering, an expert in both Dylan's work and Jewish culture, Dylan visited Israel in the summers of 1969, 1970, and 1971. "In May 1971, the Israeli newspaper *Yediot Aharonot* published a brief interview," Pickering told me. "Dylan mentioned the earlier visits, that he had friends in Israel." On May 22, 1971, Dylan and Sara walked through Old Jerusalem, and visited the Mount Zion Yeshiva, a Cabalistic training center. Several American students were introduced to Dylan by Rabbi Yoso Rosenzweig, who asked Dylan why he shied away from a personal, direct, unmistakable declaration. "There is no problem," Dylan replied. "I'm a Jew. It touches my poetry, my life, in ways I can't describe. Why should I declare something that should be so obvious?"

Through the dust of rumor, I pieced together this picture: while Dylan was listening to the silence after his accident, he was trying to plumb his own mysteries and identities. Reading Jewish writers, going to Hasidic weddings, interest in the "toughness" of the Jewish Defense League—none of this, I think, signaled any dramatic change, just a *searching*. Many Jews believe that the only way to avoid alienation in a hostile world is to assert their Jewish identity. To some this becomes tantamount to embracing Zionism. But many Jews are not oriented toward Israel. As a young man, Dylan had wanted to be part of the American experience. Jewish friends, from Allen Ginsberg to his music publisher Naomi Saltzman, might have suggested he could find some peace by identifying with Jewish culture. *All else is speculation.* Dylan wanted to take a look at Israel, without being crowded or pledged to public commitment. Although Ginsberg heard Hebrew cantillation on *Desire*, I hear flamenco and soul. So much depends on the beholder.

The controversy over Dylan's politics, apoliticism or even anti-politicism continued for years. If he didn't speak, his songs did. From 1969 on, there had been pressure on him to resume writing protest music. When he released "George Jackson" in 1971, *Rolling Stone* remarked that the song immediately "divided speculators into two camps, those who see it as the poet's return to social relevance and those who feel that it's a cheap way for Dylan to get a lot of people off his back."

But even Dylan's appearance before 40,000 people on August 1, 1971, at the Concert for Bangladesh, wasn't enough for politicos.

On May 9, 1974, Dylan appeared unbilled in New York at a Felt Forum benefit for Chilean refugees from the junta that deposed Socialist president Salvador Allende. Hosts for this Friends of Chile concert were Phil Ochs and actor Dennis Hopper. Dylan jammed with Ochs, Dave Van Ronk, Pete Seeger and Arlo Guthrie. He spent time then with Joan Jara, widow of Victor Jara, the Chilean folk singer executed in Santiago's National Stadium. Reliving her loss at rallies around the world, she was under great strain.

In London later, Joan recalled how Dylan asked if she could ever relax. "'Come down and see some nice pictures,' Dylan said to me. 'Meet me at Fifth Avenue and 54th Street tomorrow afternoon at three, and I'll take you to see some nice pictures.' I never imagined he would be there. But I showed up, and there he was, leaning against a lamppost. And he took me to the Museum of Modern Art and showed me around, said he was with us." Dylan wanted human contact with a woman who had suffered—he didn't want to picket the Chilean Embassy.

Gradually, Leftist critics realized Dylan was still on the side of the angels. Meanwhile, as late as summer 1975, there were guns on the Right. South Africa's *Transvaal Educational News* ran a story headed: BOB DYLAN, "A VOICE FOR THE REDS," alleging that Dylan had become "the most successful proponent of communism's new class war, youth versus age" and had "become a millionaire while singing lyrics about the poor overthrowing the rich." And in September 1977, *Soviet Literature Gazette* dismissed Dylan as "nothing more than a money-hungry capitalist now." Which side was he on?

The greater an artist's influence, the more various causes try to align him as a spokesman. Dylan's message was consistently misunderstood and misapplied. Perhaps the reason he chose to go in and out of "political commitment," to pick the causes he chose to support, was simply that he didn't want to be tied to people who might speak for him without permission.

Which was the greater surprise? That Princeton offered Dylan an honorary doctorate of music, or that the anti-academic college dropout accepted? Dylan arrived the night before the ceremony of June 9, 1970, with his wife, David Crosby, and Ben Saltzman, his music publisher's husband. Among the nine to be honored at Princeton's 223rd graduation ceremonies was another writer, Walter Lippmann, and another singer, Coretta King, widow of Dr. Martin Luther King Jr. At first, like twenty-five of the 1,200 graduating seniors, Bob refused to wear the traditional black robe, but he later put it on over his pin-striped suit. He wore no tie or mortarboard. Like most of the graduates, he put on a white armband bearing a peace symbol. Dylan's escort was William H. Attwood, editor-in-chief of *Look*, and a Princeton trustee.

Princeton's President Robert F. Goheen gave Dylan his DMus, writ in Latin on parchment. The more informal citation read: "As one of the most creative popular musicians of the last decade, he has based his techniques in the arts of the common people of our past and torn his appeals for human compassion from the experience of the dispossessed. Paradoxically, though known to millions, he shuns publicity and organizations, preferring the solidarity of his family and isolation from the world. Although he is now approaching the perilous age of thirty, his music remains the authentic expression of the disturbed and concerned conscience of young America."

As he was receiving his DMus, Dylan released *Self Portrait*, which remains his most contentious album. A *Rolling Stone* chorus of twelve writers voiced outrage. "What is this shit?" Greil Marcus challenged Dylan, warning, "Unless he returns to the marketplace with a sense of vocation and the ambition to keep up with his own gifts," the music of 1965–66 would dominate his career. *Record World*: "The revolution is over. Bob Dylan sings 'Blue Moon' to Mr. Jones." Dylan later said: "A lot of worse stuff was appearing on bootleg records." It was, "so to speak, my own bootleg record."

Self Portrait forced Dylan to show doubters that his inspiration still burned. His early return to the studios in autumn 1970 to tape the twelve songs of *New Morning* certainly seemed like a riposte. This album, and title song, recalled lines from his *Broadside* letter of January 1964: "An I shall wake in the mornin and try t start lovin again." Many regarded *New Morning* as his best album since *Blonde on Blonde*. The new album was unpretentious, a collection of quiet gems. *New Morning* began the seventies with a statement of serenity, proclaiming Emersonian "self-reliance," a frontier of personal freedom. Dylan's response to public disappointment in *Self Portrait* was an affirmation of life and happiness. As the drifter of *John Wesley Harding* discovered, there is an escape route from the horror.

The Greatest Concert Of The Decade
NOW YOU CAN SEE IT AND HEAR IT...
AS IF YOU WERE THERE!

apple presents

THE CONCERT FOR BANGLADESH

ERIC CLAPTON · BOB DYLAN · GEORGE HARRISON · BILLY PRESTON · LEON RUSSELL · RAVI SHANKAR
RINGO STARR · KLAUS VOORMANN · BADFINGER · PETE HAM · TOM EVANS · JOEY MOLLAND
MIKE GIBBONS · ALLAN BEUTLER · JESSE ED DAVIS · CHUCK FINDLEY · MARLIN GREENE · JEANIE GREENE
JO GREEN · DOLORES HALL · JIM HORN · KAMALA CHAKRAVARTY · JACKIE KELSO · JIM KELTNER
USTED ALIAKBAR KHAN · CLAUDIA LENNEAR · LOU McCREARY · OLLIE MITCHELL · DON NIX
DON PRESTON · CARL RADLE · ALLA RAKAH Directed by Saul Swimmer
Produced by George Harrison and Allen Klein   Music Recording Produced by George Harrison and Phil Spector   Technicolor®

G | ALL AGES ADMITTED
General Audiences   apple / 20th century-fox release   Original Sound Track Available On Apple Records

COPYRIGHT ©1972 TWENTIETH CENTURY-FOX FILM CORPORATION   STYLE B   72/135

Late in 1969, Dylan had escaped back to the Village, to a house on lower MacDougal Street, below Bleecker. For a time, he enjoyed the anonymity that he lost in the country. But not for long could he dissolve into city streets and live quietly behind closed doors. He surfaced in old haunts, seeing what was left of his old Village gang. A decade had changed the Kettle, Folk City, the Gaslight, the Bitter End.

Early in 1971, during the war in Bangladesh, millions of starving refugees flooded from East Pakistan into India. The Indian army was mobilized to fight West Pakistan, and global help for the hapless refugees began. Ravi Shankar, Indian sitar master and raga interpreter, spoke to his pupil, George Harrison, who sprang into action. On August 1, 1971, two concerts at Madison Square Garden raised $250,000 in one day. A film and recording of the concerts raised much more.

Harrison and Ringo Starr represented the Beatles. Guitar hero Eric Clapton came out of retirement. Along came Badfinger, Klaus Voorman, Billy Preston, Leon Russell, Jim Keltner, and others. Harrison enlisted Dylan with a phone call. Introducing him at Madison Square Garden, Harrison simply said: "Another friend of mine … someone we all know." Dylan walked on in a denim jacket, as though at a sixties folk club. His "Hard Rain," which followed film clips of Bangladesh, stung. In his afternoon and evening appearances, Dylan contributed "Love Minus Zero," "Just Like a Woman," "Train to Cry," "Blowin' in the Wind," and "Tambourine Man." He did "Hard Rain" and "Wind" solo, but on the other songs he was joined by Starr on tambourine and Harrison and Russell on electric guitars. There was also vocal harmony on "Just Like a Woman."

Hassles followed between Apple, Capitol, and Columbia Records over the triple album, which was finally released in January 1972, becoming a worldwide bestseller.

By spring 1970, Harrison was preparing to break out as a solo performer, releasing a triple album, *All Things Must Pass*, co-produced with Phil Spector. Dylan had written the lyrics for the first track, "I'd Have You Anytime." Also included, along with fifteen originals by Harrison, was "If Not for You." Harrison told Ray Coleman of *Melody Maker* on September 6, 1976: "Bob Dylan is still the most consistent artist there is … every single thing he does represents something that's him."

After nearly three years of listening to the silence, Dylan started listening to old musician friends and new. He made tentative moves toward the folk movement—the Guthrie concerts of 1968, the *Sing Out!* interview later that year, a meeting with Pete Seeger, a visit to a Clancy Brothers concert. Publicity agents for performers quickly parlayed any contact into accolade. It became a game of tag—Dylan was here, there, everywhere, nowhere; singing, playing, hanging out. Mick Jagger turned twenty-nine and threw a party at the St. Regis, where Dylan was photographed with Zsa Zsa Gabor. Tito Burns said he was having British tour talks with Dylan. Bob was reported to be writing a Broadway musical. *New Musical Express* carried an exclusive report that Dylan, John Lennon, and Phil Ochs were holding heavy political talks with Bobby Seale and Jerry Rubin. All proved erroneous.

ABOVE

Passing through: Dylan at the Mariposa
Folk Festival in Toronto Island Park,
Ontario, July 16, 1972.
He was vacationing nearby.

FOLLOWING PAGES

Dylan and George Harrison at the Concert for
Bangladesh. Dylan wrote the lyrics for "I'd Have
You Any Time," on Harrison's three-LP set *All
Things Must Pass*.

Whatever he did, he told me, got blown out of all proportion. Old friends were delighted to have it known that they were back in touch with "Bobby." He was just trying to be neighborly.

One of the most elusive sessions took place with Allen Ginsberg on November 14 and 15, 1971. Allen sent out word that he was recording in New York with Dylan, Happy Traum, David Amram, and poets Andrei Voznesensky and Gregory Corso. Allen had evidently put up $10,000 of his own money. Without flamboyance, Dylan lent encouragement where he could, doing what came naturally—making music.

Shot in Durango, Mexico, *Pat Garrett and Billy the Kid* seemed an ideal vehicle for Dylan's commercial film debut and it dealt with one of his favorite themes—the embattled antihero. The filming, from late 1972 to early 1973, involved a crew of super-individualists: Sam Peckinpah, the director, a great stylist; actor James Coburn, a senior Hollywood hipster; Kris Kristofferson, singer turning actor; Rudy Wurlitzer, bright young novelist making his mark as a scriptwriter. Dylan quietly upstaged nearly everyone. Reporters buzzed around, asking Mexican extras about Dylan.

Pat Garrett was the violent story of cocky William Bonney, a kid drawn into the frontier life. Death hangs over the film's sunset colors. Little happens and little is said, yet *Pat Garrett* is a classic western, fixing on the confrontation between Billy and his friend-turned-lawman, Pat Garrett. Peckinpah implies that on the pair's deep bond of affection balances the need to destroy or be destroyed. Dylan plays a modern Fool, a youngish printer's assistant who follows and helps Billy. In a

> ## He's got a presence on him like Charlie Chaplin. ... You see him on screen and all eyes are on him. There's something about him that's magnetic.
>
> ### KRIS KRISTOFFERSON

LEFT
Dylan and his "crew of super-individualists": James Coburn, "senior Hollywood hipster" (right), and singer-turned-actor Kris Kristofferson in *Pat Garrett and Billy the Kid*, 1973.

somber film, Dylan provides wistful humor. "What's your name?" Garrett asks, and he replies: "That's a good question." Later, he says his name is Alias, "Alias anything you want."

His first day's shooting was challenging, for Bob hadn't done much riding. But the turkey-chase scene came off well. Kristofferson: "I couldn't believe it. He's got a presence on him like Charlie Chaplin … you see him on screen and all eyes are on him. There's something about him that's magnetic. He doesn't even have to move. He's a natural. … He has to throw a knife. It's real difficult. After ten minutes or so, he could do it perfect. … He does things you never thought was in him. One night he was playing flamenco and his old lady, Sara, had never known him to do it at all before."

In a barn-like studio, Dylan started laying down tracks a little after 11 p.m. one Saturday night in January 1973. Trial and error, adding and cutting. Dylan was in charge in the studio, although film producer Gordon Carroll, hovered about. Dylan led Kris's band into "Will the Circle Be Unbroken," then more instrumental tracks. Kris, Rita Coolidge, and James Coburn joined in on vocals. At 3 a.m., Bob was still going strong, taping "Holly's Song." He called for his two Mexican trumpeters, cued them on "Pecos Blues." By four in the morning, the co-stars and the scriptwriter had evaporated. Dylan was still energetic, taping other versions of "Billy." By seven in the morning, the studio technicians were exhausted, but Dylan was wide awake.

When *Pat Garrett and Billy the Kid* opened in summer 1973, critical opinion was sharply divided but it became a cult movie, frequently revived at art houses. Dylan's soundtrack, a model of economy and another new departure, has been highly regarded. He had selected some ace sidemen, including Roger McGuinn and Bruce Langhorne. His understanding of the folk ethos served him well, for *Pat Garrett* is almost a folk tale, overhung by imminent death. The score comprises ten related works, including the hit single, "Knockin' on Heaven's Door." "Pilgrims toward death" are the protagonists of this frontier epic, and Dylan's music never forgets that the film is a tragedy.

Despite his impact in *Pat Garrett*, naysayers were again chanting that his career was finished. Columbia carved another epitaph with the album they rushed out just before Christmas 1973. Reflecting base record company cynicism, *Dylan* comprised scraped-together rejects from the *Self Portrait* and *New Morning* period. This dreadful album added to a growing feeling that Dylan's career was at ebb tide, yet Bob already had plans for a dramatic return to live performances. At the end of 1973 Dylan was ready to stand naked and let it bleed onstage again.

January 3, 1974: Chicago can be as heartlessly cold as Hibbing. This time Dylan didn't have to face the cold alone. He had five trusted musician friends beside him and almost twenty thousand people in the Chicago Stadium saying "Welcome back." Yet, as the moments elapsed before going onstage, he *was* alone again. Some out there would have been as delighted if he made a fool of himself as if he triumphed.

Dylan was dressed down in the same "poor boy" outfit he wore the first time he hit Chicago. To relieve the stage's impersonality, he had approved a little set, with a bunk bed, a sofa, a Tiffany lamp, a clotheshorse, and a few candles. Balloons floated through the haze of cigarettes and joints. The audience was tense and expectant. Then a blue spotlight sliced a hole in the dark, and Dylan and the Band ambled on: Dylan, unsmiling, tried to looked casual.

"One foot on the highway, and one foot in the grave," he sang—"Hero Blues" from 1963, but he'd rewritten it. Then on through some thirty songs, a career spectrum. Some three hundred reporters were present from around the world and the tour became one of the New Year's big stories. There were five million applications for 650,000 seats, a total of ninety-three million dollars. Tour '74 grossed five million dollars and turned into a media festival, a homecoming, a quasi-religious, demi-political rally for new fans and old.

After intermission, Dylan came onstage truly alone and launched into his solo acoustic set, the highlight of that and the thirty-nine shows that followed in twenty-one cities for six weeks. He and his guitar told again how the times were changing and how Hattie Carroll died. Then, in "It's Alright, Ma," he came to the line about the president having to stand naked. The link to Nixon and Watergate ignited the audience. He quit the stage leaving an uproar behind him. His encore was "Like a Rolling Stone." *Time*: "Arms linked together, swaying in unison, chanting in time to the psychic current, a generation's anthem … not finally understood until a period of adult crisis."

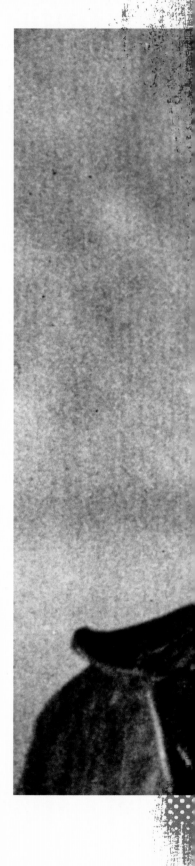

Dylan in a scene from *Pat Garrett and Billy the Kid*.

"In a somber film, Dylan provides wistful humor."

Dylan won a hero's reception, a shouting, stamping, and cheering ovation. The audience lit thousands of matches, cigarette lighters, scraps of paper, turning the stadium into an Impressionist painting. Dylan and the Band finished with "Most Likely You Go Your Way (and I'll Go Mine)," which had so much punch they used it to start the other concerts. Tour '74 caused audiences to review their last thirteen years, their own successes and failures, their direction home, or away from home. Dylan told John Rockwell of the *New York Times*: "The last tour we did, in 1965–66, was like a hurricane. This one is more like a hard rain."

In the presidential campaign of 1976, Democratic candidate Jimmy Carter, governor of Georgia, repeatedly quoted Dylan, most notably in his nomination acceptance speech: "He not busy being born is busy dying." In December 1973, in a handwritten note, Carter had invited Dylan to his home. After the first of his two 1974 concerts in Atlanta, Dylan and aides arrived at the governor's mansion. One of Carter's sons, Chip, had gone to Woodstock in late 1968, and

ABOVE

May 9, 1974, Dylan plays at Phil Ochs's Friends of Chile Benefit at New York's Felt Forum. Pete Seeger, Arlo Guthrie, and Dennis Hopper were among an electic lineup.

The final concert ended after Dylan had called tour producer Bill Graham and his aide, Barry Imhoff, on stage for bows, with "Blowin' in the Wind." There was a party at the Forum, then another at the Beverly Wilshire Hotel for just a few who were close to Dylan—David Blue, Bobby Neuwirth, Robbie Robertson, and a Minnesota friend, Lou Kemp. Tour '74 was over, for the performers and the crowds, but the impact remained.

Columbia Records had a litany for pop artists: Cut a record and tour to promote it. Dylan had resisted the formula, but no sooner were plans set for Tour '74 than he and the Band were in West Los Angeles's Village Recorder studios on November 5, 6, and 9 laying down *Planet Waves*. That done, he concentrated on the tour. During six weeks, Dylan and the Band performed fifty-three songs, only three of which came from *Planet Waves*, released in January. The title echoed a 1968 City Lights anthology of Ginsberg poetry.

The album's theme is the many faces of love—for wifely figures, for children, for various female prototypes. Even "Dirge" counterposed a love of life against death, a quality also reflected in "Going Going Gone." *Planet Waves* marked a return to stinging, aphoristic expression, free-form melodiousness, self-involvement. If considered part of a trilogy with the two subsequent albums, *Blood on the Tracks* and *Desire*, the album marked a new stylistic period. The album is strongly autobiographical, and Dylan's recurring theme is that pain has to be endured along the way to pleasure, and that pleasure is, above all, transitory. The songs "speak to each other," and certain motifs—dreams, sea, waves, mountains, hills, edges, ledges, and lonely, high places—reappear. A 1974 poll of twenty-four critics in the *Village Voice* ranked *Planet Waves* as number eighteen, with *Before the Flood*—a live double album full of new Dylan/Band interpretations—at six.

Blood on the Tracks, released in January 1975, was Dylan's third album in a year. Here was a renewed Dylan reaching fresh heights. Critical reaction ran to superlatives, calling *Blood* the best Dylan work in seven or nine years, even his best work *ever*. Dylan got this album just as he wanted it. He replaced some New York tapings

the invitation was apparently his idea. Around thirty people gathered for some of the food Dylan had requested—down-home grits, ham and eggs.

Some tour-watchers thought the January 30 Garden matinee was the high point. Wednesday night attracted musician friends and Dick Cavett, Shirley MacLaine, and Jack Nicholson. Mike Porco and the Gleasons were given tickets. A party followed at the St. Moritz. By February 11, Dylan was back in the Bay Area. Finally, Dylan and the Band wound up back where they'd started their rehearsals, at the Inglewood Forum in Los Angeles.

from September 1974 with December tapes from Minneapolis. He scrapped an elegiac liner-note essay by Pete Hamill, which later won a Grammy award, in favor of an abstract drawing.

Blood on the Tracks bore out *Planet Waves*'s forecast in "Dirge" and "Wedding Song": the artist was in torment. The new album was the spiritual autobiography of a wounded sensibility, whether the pronouns were "I," "he," "she," or "you." One of his most listenable albums, musically lustrous and varied, it contains some of Dylan's most direct, rich, emotive, and supple vocalizing. Like the mid-sixties albums, *Blood on the Tracks* shows what Wallace Fowlie called Rimbaud's "persistent theme of abandonment." The album is about the impermanence and fragmentation of remembrance and relationships.

These ten songs show high craftsmanship and control. Translucent surfaces reveal many layers beneath; abstract imagery is rendered into colloquialism. Basic elements—blood, pain, storm, rain—assume dozens of patterns. There are images of conflict—blood and barbed wire; life is a battleground and so is memory. "Rain" falls and falls again, coming with waves, flood tides, hail—"hard rain"—nature's blood, bringing life to deserts, life that is flood, tears, pain, loneliness, sensation itself. *Blood on the Tracks*, with its tears, insights, and wit, spells an end to complacency and contentment.

Dylan has been a cruel, self-centered loner. After the accident, he tried to change his ways. After his move back to the Village in 1969, he was also trying to rekindle old friendships. From the summer of 1975 onward, he made an even more concentrated effort to forge a community of singers. Dylan has wanted to be liked, but he tried to balance that need with trying to be true to his many embattled artistic selves. Years before Rolling Thunder, Dylan was pondering how to revive his old music community of the early sixties. The opportunity presented itself after he had purged his feelings, and those of many others, with the brilliant catharsis of *Blood on the Tracks*.

In early 1975, Bill Graham found a rallying point. San Francisco's beleaguered school system faced a three-million-dollar budget shortage, which would end all sorts of extracurricular activities. Graham formed SNACK (Students Need Athletics, Culture, and Kicks), reasoning: "We make our living from the youth of San Francisco. This is one way we hope to thank them." On February 4, only two weeks after his brainstorm, Graham announced that he'd signed Jefferson Starship, the Doobie Brothers, the Grateful Dead, Santana, Joan Baez, Graham Central Station, and Tower of Power. Rumored to appear: Dylan and Brando (each had five children), Neil Young, and the Band. On March 23, 1975, some sixty thousand people, mostly teenagers, besieged Golden Gate Park's Kezar Stadium. Football and baseball stars, notably Gene Washington and Willie Mays, joined the rock constellation. Radio station K-101 broadcast that "a surprise guest, the man from the Fairmont" was expected momentarily.

> **The last tour we did, in 1965–66, was like a hurricane. This one is more like a hard rain.**

OPPOSITE

Performing with the Band at the Hollywood Sportatorium in Pembroke Pines, Florida, January 19, 1974.

FOLLOWING PAGES

Bob Dylan and the Band perform at Madison Square Garden. From left: Levon Helm, Robbie Robertson, and Bob Dylan, January 29, 1974.

When Brando took the stage, many thought he was the surprise guest. "The Godfather" spoke with passion. Baez followed Brando. The man from the Fairmont Hotel was noticed backstage, heading into the tuning-up trailer. Graham announced a supersession: "On bass, Rick Danko; on keyboards, Garth Hudson; on drums, Levon Helm; on guitar, Tim Drummond; on pedal-steel, Ben Keith; on harmonica and guitar, Bob Dylan!" Roar followed roar when Graham also announced Neil Young. Nearly everyone sprang to their feet to greet the Dylan-Young-Band-Doobies set. At stage-side, Brando and Baez embraced. The concert raised $200,000. As the listeners trekked home at 6 p.m. Dylan, Brando, and Graham went to dinner at the home of Francis Ford Coppola, director of *The Godfather*.

There was Dylan sharing a stage again with the obdurately political Baez and Brando, and enjoying every minute. He was hinting that he might become identified again with social action. In the early seventies, despite his overt indifference, Dylan had been wrestling with his longing for community. His own romantic rebelliousness and social passions were cool to the point of cynicism: "The Dream is over, the Great American Dream is over. ... There are guys in prison that just can't afford to get out," he told me. Perhaps he also meant the prison of his own solitude.

That spring, Dylan was ready to talk on radio with Mary Travers, however haltingly, about the past. Tour '74 had put Dylan in touch with his old music, including the music that spoke of a certain political mood. What the seventies needed, Dylan saw, was another shot of that singular sixties zeal. Dylan has described the sixties as "like a flying saucer landed. ... Everybody heard about it, but only a few really saw it."

After Tour '74, offers for more shows flooded in, including a million-dollar guarantee for a one-day show. Amid promoters' attempts to capitalize on Tour '74, Dylan simply went visiting, socializing with people he might have written off earlier. By the time he was getting *The Basement Tapes* ready for official release in July 1975, Columbia Records was promoting its prodigal-son-returned. In March 1975, both *Greatest Hits* albums had entered the lower end of the charts again and were rising fast. Some nine years after its release, *Blonde on Blonde* reentered the album charts.

Dylan was ready to spend summer 1975 walking the streets of the Village, hanging out again, constantly on the scene, as he had been from 1961–64. He was so omnipresent that the *Village Voice* trumpeted a page one headline on July 14, 1975: JAMMING WITH DYLAN: WILL MACDOUGAL ST. RISE AGAIN? Jerry Leichtling; "You can't spit out your window these days without hitting Dylan." Over the July 4 weekend, the Other End on Bleecker Street became the site of "The First Annual Village Folk Festival." With many regulars out of town, the audience was small. All that week, Dylan had been seen around the Village wearing the same grubby outfit, black leather jacket, beige corduroy trousers, blue striped T-shirt. Monday night he'd jammed with Muddy Waters at the Bottom Line. Thursday, he'd joined Jack Elliott onstage at the Other End. Paul Colby had reopened the former Bitter End in June, after a year's darkness. On Saturday night, Dylan returned with Patti Smith, Tom Verlaine, and Bobby Neuwirth. Jake and the Family Jewels was the lead act. Dylan jammed

66

I didn't consciously pursue the Bob Dylan myth. It was given to me—by God.

99

backstage with Neuwirth, who announced "a surprise backup guitarist" and dragged the reluctant guitar-picker onstage. Dylan played piano as the talented crew joined him on "Will the Circle Be Unbroken." He remained at the keyboard while Smith sang lead on "Amazing Grace," "Banks of Ohio," and "Good Night, Irene," the old Leadbelly classic. It was like a 1961 hoot. Tastes were broader now, rock had brought riches to folk, and vice versa.

Bob came in nightly with his guitar case, piles of papers, and notebooks. Phil Ochs and Dave Van Ronk staggered by. The old hassles may not have been entirely forgotten, but Dylan was trying. The next night, Dylan backed Elliott on "Pretty Boy Floyd" and "How Long Blues" and, with Neuwirth, sang a song Dylan had been working on only that afternoon. After the time-honored finale, "This Land Is Your Land," the group moved next door to the Dugout, where the theme became "this drink is your drink." To Smith, Dylan seemed to be "exploding" with his new material for *Desire*. To Neuwirth, Dylan was "an audio voyeur, just listening to and watching people."

All of this made Dylan think about a tour of small clubs. Probably Jack Elliott suggested it, perhaps Patti Smith, perhaps Neuwirth. For a cover story in *People* on November 10, Dylan told Jim Jerome: "I didn't consciously pursue the Bob Dylan myth. It was given to me—by God. Inspiration is what we're looking for. You just have to be receptive to it. … I was locked into a certain generation. I still am. A certain area, a certain place in the universe at a certain time. … I'm not an activist. I am not politically inclined. I'm for people, people who are suffering. … Writing a song, it can drive you crazy. My head is so crammed full of things I tend to lose a lot of what I think are my best songs, and I don't carry around a tape-recorder. … We have to be able to hear that voice. I'm through listening to other people tell me how to live my life. … I'm just doing now what I feel is right for me … for my own self."

September 10, 1975: Station WTTW's National Educational Television Studios in Chicago were taping a telecast for December 13, *The World of*

John Hammond. Just before his TV tribute was broadcast, Hammond said: "Dylan changed my life, I guess." Taping of the hour-long show began at 9 p.m., but Dylan didn't appear on camera until 2 a.m., before a thinned-out audience of 150 people. Despite four heart attacks, Hammond was looking well, delighted to be honored by so many of his associates and artists. Among them were Goddard Lieberson, Benny Goodman, Jerry Wexler, former Count Basie singer Helen Humes, gospel queen Marion Williams, Sonny Terry, Hammond's son, and jazz stars Teddy Wilson, Benny Carter, Jo Jones, and Red Norvo.

Dylan was rubbing the sleep from his eyes when he arrived onstage, backed by Howie Wyeth on drums, Rob Stoner on bass and backup vocals, and Scarlet Rivera, on violin. Dylan and combo sailed into "Hurricane," jolting the tired audience. After taping "Oh, Sister" and "Simple Twist of Fate," Dylan re-taped "Hurricane," adding even more sting to his performance. His intense scowl heightened the song's anger. Before he sang "Oh, Sister," Dylan said, on camera: "I want to dedicate this to someone out there watching tonight I know. She knows who she is."

Dylan left hurriedly afterward. Observers were fascinated with the violinist in a long dress, with dark gypsy eyes and flowing hair. Some believed her to be a real gypsy Dylan had discovered walking along Second Avenue with her violin case. Some Chicagoans recognized her as Donna Shea, who had been on their local rock scene in the late sixties. Dylan later remarked: "For all John Hammond's done for me, it was worth staying late."

ABOVE

Dylan with clarinetist and band leader Benny Goodman (center), and record producer John Hammond, who is credited with discovering both. The trio met at a tribute to Hammond, portions of which were shown on PBS in *The World of John Hammond* (1975).

OPPOSITE

Maple Leaf Gardens, Toronto, January 10, 1974.

12

THUNDER, HURRICANE, AND HARD RAIN

> ## We were all very close. We had this fire going ten years ago, and now we've got it burning again.

During those hot summer nights of 1975, the idea of a "different" tour took root. Dylan put it this way: "We were all very close. We had this fire going ten years ago, and now we've got it burning again." Neuwirth: "It's gonna be a new living room every night. This is the first existential tour. It's a movie, a closed set. It's rock 'n' roll heaven and it's historical. It's been Ramblin' Jack's dream for a long time—he's the one who taught us all, and the dream's coming true."

Dylan was preparing to record *Desire* and continuing to hang out with his Village crowd. One night at the Other End, he asked Jack Elliott if he wanted to tour with him, to "play for the people." Jack's response to the buddy he'd not seen in seven years: "Let's go!" It took planning. First, Dylan went west to see his family, then popped up in Minnesota before taping the TV tribute to John Hammond, returning to New York with ideas about a rambling, tumbling tour of the north-east, with film cameras capturing it all. It wouldn't be announced, it would just "happen." Lou Kemp, the Alaska "salmon king" from Duluth, was named tour manager, assisted by Barry Imhoff and Shelly Finkel. Jacques Levy helped with stage direction. Rob Stoner organized a backup band that included Howard Wyeth, Luther Rix, Mick Ronson, Scarlet Rivera, T-Bone Burnette, and a nineteen-year-old mandolin/Dobro wizard named David Mansfield. The lead singers would be Dylan, Neuwirth, Ronee Blakley, Roger McGuinn, Elliott, and Joan Baez. Dylan phoned to ask what she was doing in November. She had planned her own tour, but this sounded more of a challenge. She said it was "irresistible" and she'd make it. Later she described the troupe as "an incredibly happy family."

One morning in October, some twenty musicians were jamming at the Other End. More signed on: Allen Ginsberg joined the chorus, fellow-poet Peter Orlovsky enlisted as a "baggage handler," David Blue and Denise Mercedes as musicians, and security people, advance men, and lighting technicians. What started as a troupe of seventy swelled to more than a hundred by Toronto.

On October 22, at the Other End, David Blue was finishing his gig. Dylan sang duets with Ronee Blakley, the country singer who starred in *Nashville*. Ginsberg sang to McGuinn's guitar. "Allen, you're the king," Dylan told him.

The following night, a little surprise for Mike Porco, who was turning sixty-one. To Mike's astonishment, four film technicians showed up at Folk City, mumbling "educational television." Under the direction of Dylan, Howard Alk, and Mel Howard, this began hundreds of hours of shooting. On hand were Phil Ochs, Patti Smith, Baez, Commander Cody members, Bette Midler, and Buzzy Linhart. A little after 1 a.m., Dylan's red Cadillac Eldorado cruised up to Folk City, and in loped Bob, Kemp, and Neuwirth. Dylan, as "the greatest star of all," went to the stage. He brought up Baez, and they sang "Happy Birthday" and "One Too Many Mornings." Mike grinned from wall to wall. He'd been waiting for this a long time.

This was a dress rehearsal for the Rolling Thunder Revue as, by twos and more, performers took to the little stage. Hours later, a hoarse Ochs did a set of his own, some traditional songs and "Lay Down Your Weary Tune." Everyone at Dylan's table stood gaping. Dylan praised Phil when he finished. (When thirty-five-year-old Ochs hanged himself on April 9, 1976, some said his exclusion from Rolling Thunder was the last in a long line of crushing events that gave him no way out. Ochs could not be signed on the tour because of his heavy drinking and unpredictability.)

That week also saw Dylan in a Columbia studio, re-taping "Hurricane." He told two top executives he wanted it rush-released. After the session, producer Don DeVito said of Dylan: "He's just totally unpredictable." All that week the troupe had been assembling at the Gramercy Park Hotel in Midtown Manhattan. Over the weekend there were intensive rehearsals at a nearby studio. Two advance men had hired the Plymouth (Massachusetts) Memorial Auditorium. On October 27, the troupe took off in three buses and some cars, most of the singers riding in a Greyhound nicknamed Phydeaux. In a few hours, they arrived at the beachside Seacrest Hotel in North Falmouth, Massachusetts, where rehearsals continued for a couple of days.

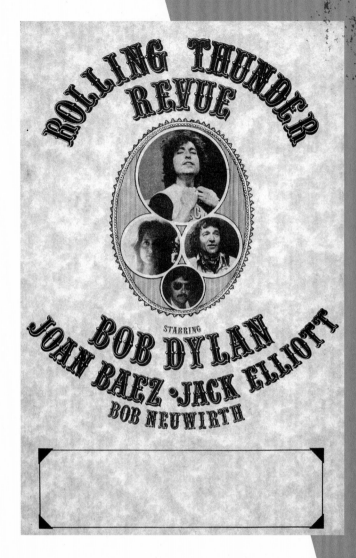

" I hadn't seen Dylan for four years. He just called me up at 4 a.m. and said: 'What're you writing? Sing it to me on the telephone. ... OK let's go out on the road. "
ALLEN GINSBERG

That night, Dylan sang in the hotel dining room and Ginsberg recited "Kaddish."

With the pilgrims landing first in Plymouth, it seemed like the grand Bicentennial gesture. It was Halloween too, so there were masks and games. With cameras rolling, the games became cinema. Elliott had once worked on the rigging of the *Mayflower* replica at Plymouth. This time, Jack climbed to the top of the mizzenmast and roared, "Ahoy!" He waved down to Dylan and Ginsberg. Allen duly proclaimed: "We have, once again, embarked on a voyage to reclaim America."

Why Rolling Thunder? Dylan said he simply looked up at the sky "and heard a boom. Then, boom, boom, boom, rolling from west to east. I figured that should be the name." He appeared pleased when someone told him that to American Indians, rolling thunder means speaking truth. Along the way, a Cherokee medicine man named Rolling Thunder joined the troupe. At Providence, he was onstage stroking a feather in time to the music. On November 5, at a beach in Newport, Dr. Rolling Thunder made some good medicine around a fire. He asked everyone to add private prayers. Dylan reportedly mumbled: "I pray we realize soon we are all of one soul."

Kemp's advance men were booking halls at a prodigious speed, often so fast the musicians didn't know the next stop. Handbills alone told the story. The autumn segment of the Rolling Thunder Revue kicked off at Plymouth Memorial Auditorium, with concerts on October 30 and 31, and closed at Madison Square Garden on December 8, with "Night of the Hurricane I." Dylan had rarely seemed more amiable, onstage and off. Sometimes he'd disappear into a room reserved for him in the name of Keef Laundry. With such voluble sources as Baez, Neuwirth, and Ginsberg, Dylan was relieved of burdensome interviews.

Baez found Dylan easier to relate to than he'd been to her in the previous ten years.

Grandiloquent Ginsberg talked volubly, most elegiacally to Peter Chowka of *New Age Journal*: "I hadn't seen Dylan for four years. He just called me up at 4 a.m. and said: 'What're you writing? Sing it to me on the telephone. … OK let's go out on the road.' … Rolling Thunder will be one of the signal gestures characterizing the working cultural community that will make the seventies." Dylan brought his mother along, Ginsberg continued, adding that "the 'mysterious' Dylan had a chicken soup Yiddish mama, who even got onstage at one point [Toronto]. … Sara and his children came. Sara met Joan Baez and they all acted in the movie together and Baez brought her mother and children [*sic*: she has only one son, Gabriel Harris], and Jack Elliott had his daughter. So there was a lot of jumping family. … Dylan is now exploring his kingdom, with a new majesty about him. He alone has the clear, clean authoritative strength to take his own monumental images, unbuild and rebuild them. This is instant teaching to a younger generation. This means he has the power to re-create America, too. All the shit he has gone through—arguments with himself—he has turned to gold. He is more a citizen than ever. And in the Bicentennial tradition, that is political, to be a hard-working citizen. … There are very few moments in my experience where I have felt the heart of history touched."

Right through the spring segment of Rolling Thunder, significant changes in Dylan were seen. Onstage he displayed great mobility, moving about like a cross between a seventies rocker and a football coach, driving his "team" onward. Dylan had his face painted white. He dressed in multi-colored scarves and different hats. He called it all "*commedia dell'arte.*" At the first show in Plymouth, the backup band's masks also recalled that sixteenth-century Italian theater form in which stock characters improvised freely. Those less historically minded saw Dylan's new face as theatrical rock à la Bowie or Peter Gabriel.

Spontaneity dominated the tour, including itinerary changes, improvisation, and guest appearances. Mimi Baez, once so critical of Dylan over what she regarded as his pro-Zionism, showed up. Joni Mitchell did two New Haven shows and reappeared later. Arlo Guthrie dropped in at Springfield. Old friends David Blue, Gordon Lightfoot, and Robbie Robertson popped up. Roberta Flack was at the prison and New York concerts. Joan said she'd never seen such a spirit.

ABOVE

Dylan in makeup before a
Rolling Thunder show in
Cambridge, Massachusetts,
December 1975.

Even after arduous shows, the cast would sing their way along on the bus: "We all sing and sing and laugh until we pass out. For us, it makes no difference if we just play for fifteen people or fifteen thousand." Love and kisses onstage, as well, with songs dedicated to Hurricane Carter, Kerouac, Sam Peckinpah, and Gertrude Stein.

Joan told Nat Hentoff of *Rolling Stone*: "The feeling is good, because everybody has some room onstage … Bob has so powerful an effect on so many lives. … I'm still deeply affected by his songs … by that presence of his. I've seen nothing like it, except in Muhammad Ali, Marlon Brando, and Stevie Wonder. Bob walks into a room and every eye in the place is on him. There are eyes on Bob even when he's hiding. … I used to be too hard on him. … I don't expect Bob to champion my causes any more. I've learned he's not an activist, which does not mean he doesn't care about people."

With Baez and Dylan doing eye-to-eye duets again on stage, some thought they were witnessing a romantic reunion. Dylan even asked her to sing "Diamonds and Rust," although, playfully, she wouldn't concede that it was about *him*. Joan told *People*: "Dylan has been a big element in my life, and he always will be. But we are different things to each other at different times. So much for Bob."

Some of the most affecting moments of the autumn tour were visible only to the camera crew. By Jack Kerouac's grave at Lowell, Massachusetts, Dylan and Ginsberg improvised a scene. Allen leafed through Kerouac's *Mexico City Blues*. Dylan told him he'd first read it in Minneapolis. At the graveside, Dylan played harmonium or guitar, while Allen improvised blues.

The Rolling Thunder Revue gathered momentum. Jerry Leichtling of the *Village Voice* said of the opening Plymouth concert: "This is one of the greatest shows I've ever seen. … This tour is Dylan's masterpiece." Fans, press, and participants dubbed it: minstrel show, medicine show, magical mystery tour, a floating musical crap game. Some were reminded of Joe Cocker's Mad Dogs and Englishmen tour, while others regarded it as a traveling electric hootenanny. Some heard echoes of Ken Kesey's Acid Test. Ginsberg told Nat Hentoff that "Dylan's getting all his mysteries unraveled," but Hentoff thought otherwise: "If he has a mania, it is for survival. … And part of the way of survival is keeping some of his mysteries damn well raveled." Jon Landau in *Rolling Stone*, January 15, 1976: "From a myth-making point of view, this is all astonishingly effective stuff. … This is one rock star who still knows the importance of mystery in creating art and in calling attention to the artist."

Dylan brought his troupe to halls where folk purists had once booed him. John Rockwell saw the Revue as a summation of all Dylan's musical influences, plus "politics and ballads fused … into something higher and more personal … Rolling Thunder … is Dylan's Bicentennial gesture to this country's true spirit."

On November 16, at the Tuscarora Indian Reservation north of Buffalo, Chief Arnold Hewitt received a telephone call—could the Rolling Thunder troupe drop in for a visit? Without speakers or amplifiers, troupe musicians showed up at the Indians' community house. Tuscaroras did traditional songs and dances to drumbeating. While Dylan sang, a few of the younger Indian children played tag around the community house. The Rolling Thunder people and their hosts then feasted on corn soup, corn bread, and venison.

All of this was filmed, including five complete concerts and assorted improvised scenes. Ginsberg saw the tour as a reaffirmation of what was actually achieved in the sixties. He also saw the film and tour as having a dominant theme of "respect for mother-goddess, eternal-woman, earthwoman principles." Dylan told him that the film's "thread" was simply "truth and beauty."

Each of the two hundred male and female convicts who heard Dylan and the Rolling Thunder troupe on Sunday, December 7, 1975, was waiting for some ship to come in. These prisoners at the medium-security New Jersey State Prison at Clinton listened to Ginsberg chant poems, and to Joni Mitchell, Roberta Flack, and Dylan sing. Among the convict-listeners was a former middleweight boxer who'd been inside for nine years on a life sentence for a triple murder in Paterson, New Jersey, in 1966. In 1974, a New Jersey investigator and a *New York Times* reporter heard two small-time thieves, Alfred Bello and Arthur Bradley, say they'd lied in fingering the man and his "accomplice" because the police had offered help with cases pending against them.

Rubin Hurricane Carter had long insisted that he and John Artis were framed; a growing number of people believed him. In summer 1975, Carter had sent his autobiography, *The Sixteenth Round*, to Dylan. Bob's reaction: "I realized Hurricane and I were coming from the same place spiritually. He's a brilliant man, one of the most truthful I have ever met. He is a perfect citizen in every way. I love him as a brother. It just isn't fair. He must get out. *Today*." In Carter, Dylan found a renewed focus for his involvement with victims and outsiders, especially black recipients of white "justice." "Hurricane" is Dylan's *J'accuse* of the American judicial system

The Hurricane Trust Fund was formed, quickly attracting the support of celebrities. Although Dylan was never listed on the fund's letterhead, his song and presence at two benefits gave the Carter-Artis appeal its greatest impetus. The night after the prison concert, "The Night of the Hurricane I" went to Madison Square Garden, where there were as many notables in the capacity audience as on stage. First came an hour of music from Neuwirth, Blakley, Joni, and the Rolling Thunder Revue Band. Then, for twenty minutes, the Hurricane cause was expounded. Heavyweight Muhammad Ali told the largely white audience: "You've got the connections and the complexion to get the protection." Hurricane, listening to the concert by telephone, said: "I thank you from my heart. I love you all madly."

Then followed nearly four hours of performances from Roberta Flack, Richie Havens, Joni and Joan, the Rolling Thunderers, and Dylan. The shortened single version of "Hurricane," even with one expletive deleted, had already made its mark. To the song's accompaniment, legal moves quickened. On November 6, the New Jersey Supreme Court announced it would review the appeal. A month later, Carter and Artis withdrew their application for pardon, seeking "complete vindication" in the courts and asking executive clemency pending a new trial. On January 12, 1976, the top Jersey court heard the appeal, and in March unanimously threw out the convictions. Carter and Artis were freed on bail and promised a new trial.

> This is one of the greatest shows I've ever seen. … This tour is Dylan's masterpiece.
>
> JERRY LEICHTLING, *VILLAGE VOICE*

Meanwhile, plans were afoot for a "Night of the Hurricane II." First planned for the New Orleans Superdome in December, it was moved to the Houston Astrodome on January 25, 1976. This promised to be the biggest rock benefit ever, with Dylan's troupe joined by Stevie Wonder, Stephen Stills, Ringo Starr, Dr. John, Santana, and others. Because of strange machinations behind the promotion, this super-concert was a curious box-office fiasco, attended by 30,000, half as many as expected.

Then came the anti-climax. Just before Christmas 1976, after jurors at the new trial had listened to seventy-six witnesses for thirty-one days, Carter and Artis were found guilty again. Bello withdrew his recantation, and all the high expectations of the previous months began to

wane. Two former defense witnesses also testified that they were not with Carter at the time of the shooting. On February 9, 1977, Carter received two consecutive and one concurrent life terms. Artis received three concurrent life terms. (In November 1985, Hurricane Carter was released without bail. Federal Judge Lee Sarokin cited "grave constitutional violations" by prosecutors and ruled that the 1976 convictions had been based on "an appeal to racism rather than reason, concealment rather than disclosure.")

Desire, released in January 1976, was an eclectic musical statement, a marriage of legendary themes and contemporary meaning. It initially struck me as spare, almost rudimentary yet, beneath its simple surfaces, *Desire* has proved alive and deep, the culmination of the trilogy

Rubin "Hurricane" Carter greets
Bob Dylan following a Rolling Thunder
benefit concert at Clinton State Prison,
New Jersey, December 7, 1975.

that began with *Planet Waves*. In some ways, this album is the real self-portrait.

Desire was the name of a New Orleans streetcar, and a western starring Marlene Dietrich. But many poets have been lured by desire. To Blake, it was man's ladder to the stars. Eliot's "Four Quartets" orchestrated themes that also intrigue Dylan—time, justice, roles, rebirth, redemption, and desire. Blake illuminated his manuscripts. Eliot used footnotes. Dylan plays his cards more slyly. His brief liner notes and carefully positioned visual symbols on album jacket and songbooks use the symbolism of tarot cards. Other clues lead to Robert Graves's *The White Goddess*, a complex *Historical Grammar of Poetic Myth*. Graves showed how the patriarchal structure of Judeo-Christian religion attempted to erase the ancient worship of the Goddess. Graves advised the poet to "achieve social and spiritual independence at whatever cost," for the poet must "learn to think mythically as well as rationally."

Dylan had been "thinking mythically" since he was a boy at the movies. *Desire*, however, is a giant step forward in the breadth of his mythological thinking, moving toward a summation of themes that have long absorbed him: apocalypse, personal or societal; identity; the hero's quest for love, knowledge, redemption, liberation. He deals here with manifold myths—of justice and the outsider ("Hurricane" and "Joey"); of the woman who suffers love and offers renewal ("Isis" and "Oh, Sister"); and of life as a movie ("Romance in Durango" and "Black Diamond Bay").

Two keynotes of the album lie in the lyrics of "Oh, Sister": "We died and were reborn and then mysteriously saved" and "Time is an ocean but it ends at the shore/You may not see me/Tomorrow." Death and rebirth, and time lost, stolen, or threatened, are the Faustian questions of the alchemist who seeks spiritual perfection and redemption.

Dylan's search for redemption stretches back to *Blonde on Blonde* and *John Wesley Harding*. In everyday language, redemption means deliverance, reclamation, or salvation; in Christian terms, it is deliverance through Christ's atonement. In his 1936 essay, "Ideas of Redemption in Alchemy," Jung declared: "After the resurrection man becomes stronger and younger than he was before" —echoed in Dylan's celebrated line, "I'm younger than that now." Jung tied the alchemist's search to the Messianic element of Hebrew prophecy, and to the myth cycles of Osiris, Orpheus, Dionysus, and Hercules, who all died and were mysteriously saved or redeemed. Jung found the epitome of artistic alchemical thinking in Goethe's *Faust*. What would Jung have made of Dylan's "chain with the devil" from his early Hibbing days until his redemption through love and through battling social injustice? Dylan's long search for redemption through alchemical identification with mythic characters culminates in *Desire*.

He refers to "the songs of redemption," which Ginsberg's notes to *Desire* take as a title. Ginsberg's essay recalls that he and fellow 1950s Beats dreamed of a quest for liberation, and of the marriage of poetry to music. He described *Desire* as "another great surge of prophetic feeling," hearing Hebraic cantillation in "One More Cup of Coffee." I hear Tex-Mex and

ranchero music, and the mélange of flamenco and soul that Otis Redding and others explored and Van Morrison developed.

Dylan's melodic resources have full sway, from the declamatory, rallying verse of "Hurricane" to the playful tune of "Mozambique," from the keening of "Sara" to the otherworldly cast of "Valley Below." "Hurricane," the album's opening track and best-known song, sets tone and texture, tolling again those freedom chimes, previewing some of the album's major themes. The Isis-Osiris relationship in "Isis," "Oh, Sister," and "Sara" continues *Desire*'s implicit struggle— against false "Justice," against false love, against false labeling. Ginsberg calls them "cameo novels." Dylan's dramatic-cinematic vision was never stronger.

Desire is dominated by women deities and women colleagues. Scarlet Rivera's violin is a genuinely innovative sound, blending melancholy and exoticism. Emmylou Harris's harmony is also an important new element. (She was on the first version of "Hurricane," but Ronee Blakley sings harmony on the released version). The women's voices against Dylan's are another experiment in texture. Although Harris is a perfectionist about intonation and polish, she acceded to Dylan's imperatives of spontaneity and urgency. Some rough-and-ready cuts were released. There is fine instrumental support from six others, most of whom were with the Rolling Thunder Revue.

Desire was unique in the presence of Jacques Levy as co-lyricist on all tracks except "Sara" and "Valley Below." Levy, a PhD in psychology, is well

ABOVE

At Clinton State Prison, Joan Baez, Bob Dylan, Allen Ginsberg, and Roberta Flack are among those performing for Rubin "Hurricane" Carter and fellow inmates. Carter was seeking a retrial after key witnesses recanted their original testimonies.

ABOVE

Thanksgiving
1976, and the
Band bows out at
the Last Waltz
at the Winterland
Ballroom in San
Francisco. On-
stage with Dylan
are Van Morrison
(left) and Robbie
Robertson.

imbued with Jungian thinking. He's also a theatrical
handyman, director of *Oh! Calcutta!* and a seasoned
lyricist. Dylan met Ramblin' Jacques on Bleecker
Street after Tour '74. A year later, after another
chance Bleecker Street encounter, Bob suggested
they try to "write some stuff together." He also
turned to Levy for ideas for Rolling Thunder.
McGuinn has attested that Levy's encouraging
manner and style bring out the best in his partners.

Before arriving at his final *Desire* team, Dylan
experimented with Eric Clapton, Kokomo, and
the Dave Mason Band, looking for a compatible
combination. Then he ran into a Lower East Side
bar band, Rob Stoner and the Rebels, with whom
Mick Ronson often sat in. Here Dylan found
sidemen for the Rolling Thunder Band and for the
final *Desire* sessions.

Primarily to raise money for his film *Renaldo and
Clara*, a second segment of Rolling Thunder was
added in 1976. What I call Distant Thunder was
more muted than the northeastern tour, because
the novelty and the gaze of the major media had
left. After Night of the Hurricane II there was a
break. The tour resumed in Florida on April 18
at the Lakeland Civic Center, the first of eight
concerts during the Easter college break. By then,
the backing group was calling itself Guam. They
opened with a dozen songs, followed generally by
Dylan doing two acoustic selections, then a set
backed by Guam. McGuinn and Baez had solo
stints, then Bob and Joan sang together, ending with
ten or so songs from Dylan/Guam.

A group of documentary-makers called Top
Value Television filmed the May 23 concert at

Hughes Stadium, in Fort Collins, Colorado, broadcast on NBC-TV on September 10 as *Hard Rain*. That day also saw the live album released, with additional tapes from the Tarrant County Convention Center, Fort Worth, Texas.

The TV show was, appropriately, under raining, cloudy skies. Bob looked very tense, and what Joan later called "his viper eyes" darted around a lot. It came to be called "an anti-special," with most mainstream TV critics panning it, as "painfully artless" and "a mess … a debacle." The underground *Boston Phoenix* called it "perhaps the most extraordinary and moving film of a concert ever made."

Warming up for what was to become his most sustained period of visibility in the American press, Dylan provided a cover story for the most widely circulated magazine in the US, *TV Guide*, on September 11. He ducked questions about Jimmy Carter, praising instead Jefferson and Ben Franklin. Since the credits of the show thanked, among others, Herman Melville and Rimbaud, Dylan explained his debts to them and to Conrad, Joyce, and Ginsberg. Asked how he imagined God, Bob replied: "I can see God in a daisy … in the wind and rain. I see creation just about everywhere. The highest form of song is prayer." Dylan had praise for the Beatles and the Stones. "And Joan Baez means more to me than a hundred of these singers around today."

Back in LA, Dylan began editing *Renaldo and Clara*. He finished a new song, "Sign Language," which Eric Clapton taped in September, for his album *No Reason to Cry*. Phil Spector finally talked Dylan into a studio, to join backup singers on the song by Leonard Cohen and Spector, "Don't Go Home With Your Hard-on."

Thanksgiving Day 1976 was chosen as the day the Band would say a long goodbye to touring, at San Francisco's Winterland Palace. The rising director Martin Scorsese decided to direct a major film of the event, which also spawned a live album. To close out sixteen years of hard traveling, they planned perhaps their greatest performance. With a three hundred-page shooting script, the director had a forty-five-member crew running seven cameras on the thirty-seven programmed songs.

The guest roster included Dr. John, Joni Mitchell, Neil Diamond, Van Morrison, Neil Young, and Dylan. For visual opulence, Bill Graham rented sets from the San Francisco Opera's *La Traviata*. The five thousand listeners not only heard a great concert but also consumed two hundred turkeys and three hundred pounds of salmon. The Berkeley Promenade Orchestra provided the waltzes, foreshadowing the New Romantics by a decade. Ronnie Hawkins, who had organized the Band as the Crackers in 1960, was there, and so were Bobby Charles, Paul Butterfield, Muddy Waters, and Eric Clapton.

Emmett Grogan was the MC for the Last Waltz. He brought on some West Coast poets at intermission, among them Michael McClure and the dean, Larry Ferlinghetti. Robbie Robertson had only finished the signature tune, "The Last Waltz," that morning. He brought on "one more friend." Dylan plugged in for "Baby, Let Me Follow You Down." Grogan said Dylan, hamming it up in a high-crowned white hat, "swaggered his lyrics" in "Hazel," "I Don't Believe You," "Forever Young," and then repeated his opener.

"THE FINEST OF ALL ROCK MOVIES!"
-Newsweek

A MARTIN SCORSESE FILM

THE LAST WALTZ

It Started as a Concert. It Became a Celebration.
Now it's a Legend.

Featuring a digitally remixed and remastered soundtrack,
personally supervised by Robbie Robertson.
For the first time in state-of-the-art 5.1 stereo surround sound.
Newly restored color corrected prints approved by Martin Scorsese.

A MARTIN SCORSESE FILM THE LAST WALTZ

STARRING
THE BAND

RICK DANKO
LEVON HELM
GARTH HUDSON
RICHARD MANUEL
ROBBIE ROBERTSON

FEATURING
BOB DYLAN
ERIC CLAPTON
NEIL YOUNG
JONI MITCHELL
VAN MORRISON
NEIL DIAMOND
EMMYLOU HARRIS

MUDDY WATERS
THE STAPLES
RINGO STARR
RON WOOD
DR. JOHN
PAUL BUTTERFIELD
RONNIE HAWKINS

PRODUCTION DESIGNED BY BORIS LEVEN EXECUTIVE PRODUCER JONATHAN TAPLIN PRODUCED BY ROBBIE ROBERTSON
DIRECTED BY MARTIN SCORSESE www.unitedartists.com

Deluxe 4-CD box set of THE LAST WALTZ available from Rhino/Warner Bros. Records

IN THEATERS THIS SPRING

ABOVE

Film poster for
Martin Scorsese's
The Last Waltz
(1978), the Band's
"long goodbye
to touring."

He remained stage-center for the grand finale of "I Shall Be Released," with Ringo Starr and Ronnie Wood joining in the jam. Scorsese, who had been on the crew of the *Woodstock* film, managed to make the movie retain a dignity rare in rock. Wrote Terry Curtis Fox in the *Village Voice*: "While ostensibly … about the Band, Scorsese's editing makes no bones about how much a Dylan event it became. … Everything else disappears behind his presence."

Another film director spent most of 1977 on a film about aspects of the music life that was to be even more personal. Dylan helped edit down 240,000 feet—some one hundred hours—for his film, *Renaldo & Clara*. The finished movie, running nearly four hours, became a candidate for commercial suicide. Complex, often non-

communicative, it was a musical triumph but a dramatic failure. Critics had a field day.

Dylan was most hurt by the reaction from his old neighborhood paper, the *Village Voice*. "Did you see the firing squad of critics they sent?" he asked me in summer 1978. The *Voice* published seven reviews on January 30, 1978. Karen Durbin called it "The coup de grâce in his de-adulation campaign," resenting his comparisons of himself to Jesus. Referring to confused scenes among Dylan, Baez, and Sara, she wrote: "Dylan could love no one like he loves himself." James Walcott said the film sank so many reputations, "it's like watching the defeat of the Spanish Armada," and considered it the spiteful revenge of "an artist on his groupies." That tough professional, Pauline Kael, in the *New Yorker*, said that "despite all his masks and camouflage," he's "still the same surly, mystic tease … more tight close-ups than any actor can have had in the whole history of movies. He's overpoweringly present, yet he is never in direct contact with us. … We are invited to stare … to perceive the mystery of his elusiveness – his distance." Her review was headlined THE CALVARY GIG.

Not every comment on the Thunder/Renaldo experience came from the press. Some observations were made by the playwright Sam Shepard, by Joan Baez in song, and by Sara Dylan in a law court.

Shepard was already esteemed as a playwright when he joined the *Renaldo* crew to write some dialogue. Not much happened there but, in his *Rolling Thunder Logbook*, he had much, positive and negative, to record. He felt himself "a collaborator in a whirlpool." He meets Dylan, finds him "all blues" and making surrealist talk about French films. When he watched Dylan at the piano playing "Simple Twist of Fate," Shepard was touched: "Here is where it's at. The Master Arsonist. The place is smoking within five minutes. … This is Dylan's true magic. Leave aside his lyrical genius for a second and just watch this transformation of energy which he carries … the kind that brings courage and hope and above all brings life pounding into the foreground. … It's no wonder he can rock the nation."

In a provocative essay, "Changing Trains," in the *Threepenny Review*, Irene Oppenheim traced the curious pasts of Dylan and Shepard, using Camus's *The Myth of Sisyphus* as a guidepost on the question of how one lives without a knowledge of the meaning of existence. The essay found both writers sharing the self-wasting process by cannibalizing themselves for material. Right after Rolling Thunder, Shepard wrote *Suicide in B-Flat* about the death and potential rebirth of an artist. The central character is a musician being driven mad by inner voices. Oppenheim thinks both writers retreated from the crest in life-preserving moves. "Dylan, after a long flirtation, and pushed to the edge by bitter marital problems, has made a leap of faith." Shepard, "mercilessly tortured by his creative demons, has opted, in desperation for a kind of suicide." By 1984, Shepard was reborn as a writer and an actor, a Hollywood figure of stature.

Baez told me she was embarrassed by some of the footage and yet it didn't change her warm feelings toward Dylan. She did a little bit of mimicry of how Bob had called her in Europe at three in the morning and got her approval to let it all go as he chose. On her 1976 album, *Gulf Winds*, "Time Is Passing Us By" and "O, Brother!" offer some amazingly frank revelations of her feelings toward Dylan.

Sara had already had her say on the failing marriage with Dylan in the divorce action of 1977. How ironic that after the bitter marital strife should come the film, with Sara as another of Bob's dark-haired women. The woman had been so much a part of Dylan's life, of his retreat from stage life to be husband and father, of the shape of some of his work from *John Wesley Harding* to *Street-Legal*. By 1978, getting so deep into opening up for the press to push *Renaldo and Clara*, he opened up about marriage: "Marriage was a failure. Husband and wife was a failure, but father and mother wasn't a failure. I wasn't a very good husband …" He said that no one in his family gets divorced and that he "figured it would last forever."

How costly the marriage was emotionally comes through in the albums. How costly it was to prove financially is not known, but there's no doubt the divorce settlement was expensive. On March 1, 1977, Sara's divorce petition was filed in Superior Court in Santa Monica. She sought permanent custody of Maria, fifteen, and her children by Dylan: Jesse, eleven; Anna, nine; Samuel, eight; and Jacob, six. She also sought child support, alimony, and court-supervised disposition of the couple's community property. Assets involved included real estate in four states, plus Dylan's holdings in publishing companies, recordings, and literary copyrights.

Sara was granted temporary custody of the children and exclusive use of the Malibu house, known as Dylan's Taj Mahal because it was crowned with a huge onion-shaped copper dome, which cost $16,000. Dylan's lawyers won a ruling to have certain legal documents closed to the public, including the size of the settlement. But that it cost Dylan a very large amount of money seems clear.

> " Marriage was a failure. Husband and wife was a failure, but father and mother wasn't a failure. "

ABOVE

Dylan with
Sara, his "radiant
jewel, mystical
wife," in 1976.
They divorced
in 1977.

Although use of the Malibu house reverted to Dylan, it was really more of a house than a home. The famed beach colony of the stars was known for the privacy it once afforded its residents, but as its glamour spiraled, it became increasingly a fishbowl, like Woodstock.

By the end of 1977, his family life in tatters, with battles between him and Sara over the children still unresolved, Dylan seemed at a low ebb. He was about to launch a film he anticipated would be demolished by critics, although he hoped that audiences would support it. He made plans to undertake a world tour and another recording. It was the beginning of the end of another phase, another career. With the American audience's backlash at *Renaldo & Clara*, and the rest of the world still enthusiastic about him, it looked as if, again, there was no direction home.

POSTLUDE:
JOURNEY THROUGH DARK HEAT

While Dylan scaled new heights around the world in 1978, he reached new depths in America. In one year, he played to 115 audiences in ten countries, encountering resistance only in his native land. As usual, some grumbles were to be heard everywhere: his look and new band suggested "the route to Las Vegas," the new album, *Street-Legal*, sharply divided opinions. And someone's catchphrase, "the alimony tour," was picked up pervasively. No matter how it tapered off in America as Dylan played while fighting a virus, the year still seemed a strong expression of will, stamina, and artistic growth.

By the end of 1977, Dylan had signed on as his business manager Jerry Weintraub of Management III. He had worked with John Denver, Frank Sinatra, Neil Diamond, and Tom Paxton to apparently good effect. "At the time I got Jerry to manage me, I almost didn't have a friend in the world. We were working on that movie. … I was being thrown out of my house. I was under a lot of pressure, so I figured I better get busy working," Dylan said.

Weintraub organized a flying squad of forty sound technicians, security people, and administrators. On the agenda were concerts in Japan, Australia, New Zealand, five countries of Western Europe, and, for autumn, America and Canada. Dylan had recruited a new eight-piece band and a female gospel-style vocal trio, which yielded a radically new sound. They rehearsed seventy songs, many in startlingly new arrangements. When I asked Bob who had done the new charts, he said proudly: "There's nothing that band does that can't be worked out on my guitar. I started recruiting this band in January [1978]. It was difficult, hard. A lot of blood has gone into this band. They understand my songs. It doesn't matter if they understand me or not."

The chief novelty was the presence of an edgy, mercurial *Blonde on Blonde* texture, achieved partially by Steve Douglas on saxophone and flute, with David Mansfield's manic mandolin and fiddle playing a bubbly embellishment. A vocal trio, Helena Springs, Jo Ann Harris, and Carolyn

Dennis, provided the backing voices. Some saw this as commercialism, but they simply weren't conversant with the black music style from which it came.

The troupe began with eleven concerts in Japan on February 20, 1978. In Tokyo and Osaka, more than 100,000 attended. Although it is the custom to react with polite restraint in the concert hall, the press reflected excitement. During two of the Tokyo gigs, Dylan recorded the *Bob Dylan at Budokan* album, originally designed solely for the Japanese market. The somewhat sterile sound didn't really reflect what the tour sound was to become but, because of its immaculate pressing, the album quickly became a collector's item. So many in Europe and America were buying *Budokan* at import prices it was decided to remaster it in the West, with some inevitable technical losses.

A dozen well-received Australian and New Zealand concerts followed, with some hints that a sixties level of passion was being felt on both sides of the footlights. Dylan went into a Santa Monica studio for a week in April to tape *Street-Legal*. With the momentum of the world tour, the album did well around the globe, but American critics admonished him to "get a producer."

Street-Legal is one of Dylan's most overtly autobiographical albums, telling of loss, searching, estrangement, and exile. It also clearly foreshadows the Christian conversion ahead. It is peopled by a group of narrators who are oppressed, wandering, and lonely, traveling in a foreign country of the spirit. The Tarot card imagery of "Changing of the Guard" has confounded some, though it is difficult not to ascribe it either to his years with Sara or with the Band, or both.

But the album is generally strong on communication, rather than on code. I call attention to two minor gems and a masterwork on the album, which have not been fully appreciated: "New Pony" has a scathing blues riff on which the women's voices drive home the repeated phrase "How much longer?" out of the Bible, yet in a song that seems to be pure sexuality. "Señor (Tales of Yankee Power)" is a strong and rueful political statement that finds American foreign policy confused and unjust. More biblical language is sandwiched between American folk language, with the reference to overturning the tables from the passages describing Jesus and the money-changers. I hear many echoes of Robert Johnson, the blues giant, especially on "Is Your Love in Vain?" Powerful, raw stuff amid tenderness in "Baby Stop Crying," "True Love Tends to Forget," and "We Better Talk This Over." I hear some fine Stevie Wonder echoes on the cataloging of "No Time to Think."

The masterwork is the final song of anguish and prophecy, a song with the sweep of "Like a Rolling Stone"—"Where Are You Tonight? (Journey Through Dark Heat)." Here we can discern the move toward Christianity, foreshadowing major changes after the hellish disorder the narrator has gone through. This is catharsis and resolution as he steals off into a troubled night with such companions as St. John of the "Book of Revelation." There are technical raw spots on the album, but Dylan clearly wanted to tape it red-hot and from the heart, and he had allowed himself only a week before hitting the road again.

Dylan's return to Britain for six concerts at Earls Court, from June 15 to 20, took the country by storm. The 100,000 tickets sold briskly, fans in London and some provincial cities having to wait in line all day. Media pictures of the weekend queues helped build anticipation, and Dylan's opening-night concert ranks as one of his greatest.

Tokyo, February 1978: Dylan at a press conference on
his first visit to Japan. The dates launched his world tour.

Working with the CBS press woman Ellie Smith, an American based in London, Dylan cordially greeted the press, with a kind word for most, unless they happened to break protocol by taking notes on what was said informally. I received the royal summons the second night, and was sitting in the backstage area with Michael Gray and Gabrielle Goodchild, trying to hold a conversation with Jack Nicholson, then in London with Stanley Kubrick for the filming of *The Shining*. We saw Dylan poke his nose into the enclosure, then back away. Later he explained to me: "I saw you there, but it was too emotional a thing to go in there among all those people."

When the three of us went out to chat with Bob, he was standing beside Helena Springs, and he started to tell her about the old days at Folk City and the nearby Troubadour. Clearly sensing the triumph of the evening, Bob asked me whatever happened to the Greenbriar Boys, who had topped the bill with him at Gerde's. Bob promised more time with me, so I raced off to find Ellie to make arrangements. Before I did, I told him the band was impressive, and asked where he had got them together. "It's about the only thing I have got together now," he said candidly.

The next night, backstage, Dylan was a bit more relaxed, and he told Gabrielle, me, and his old Woodstock friend, Happy Traum, about how England had once been so lavish with honors for Big Bill Broonzy and other black American bluesmen "when they were just working as janitors in the States." Seeing old friends in London after the post-divorce depression and the trashing of *Renaldo & Clara* by the American critics seemed to bring Bob great joy and relief. He suggested another night for supper and an interview, since he had to talk to a reporter from *L'Express*, Paris, which had a cover story planned.

We showed up at a smart Knightsbridge restaurant, San Lorenzo, where the concert promoter, Harvey Goldsmith, was hosting the crew and local staff with a dinner after the final concert. Gabrielle and I got there early, and I sized up the room. "I think he'll probably want to sit in a corner where he can watch the door," I remarked. A few minutes later, Bob walked in and headed straight for the corner table before he even saw us there.

Dylan wanted to make it clear he was "subservient to those songs. I'm not out there as a performer underneath a dance team. The writing part is a very lonely experience, but there's strength in that loneliness. But I'm a performer too, and that's an outward thing. One is the opposite of the other, and it makes me crazy sometimes, because I can't write with the energy that I perform with. I can't perform off the energy that I write with. There just has to be time for both." Was he any more comfortable now being called a poet? "Very much so. I consider myself a poet first and a musician second." (In his first American interview of the autumn 1978 tour, he told a reporter: "I'm a musician first and a poet second.") Bob went on: "I live like a poet and I'll die like a poet. I've always liked my stuff. All you really have to please is yourself in any arena of life."

I asked him if he were able to relax on the tour. He had been going up each day to a pool in North London for a swim, he told me, and was not recognized. How had he taken the news of Presley's death? He downed a shot of Courvoisier. "I broke down. One of the very few times. I went over my whole life. I went over my whole childhood. I didn't talk to anyone for a week after Elvis died. If it wasn't for Elvis and Hank Williams, I couldn't be doing what I do today."

ABOVE

July 1978, at the Pavillion de Paris, towards the end of the European leg of his world tour.

EARLS COURT, LONDON
(Opposite Warwick Road Exit, Earls Court Tube Station)

HARVEY GOLDSMITH ENTERTAINMENTS
proudly present

BOB DYLAN
in concert

1

BLOCK
78

Thursday, 15th June
at 8.00 p.m. Doors open 6.30 p.m.

GALLERY
£5.00
(including V.A.T.)

No cameras, tape recorders or bottles allowed in Auditorium

WARNING: Official souvenirs are on sale within the auditorium only

D 43

For Conditions of Sale see over

To be retained

> "I feel at home in America, because, as primitive as it is, I still can create from America. All my feelings come out of America."

At that final concert, Bob had told his audience, "I'm thinking about moving up to Liverpool." Would he consider living outside America? He told me about time spent in Corsica and France around *Blood on the Tracks*, marvelous, haunting times, with and without Sara. Would he seriously consider the expatriate life? "Yes, I would. But creatively, I couldn't live anywhere but America, because I understand the tone behind the language there. I'd love to live somewhere else, but only for a while. I lived in Mexico for three months. I wrote my fourth album in Greece, but that was an American album." He spoke with animation about "two birthdays ago" and a gypsy festival at Saintes-Maries-de-la-Mer en Carmargue, France, with all the flamenco in the air, and the wildness of Corsica. But he always brought the raging beauty back home.

"I feel at home in America, because, as primitive as it is, I can create from America. All my feelings come out of America. When you leave, you get peace. America is a very violent place, so when you leave, you get that peace to create. In America, everybody's got a gun. I've got a few of them!" It sounded like Dylan was loading up for some target practice, so I threw up the bull's-eye, the talk about "the alimony tour." Dylan replied: "The myth of the starving artist is just that—a myth!

"I earn everything I make! I'm not getting nothing for nothing. Reggie Jackson of the New York Yankees gets three million dollars a year, for striking out! For every dollar I make, there's a pool of sweat on the floor. I feel we are all underpaid—my band, my singers. I put in an eight-hour day in two hours onstage." Mentioning a few of the other rock veterans "who had come through," Dylan declared: "It's a question of how much of it you can stand. How much can you stick it out."

According to Goldsmith, Dylan had originally wanted only three or four large outdoor arenas for the whole European tour, but Harvey had talked him into the six nights at Earls Court. Advance ticket sales were so great that Goldsmith undertook to convert the old Blackbushe Aerodrome, ninety minutes south of London, into a site for an audience of 100,000. When Saturday, July 15 burst fair, a lot of people who hadn't bought tickets decided to spend the day in the country listening to Dylan, Eric Clapton, Joan Armatrading, and others. The official police figure was 200,000, though estimates put it 20 percent higher than that. It was described as Britain's largest rock audience of all time, and even made news on American TV. Flushed with excitement, Dylan donned a top hat throughout his three hours onstage, and sang thirty-

ABOVE

Dylan's six-night season at Earls Court, his first British concerts since the Isle of Wight in 1969, prompted overnight queues for tickets in many cities and the concerts quickly sold out.

BELOW

Dylan en route
to Earls Court
from the Royal
Garden Hotel,
June 15, 1978.

three songs in a general mood of euphoria. As he had throughout the tour, he mostly reworked his old hits into startling new arrangements. Many were finding fresh insight into the lyrics when, as in "Tangled Up in Blue," he gave new emphasis and shape to songs long since taken for granted. As Russell Davies wrote in the *Sunday Times*, it was the best "creative re-vamping since Duke Ellington stopped coming round with savagely recycled oldies." Blackbushe soon entered the language of the British rock fan, as Woodstock had. It was more than a concert; a community, really.

By July 15, Dylan would have sung to more than 800,000 people in fifty concerts. The Continental leg of the 1978 tour took him to the Netherlands, West Germany, France, and Sweden. Still, I saw some tension I couldn't identify, and urged him to expand on something he'd been saying for the past year or so: "No man can fight another like the man who fights himself. Who could be a stronger enemy?"

"It's true," Bob said, "that a man is his own worst enemy, just as he is his own best friend. If you deal with the enemy within, then no enemy without can stand a chance." What was his enemy within? "Suspicion," he replied, as if he could answer all those allegations of paranoia in one word. Could he put his finger on the enemy within? He pointed his index finger toward his heart. Cautiously, he continued: "It's all in those two verses of that last song." In "Where Are You Tonight?" he directed me toward the moral battle with his alter ego.

Typical of his ambiguity, the twin Dylans have so many paired faces: the Gemini polarities of strength versus weakness, kindness versus cruelty, optimism versus pessimism, life versus death, suspicion versus friendliness. If any word alone can be found to characterize the contradictions in Bob Dylan, it would have to be *ambivalence*. If you're not being born, you're dying.

Bob nibbled at his food and kept working on the bottle of Courvoisier that was near him. He was better at small talk than I could ever remember, but he also wanted to get into the interview. "It's for your book, but you can do whatever you want to with it," he said. I teased him with his famous question, "How does it *feel?*" Dylan insisted that the ovations and

"It's not me. It's the songs. I'm just the postman. I deliver the songs. That's all I have in this world are those songs. That's what all the legend, all the myth is about—my songs.""

ABOVE

Tour '78 concluded with
the Picnic at Blackbushe
Aerodrome in Camberley,
Surrey. The audience was
estimated at 250,000 and as the
sun set on a perfect summer's
day Dylan sang for three hours,
wearing a top hat purloined
from his hotel doorman.

rave reviews were for his work: "It's not me. It's the songs. I'm just the postman. I deliver the songs. That's all I have in this world are those songs. That's what all the legend, all the myth is about—my songs. I started writing those songs before I could walk. George Harrison told me last night I'd be singing 'It's Alright, Ma' when I'm ninety. Nobody else gives those songs life. It's up to me to do it. But those songs have a life of their own too. Jimi Hendrix sang them. Stevie Wonder, Van Morrison, and Elvis Presley have sung them."

In the notes to *Biograph,* Dylan said he was "amazed that I've been around this long, never thought I would be" and that he tried "to learn from both the wise and the unwise, not pay attention to anybody, do what I want to do. … No matter how big you think you are history is gonna rollover you. Sound like a preacher, don't I? To the aspiring songwriter and singer I say disregard all the current stuff, forget it, you're better off, read John Keats, Melville, listen to Robert Johnson and Woody Guthrie."

We can't put a price on those rhythms, cadences, and images from Bob Dylan that have re-entered our everyday speech from which he first mined, then refined them. We know Mister Jones as the arch-Philistine who is unaware that something is happening. Even though we're stuck inside Desolation Row, we keep on keeping on. There may be blood on those tracks and nothing is revealed, yet he's told us there must be some way out of here. There may be no direction home for him or for us, but with one foot on the highway and the other in the grave, we try to get outside the empty cage that holds us. Desperation and hope fight in the captain's tower, a pair of warring twins. Although it's all over now, we renew ourselves by leaving the dead behind us. We're younger than all that now. Death and rebirth. For every seven people dyin' there's seven new ones busy being born. We forget where Dylan's lines end and our own begin.

Even though he denied being in "the teachin' business," there's a world to learn by following his road of self-made culture, of self-education. When he hopped off the subway from America's heartland in Greenwich Village, we were all looking for answers, only he probed deepest, knowing the question itself might unlock the answer. We turned to him for his vision, wit, fresh ideas, but mostly for his daring to try what hadn't been tried. Find your own answers, man, and you'll value them more, he said to us, time and again. Even when we insisted, he didn't want to play guru. He was too skinny then to carry a cross, and too wary to let his manager carry it for him.

"There's so many sides to Dylan, he's round," said his Woodstock friend Bernard Paturel. And he's been so many different people that this wasn't a biography of one man, but of several. Long before Dylan met or read Robert Graves, he was following the old poet's admonition that a poet must think mythically as well as rationally. He's a disturber of the peace—ours, as well as his own.

The past could be prelude or postlude. He's already poured five lifetimes into one. He may follow Rimbaud's route, having articulated more of the language of revolt than the world was then ready for. Or he may follow Yeats's route of more seeking and more finding and even greater creativity toward old age. Knowing Dylan as much as the mystery of genius will reveal to us, he'll probably do it his own way. He always has.

AFTERWORD

OPPOSITE

"To listen to *Theme Time Radio Hour* is to rediscover the sense of musical adventure that old-fashioned disc jockeys with strongly individual personalities offered in the days before big-money stations pinned their fiscal hopes to the rigid Top 40–style playlists that took the fun out of radio"—*Wall Street Journal*. Dylan hosted three series on Sirius XM between May 2006 to April 2009.

Bob Dylan's career is now in its seventh decade and shows little sign of slowing down. By spring 2019, he had notched up some three-thousand shows that have taken him back and forth across continents, and to China, South Korea, and Vietnam, in the so-called Never-Ending Tour, a description he typically disdains. "Critics should know that there's no such thing as forever," he told Douglas Brinkley of *Rolling Stone*, between concerts in Paris in 2009—with Nicholas Sarkozy and Carla Bruni, and Charles Aznavour, among backstage guests—and in Amsterdam. Dylan asked rhetorically if the label had been applied to Henry Ford or Billy Graham, Rupert Murdoch or Duke Ellington, adding that everything today had to be broken down into "simplistic terms" and, as usual, critics "apply a different standard to me for some reason." In words of which his parents and grandparents would have approved, he advised: "Every man should learn a trade. It's different than a job. My music wasn't made to take me from one place to another so I can retire early."

So, Dylan regards himself as "a tradesman," not a moniker many musicians would wish to claim; perhaps only the old bluesman to whom he has always vowed fealty. The Never-Ending Tour (halted only by a personal health scare in 1997, and by the coronavirus pandemic in 2020) has encompassed everything from small clubs and sports arenas to a presidential inaugural (Bill and Hillary Clinton looked thrilled, daughter Chelsea perplexed) and, most bizarrely, the 23rd Italian National Eucharistic Congress over which Pope John Paul II presided.

Since the original 1986 publication of Robert Shelton's biography, Dylan has released over a dozen studio albums, alongside the *Bootleg Series*, which has put truly landmark material officially out into the world.

In 2009, there was a Christmas album—once unthinkable—followed by three in which Dylan covered (or, as he put it, "uncovered") classics from the Great American Songbook. The material featured prominently in concert and in his *Theme Time Radio Hour* series. It began to look as if *Tempest* (2012) marked the close of Dylan's career as a songwriter.

In *Chronicles* (2004), the picaresque memoir that was supposed to launch a trilogy, Dylan wrote about what sounds like a mid-life crisis. He'd been on the road, but it felt like a road to nowhere: "It's nice to be known as a legend, and people will pay to see one, but for most people, once is enough." There was "a missing person inside of myself." He felt "done for, an empty burned-out wreck … a sixties troubadour, a folk-rock relic, a wordsmith from bygone days." He decided his upcoming tour with Tom Petty would be his last. But when it finished Dylan felt that "instead of being stranded somewhere at the end of the story, I was actually in the prelude to the beginning of another one." Thoughts of retirement were abandoned, another tour planned.

Fate intervened, according to *Chronicles*: Dylan found himself becalmed at home, his arm in a cast. He began writing again, the songs that would become *Oh Mercy* (1989), an album produced by Daniel Lanois which ranks among his best. But then once again Dylan lost his mojo: seven lean years followed until *Time Out of Mind* (1997)—an album of existential crisis, Lanois once more producing— began Dylan's creative renaissance: *"Love and Theft"* (2001), *Modern Times* (2006), *Together Through Life* (2009), and *Tempest* were each a critical and commercial success.

In a 1991 interview with Paul Zollo, Dylan acknowledged that writing was no longer easy, as it had been thirty years earlier, "when the songs would come three or four at the same time. … Once in a while, the odd song will come to me like a bulldog at the garden gate and demand to be written. But most of them are rejected out of my mind right away. You get caught up in wondering if anyone really needs to hear it. Maybe a person gets to the point where they have written enough songs. Let someone else write them." Besides, "playing music is a full-time job."

At some point, the bulldog had nudged open the gate: in spring 2020, without fanfare, Dylan released three new songs. "Murder Most Foul," a *Billboard* number one, which addressed the 1963 Kennedy assassination, was accompanied by a short message to a world in lockdown: "Greetings to my fans and followers with gratitude for all your support and loyalty across the years. This is an unreleased song we recorded a while back that you might find interesting. Stay safe, stay observant and may God be with you." It was followed by "I Contain Multitudes," and then by "False Prophet," released on May 8, the same day Dylan announced his 39th studio album, the all-original *Rough and Rowdy Ways*.

The album dropped five weeks later, making its debut on America's *Billboard* chart at number two, and taking the top spot in ten countries. It was, according to Spencer Kornhaber in the *Atlantic*, "a work of pessimistic Americana." In another interview with Brinkley, for the *New York Times*, Dylan talked of his "trance" and "stream-of-consciousness" approach to songs that "kind of write themselves and count on me to sing them." *Rough and Rowdy Ways* won widespread critical acclaim. In the *New Yorker*, Amanda Petrusich saw it as a "reckoning with the vastness and immediacy of American culture." In the *New York Times*, Jon Pareles summed up: "For all he has seen and sung, on *Rough and Rowdy Ways* Dylan refuses to settle down, or to be anything like an elder statesman. He sees death looming, but he's still in the fray."

Dylan has found other outlets for his creativity. He has always drawn and painted, as a clutch of album sleeves testify, and in 2007 he made his formal debut as a visual artist with *Drawn Blank* at the Kunstsammlungen in Chemnitz, Germany. Several exhibitions followed, each themed; and in 2013, *Mood Swings* showcased Dylan in yet another medium— ironwork, using materials picked up in junkyards and created in his Black Buffalo Ironworks. He explained: "I've been around iron all my life ever since I was a kid. I was born and raised in iron ore country, where you could breathe it and smell it every day. Gates appeal to me because of the negative space they allow. They can be closed but at the same time they allow the seasons and breezes to enter and flow. They can shut you out or shut you in. And in some ways there is no difference."

Then in 2018, Dylan launched a range of bespoke whiskeys, Heaven's Door Spirits, distilled in a deconsecrated Tennessee church. "You don't always find inspiration. Sometimes it finds you. We wanted to create a collection of American whiskeys that would each tell a story." Bottles feature artworks based on his sculptures.

Other ventures raised eyebrows: the licensing of "The Times They Are a-Changin'" to the Bank of Montreal for a television advertisement, a move that once again drew charges of sellout, and of "Love Sick" to Victoria's Secret for a campaign in which Dylan himself appeared. (Asked in 1965 what might tempt him to sell out, he famously replied: "Ladies garments.") An advertisement for a Cadillac ("Good car to drive, after a war") was a cross-promotion for Dylan's much-praised *Theme Time Radio Hour*, which ran for three years on XM Satellite Radio and can still be accessed online. In 2014, during the Super Bowl, a primped and permed Dylan starred in an ad for Chrysler, one American icon promoting another: "You can't import original, you can't fake true cool," he intones, "Things Have Changed" bowling along in the background. The appeal, fundamentally, is not only to American values but for support of American workers, as it had been in "Union Sundown" thirty years earlier.

In his Nobel Prize acceptance speech, Dylan wrote that "I've been doing what I set out to do for a long time, now. I've made dozens of records and played thousands of concerts all around the world. But it's my songs that are at the vital center of almost everything I do. They seemed to have found a place in the lives of many people throughout many different cultures and I'm grateful for that."

Not only in many lives, but through many mediums. In 2017, *Girl from the North Country* opened at London's Old Vic, later transferring to the West End, and thereafter crossing the Atlantic. It was written by the distinguished Irish playwright Conor McPherson, who was approached by Dylan's management to create a project around his vast songbook. Set in Duluth amid the depths of the Depression, *Girl from the North Country* drew comparisons with Eugene O'Neill and Arthur Miller. The *New York Times* noted that "the songs exist in self-sufficient independence of their creator's gravelly, much imitated voice. You hear them ripening into new fullness. Those who scoffed when Mr. Dylan received the Nobel Prize in Literature in 2016 may find they have to think again."

While Dylan's greatest gift may be his poetic facility, his legacy is most apparent in the work of the legions of "composers" who endeavor to create intelligent, meaningfully emotive rock songs to be sung with a drummer nearby, emphasizing the downbeat. As Robert Shelton wrote in "Trust Yourself," an essay published five years after his original book in *The Dylan Companion*: "Dylan could have died in 1966, or after, and still have changed the face of popular music, and its metabolism."

A self-described "musical expeditionary," Bob Dylan will surely play on until his final breath, like the old bluesmen he so reveres. Like Dylan Thomas, who took his last drink at the White Horse Tavern in Greenwich Village, a decade before Dylan and Shelton propped up the bar, he will rage as life's candle gutters. The fierce glow of his songs which have illumined our grievances and our grieving will however never be extinguished.

Author's acknowledgments

Because this book was always designed to reflect many voices commenting on the life and music of its subject, a vast number of people helped me to assemble it. Especial thanks to Liz Thomson, Gabrielle Goodchild, and Roger Ford for being the stalwart trio who helped me most directly. A variety of doors were opened up to me at the Dylan Revisited conventions in Manchester in 1979 and 1980, for which I especially thank its chief organizer, Richard Goodall.

The collectors and/or discographers Steven Goldberg, Stephen Pickering, and Jacques von Son were especially helpful. I actively corresponded with a dozen academics, mostly in America, who were carrying forward multidisciplinary "Dylan Studies" in their own classrooms and research. I traveled many thousands of miles to research the work, and want to express my thanks for the help extended to me by the subject's mother and brother and late father. Tony Glover was especially conscientious in pulling together the chaotic, stimulating days in Minneapolis–St. Paul. In New York, I was given detailed historical/ emotional reconstructions by Suze Rotolo and her sister, Carla. Sis and Gordon Friesen were, as ever, generous with their recollections of the heady Broadside days. Special thanks to the author of the first serious book on Dylan, Michael Gray, for strong support over a number of years, and for his work in assembling my material on the Band, the first Australian tour, and the thorny question of bootleg recordings. For technical musical advice, thanks to the singer-guitarists Carol Crist and Barry Tomlinson.

Editor's note and acknowledgments

This 2021 illustrated edition of Robert Shelton's classic firsthand account is based on the 2011 edition, which restored crucial parts of Shelton's original text excised from the 1986 edition, which the author felt had been "abridged over troubled waters." Published by Omnibus Press (UK), Backbeat Books (US) and Hardie Grant (Australia), as well as in German, Brazilian, Korean and Chinese translations, the 2011 edition should be regarded as the urtext, because it was faithful to the manuscript Shelton sent to his publisher in 1979. The crucial restorations took place around the interview with Dylan's parents, to whom Shelton alone was granted access; the formative Greenwich Village years, to which he was privy; and the 1966 interviews en route from Lincoln, Nebraska to Denver, Colorado, where their conversation continued late into the night and picked up the next day. That book can still be found, for those seeking the last word. From its 244,000 words, this more manageable new edition has been hewn: it retains those crucial sections but dispenses with lengthy interview transcripts, the album reviews, and the chapter making the case for Dylan as poet. After all, the award of the Nobel Prize for Literature in 2016 surely settles that argument.

Robert Shelton's sisters, Ruth Kadish and Leona Shapiro, and brother-in-law Morrie Kadish, have sadly now all passed away, and I'm grateful for the continued friendship and support of Robert's nephew, David Kadish, and his husband Michael Norton.

Thanks, also, to Rob Nichols and Team Palazzo, and to designer Sarah Pyke.

And finally to Robert Shelton himself, a friend and mentor without whom… I hope he would approve of what's been done in his name to ensure his life's work lives on. Unlike most of those who have written about Bob Dylan, Robert was actually there, with him when there really was "music in the cafés at night and revolution in the air."

Credits

DYLAN LYRIC PERMISSIONS

Copyright © Bob Dylan: "One Eyed Jacks" by Bob Dylan (unpublished); prose poem from *In the Wind* liner notes by Bob Dylan (1963); "11 Outlined Epitaphs" by Bob Dylan (1964); "away away be gone all you demons" by Bob Dylan (open letter); "An I shall wake in the mornin an try t start" by Bob Dylan (open letter); Lyrics from "Last Thoughts on Woody Guthrie," words and music by Bob Dylan (unpublished). **Copyright © Special Rider Music:** Lyrics from "Subterranean Homesick Blues," words and music by Bob Dylan (1965); "My Life in a Stolen Moment" by Bob Dylan (1973); Lyrics from "It's Alright, Ma (I'm Only Bleeding)," words and music by Bob Dylan (1965); Lyrics from "My Back Pages," words and music by Bob Dylan (1964). **Copyright © Dwarf Music:** Lyrics from "Pledging My Time," words and music by Bob Dylan (1966). **Copyright © Ram's Horn Music:** Lyrics from "Oh, Sister," words and music by Bob Dylan and Jacques Levy (1975); Lyrics from "Tangled Up in Blue," words and music by Bob Dylan (1974). **Copyright © Big Sky Music:** Lyrics from "When I Paint My Masterpiece," words and music by Bob Dylan (1971); Lyrics from "I Threw It All Away," words and music by Bob Dylan (1969).

PICTURE CREDITS

Courtesy of Alamy Alice Ochs/Michael Ochs Archives: 200; Archive PL: 59, 217; Arnie Sachs/CNP/MediaPunch: 31l; CBW: 139; Dale Smith: 187; David Cornelius: 256; Everett Collection Historical: 6, 9, 16c, 21, 23t, 40, 51, 248, 257; Granamour Weems Collection: 55; Granger Historical Picture Archive: 64; Granger, NYC: 105b; Ivy Close Images: 32b; JRC/The Hollywood Archive/PictureLux: 25; Keystone Press: 17, 18, 19t, 290; Landmark Media: 171; Landmark/MediaPunch: 10, 166; Neil Setchfield: 297; Philippe Gras: 295; Pictorial Press: 23b, 28, 44, 174, 213; Richard Busch/Granger, NY: 20; Ron Harvey/Netflix/Everett Collection: 270; ScreenProd/Photononstop: 36l; Simon Robinson: 31r; Tony Gale/Pictorial Press Ltd: 4, 13, 199; Trinity Mirror/Mirrorpix: 170; United Archives GmbH: 14; Walter Bibikow/Danita Delimont: 16; ZUMA Press: 48

Courtesy of Getty Alice Ochs/Michael Ochs Archives: 178, 196; Alvan Meyerowitz/Michael Ochs Archives: 267; Bettmann: 74, 207, 280, 282; Bill Ray/The LIFE Picture Collection: 246, 254; Blank Archives: 86, 90, 100, 105t, 111, 135, 139, 230; Blank Archives/Hulton Archive: 274; Brian Shuel/Redferns: 113, 115; CBS Photo Archive: 118; Charlie Steiner/Highway 67: 194, 221, 231; Columbia Records: 121; Daily Mirror/Mirrorpix: 147, 162, 173; David Gahr: 80, 102, 107, 124, 127, 150, 152; Dick Kraus/Newsday RM: 82; Ed Perlstein/Redferns: 285; Elliott Landy/Redferns: 228; Eric Schaal/The LIFE Picture Collection: 70; Evening Standard/Hulton Archive: 296; Fiona Adams/Redferns: 201; Frank Lennon/Toronto Star: 279; Fred W. McDarrah: 93, 272; Gai Terrell/Redferns: 148; Gene Lester/Metronome: 60; GHI/Universal History Archive: 84; Gijsbert Hanekroot/Redferns: 264; Graham Bezant/Toronto Star: 269; Hulton Archive: 146; Ivan Dmitri/Michael Ochs Archives: 47; Jack Riddle/The Denver Post: 76; Jean-Louis Atlan/Sygma: 241; Jim Steinfeldt/Michael Ochs Archives: 39; John Byrne Cooke Estate: 129; Keith Beaty/Toronto Star: 253; Ken Regan/Camera 5 via Contour: 276; Koh Hasebe/Shinko Music: 293; Larry Hulst/Michael Ochs Archives: 283; LMPC: 251; Mark and Colleen Hayward/Redferns: 168; Metro-Goldwyn-Mayer: 259; Michael Ochs Archives: 67, 72, 91, 95, 96, 125, 136, 140, 164, 177, 180, 183, 189, 190, 229, 232, 235, 244, 289; Milton Glaser/Michael Ochs Archives: 222; Mirrorpix: 298; Mitch Greenhill: 133; Movie Poster Image Art: 224, 226; Patrice Habans/Paris Match: 242; Paul Popper/Popperfoto: 236; Paul Slade/Paris Match: 78; Raeburn Flerlage/Chicago History Museum: 103; RB/Redferns: 43; Rick Diamond/WireImage: 263; Rolls Press/Popperfoto: 238; Rowland Scherman: 116, 123, 131; Sigmund Goode/Michael Ochs Archive: 88; Steve Morley/Redferns: 260; Thomas S. England/The LIFE Images Collection: 268; Tony Evans: 142; Trinity Mirror/Mirrorpix 144

Courtesy of Theme Time Radio Hour Jaime Hernandez: 300

Albums © Columbia Records/Sony Music Entertainment Daniel Kramer: 19; Don Hunstein: 90, 111; Barry Feinstein: 139; **© Folkways Records** Ronald Clyne: 100; **© Spivey Records** Bobbie Hickey: 105